WINDOWS
3.0 and 3.1

Helmutt Erlenkötter, Volker Reher

WINDOWS
3.0 and 3.1

PRISMA COMPUTER COURSE

Prisma Computer Courses first published in Great Britain 1992 by

McCarta Ltd
15 Highbury Place
London N5 1QP

Translation: George Hall
Production: LINE UP text productions

© 1991 Rowohlt Taschenbuch Verlag GmbH, Reinbek bei Hamburg
For the English translation
© 1992 Uitgeverij Het Spectrum BV, Utrecht

No part of this book may be reproduced in any form, by print, photoprint, microfilm or any other means without written permission from the publisher.

ISBN 1 85365 345 4

British Library Cataloguing-in-Publication Data.
A catalogue record for this book is available from the British Library.

Contents

Foreword 13

1	Basic skills	15
1.1	Mouse and keyboard	16
1.2	Starting and quitting Windows	19
1.3	Windows	20
1.3.1	Moving a window	22
1.3.2	Enlarging and reducing windows	23
1.3.3	Reducing windows to icons	23
1.3.4	Restoring windows	24
1.3.5	Maximum window	25
1.3.6	Exercises 1 and 2	25
1.3.7	Using Scroll bars	25
1.3.8	Exercise 3	27
1.3.9	Closing windows	27
1.4	Menus	28
1.4.1	The Control menu	29
1.4.2	Other menus	32
1.4.3	Exercises 4 to 7	33
2	The Program Manager	35
2.1	Groups	35
2.1.1	Opening and closing group windows	37
2.1.2	Arranging group windows	37
2.1.3	Arranging icons	40
2.1.4	Exercises 8 and 9	41
2.1.5	Changing descriptions and setup	42
2.1.6	Creating and deleting groups	43
2.1.7	Summary	47
2.1.8	Associating documents with programs	48
2.1.9	Other program properties	49
2.1.10	Other options for operating groups	50
2.2	Starting up programs	51
	The Startup group window	52
2.3	Exiting the Program Manager	53
3	Paintbrush	55
3.1	The window	56
3.2	The first drawing	58

3.3	Saving and opening	61
3.4	Correcting mistakes	65
3.4.1	Erase	66
3.4.2	Undo	67
3.4.3	Using Backspace	68
3.4.4	Enlarging screen sections	69
3.4.5	Summary	70
3.5	Exercises 10 to 12	71
3.6	Scissors, pick, brush, line and box	71
3.6.1	Drawing a window	71
3.6.2	Summary	74
3.7	Showing the cursor position	75
3.8	Making a map	75
3.9	The text tool	76
3.10	Using Circle/Ellipse and Curve	79
3.11	Special functions	80
3.12	Printing	82
3.12.1	Printing a drawing	82
3.12.2	Specifying the page setup	84
3.13	Other tools and options	85
3.13.1	The polygon	85
3.13.2	The filled boxes	86
3.13.3	Image attributes	86
3.13.4	Determining the shapes and colours	87
3.13.5	Loading and saving parts of a drawing	89
3.14	The letterheading	90
3.15	Summary of all tools	90
4	Write	93
4.1	Starting up Write	93
4.2	Compact summary	94
4.3	Moving the cursor	95
4.4	Correcting text	96
4.5	Exercise 13	96
4.6	Selecting text	97
4.7	Processing text blocks	98
4.7.1	The Clipboard	98
4.7.2	Cutting, copying and pasting	99
4.8	Find and Replace	101
4.8.1	Finding text	101
4.8.2	Replacing text	102
4.8.3	Exercise 14	104

4.8.4	Possible mistakes using Find and Replace	104
4.9	Document layout	105
4.9.1	The ruler	105
4.9.2	Character styles	105
4.9.3	Subscript and superscript	106
4.9.4	Font and font size	106
4.9.5	Formatting paragraphs	107
4.9.6	Using tabs	109
4.9.7	Hyphenation	111
4.9.8	Exercise 15	111
4.10	Determining the page layout	113
4.10.1	Entering text in headers and footers	113
4.10.2	Page endings	114
4.11	Saving and printing documents	115
4.12	Combining text and pictures	117
4.13	Exercise 16	118
4.14	OLE technology	118
5	Operating Windows	119
5.1	The Task List	119
5.2	The Control Panel	121
5.2.1	Colour	122
5.2.2	Fonts	126
5.2.3	Ports	127
5.2.4	Mouse	128
5.2.5	Desktop	128
5.2.6	Keyboard	132
5.2.7	Printers	132
5.2.8	International	137
5.2.9	Date/Time	138
5.2.10	Network	139
5.2.11	386 Enhanced	139
5.2.12	Drivers	142
5.2.13	Sound	143
5.3	The Print Manager	143
5.3.1	The Print Queue	144
5.3.2	Processing the print queue	145
5.3.3	Commands from the Print Manager	145
5.3.4	Printing to a file	146
5.4	The PIF Editor	147
5.4.1	Specifying operating modes	149
5.4.2	Entering program information	150

5.4.3	Advanced options	. 153
5.4.4	Exercise 17	. 157
6	File Manager	. 158
6.1	Working with directory windows	. 158
6.2	Copying, moving and deleting files	. 166
6.3	Exercise 18	. 169
6.4	Editing directories	. 169
6.5	Exercises 19 to 21	. 171
6.6	Editing disks	. 171
6.7	Associating documents and	. 172
6.8	File Manager settings	. 173
6.9	Summary	. 174
7	Clock	. 175
7.1	Application and appearance	. 175
7.1.1	Icon	. 175
7.1.2	Window	. 175
7.1.3	Analogue	. 176
7.1.4	Digital	. 177
7.2	Setting the Clock	. 177
7.3	Exercises 22 and 23	. 178
8	Calendar	. 179
8.1	Application and appearance	. 179
8.1.1	Icon	. 179
8.1.2	Window	. 179
8.1.3	Calendar with daily schedule	. 180
8.1.4	Calendar with Month view	. 181
8.2	Some remarks concerning calendar planning	. 182
8.2.1	Schedule	. 182
8.2.2	The start of the working day	. 183
8.3	Defining special days	. 184
8.3.1	Marking symbols	. 184
8.3.2	Introducing commentary	. 185
8.4	Registering appointments	. 186
8.4.1	Appointments conforming to the schedule	186
8.4.2	Appointments which deviate	. 186
8.5	Setting an alarm	. 187
8.6	Managing appointments	. 188
8.7	Saving the calendar	. 189

8.8	Printing the calendar	190
8.8.1	Layout	190
8.8.2	Printing	191
8.9	Exercises 24 to 29	192
9	Cardfile	193
9.1	Application and appearance	193
9.1.1	Icon	193
9.1.2	Window	193
9.1.3	Card View	194
9.1.4	List View	195
9.2	Organization of the Cardfile	195
9.2.1	The index line	196
9.2.2	The information area	197
9.2.3	Telephone numbers	197
9.3	Creating a cardfile	198
9.3.1	Processing a blank card	198
9.3.2	Adding new cards	199
9.3.3	Text cards	200
9.3.4	Picture cards	201
9.3.5	Mixed cards	202
9.3.6	Working with pictures and objects	203
9.4	Saving a cardfile	204
9.5	Printing a cardfile	204
9.5.1	Check the printer settings	204
9.5.2	Adjusting the layout	204
9.5.3	Printing	205
9.6	Searching in a cardfile	205
9.6.1	Searching through the index	205
9.6.2	Searching in the information area	206
9.7	Dialling automatically	207
9.8	Editing a database	209
9.8.1	Altering the index line	209
9.8.2	Altering the information area	209
9.8.3	Restoring cards	210
9.8.4	Deleting cards	210
9.8.5	Duplicating cards	210
9.8.6	Merging cardfiles	211
9.9	Exercises 30 and 31	211
10	Notepad	212
10.1	Application and appearance	212

10.1.1	Icon	212
10.1.2	Window	212
10.1.3	Notepad files	213
10.2	Creating a file	213
10.3	Saving files	214
10.4	Searching in the Notepad	215
10.5	Printing a file	216
10.5.1	Checking the print settings	216
10.5.2	Specifying the page setup	216
10.6	Altering text	217
10.7	Limits to the file size	218
10.8	Logbook files	218
10.9	Exercises 32 and 33	219
11	Terminal	220
11.1	Starting up Terminal	220
11.2	Hardware requirements	221
11.3	Other preconditions	222
11.4	Preparing a session	223
11.5	Realizing a computer connection	225
11.6	Session procedure	226
11.6.1	Logging in	226
11.6.2	Dialogue	227
11.6.3	Exchanging files	227
11.6.4	Logging out	228
11.7	Printing	229
11.7.1	Printing incoming messages immediately	229
11.7.2	Printing text fragments	230
11.8	Advanced options	231
11.8.1	Registering telephone numbers	231
11.8.2	Terminal emulations	232
11.8.3	Terminal Preferences	233
11.8.4	Communication parameters	235
11.8.5	Modem commands	238
11.8.6	Data transmission	240
11.8.7	Assigning commands to function keys	243
11.9	Saving Terminal files	245
11.10	Working with Terminal files	245
11.11	Exercise 34	246
12	Multimedia	247
12.1	The Media Player	248

12.2	The Sound Recorder	249
13	Calculator	252
13.1	Application and appearance	252
13.1.1	Icon	252
13.1.2	Window	252
13.2	The standard calculator	253
13.2.1	Calculating using the keyboard	254
13.2.2	Calculations using the mouse	256
13.3	The scientific calculator	256
13.3.1	Simple calculations using the keyboard	256
13.3.2	Calculations using the mouse	259
13.3.3	Statistical calculations	261
13.4	Automatic calculation	264
13.5	Exercises 35 to 38	265
14	Recorder	266
14.1	Application and appearance	266
14.2	Macro planning	267
14.3	Recording macros	268
14.4	Playing back macros	271
14.5	Changing macros	271
14.5.1	Changing options	272
14.5.2	Deleting macros	273
14.5.3	Merging macros	273
14.6	Creating macros to use as demos	274
14.7	Exercise 39	275
15	Integrating Windows applications: working with OLE technology	276
15.1	Linked and embedded objects	276
15.2	The Object Packager	277
15.3	A familiar example: the letterheading from Paintbrush and Write	280

Appendices

A	Installation	283
B	Practical tips	285
C	ASCII character set	296
D	ANSI character set	298
Index		299

Foreword

It is beginning to look as though the Windows user interface is growing to become the standard it was originally developed to be. The ease of operation and the program speed have increased considerably with the appearance of version 3.1 in 1992. The simple installation, the fine graphic design, the extensive help function and the sophisticated memory management are particularly striking.

Small imperfections in the 3.0 version have been corrected and this, in general, leads to a more satisfactory way of working. The increased operating speed is also reflected in the minimum demands which are placed on the hardware: an IBM compatible AT with an 80286 processor and at least 2 Mb RAM. In systems with a more powerful processor (for example 80386 or 80486) more RAM is required (4 Mb is perfectly sufficient) in order to work optimally with Windows.

The real virtue of Windows is, however, actually expressed in the use of programs which have been specially developed for this interface. Although normal DOS programs can also run with Windows, the benefit of running these programs with this interface is mostly limited to the multi-task function and odd cutting and pasting possibilities.

The OLE technology is integrated in the 3.1 version and this makes it a pleasure to work with the applications which have been specially developed for Windows. It is now almost child's play to link data from different programs. The dynamic data exchange (DDE) in Windows 3.0 has been replaced by the greatly improved OLE technology which makes it possible to couple elements from different programs to each other.

Now that the 3.1 version has come on to the market, the number of Windows applications, which is already substantial, will rise even more. Many traditional DOS programs, for which there are now Windows versions such as Word for Windows, belong to this category. In addition to Windows' own spreadsheet, Excel, Lotus has also introduced a Windows version of 1-2-3. The computer languages also make their presence felt; there is already a Windows version of Turbo C++. It seems that Windows will be *the* user interface for the coming years; it appears ever more likely that Windows will replace DOS as operating system with the passage of time.

This book deals with the possibilities within Windows 3.1 in the light of examples geared to practice. That is why this book is designed in such a way that you can try out the examples and exercises on your computer immediately. Place this book next to your computer and go through it step by step. Although all the chapters deal with different topics, there is a continuing thread and we shall occasionally refer back to a subject which has been mentioned earlier.

This book is not primarily a reference book; it is more of an instruction manual which teaches you to work with Windows step by step. That is why, as a rule, certain methods and techniques are explained at those places where you first require them. Nevertheless, in order to offer you the possibility of finding a certain topic quickly, an extensive reference index has been included at the end of this book.

1 Basic skills

Windows' graphical user interface simplifies working with a personal computer considerably. You do not have to immerse yourself anymore in complicated exercises and the corresponding syntax. Instead, you can select functions from menus or use **icons**.

In Windows, the screen is called **desktop**. On this desktop you will find rectangular work areas called **windows**. These can be enlarged, reduced, moved and closed again. Everything that you wish to do in Windows takes place within these windows.

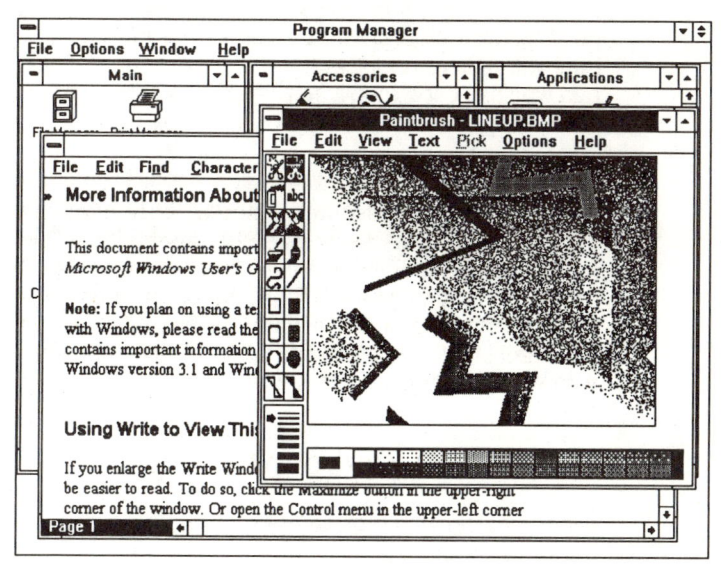

Mostly you operate Windows using the **mouse**. This handy pointing device transforms the movements of your hand on the worktop into movements of the **cursor** upon the screen. Accordingly, you can start up a program, for example, by selecting the corresponding icon using the arrow pointer and subsequently clicking on the mouse button.

In principle, Windows can also be operated using the keyboard, but using the mouse is much more efficient. That is why, in general, we have confined ourselves in this book to operation using the mouse. If you do not already have a mouse, it is advisable to acquire one. It does not have to be expensive, but in order to prevent unnecessary problems, it is sensible to purchase a mouse which is compatible with the Microsoft mouse.

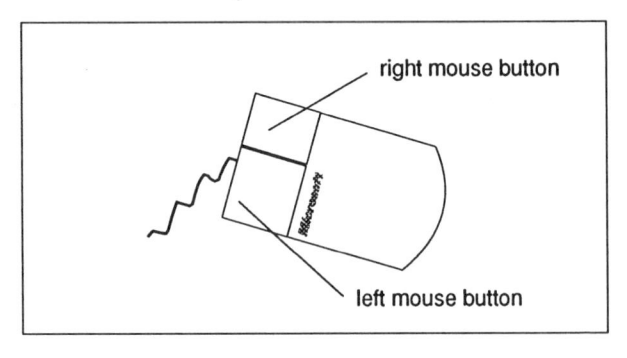

![Diagram of a mouse with labels pointing to "right mouse button" and "left mouse button"]

If you are not yet familiar with Windows procedures, you should first work your way carefully through the following chapter. This will make everything much easier. In addition, you only need to learn the procedures once, since all the programs which work within Windows are operated identically. We shall begin working creatively with Windows from chapter 3 onwards.

1.1 Mouse and keyboard

When dealing with **mouse operations** we use the following terminology:

Mouse pointer   Small symbol on the screen which, depending upon the application, assumes various forms (arrow, line, cross etc.).

Mouse and keyboard

Click Pressing down one mouse button (mostly the left-hand one) and then releasing it again.

Double click Pressing the mouse button twice in rapid succession and then releasing it.

Dragging Pressing the mouse button, holding it down and moving the mouse. In this way, you can relocate, for instance, icons or windows.

Cursor A mark on the screen which indicates where the following character will appear. Another name for cursor is **Insertion point**.

If your mouse has more than one button, you should, as a rule, use the left-hand button. However, with help from the Control Panel (see section 5.2), you can personally determine which mouse button you wish to use. With a few exceptions, this single mouse button is sufficient for operating Windows.

If in a specific case the **keyboard** must be used, the required keys and key combinations are shown as follows:

Key1-key2
A hyphen means that both keys should be pressed down simultaneously. In the key combination Alt-Spacebar, you should first press the Alt key and then the Spacebar. Keep in mind that you only have to press most keys down for an instant. If you hold a key down for any longer, the character in question will be entered several times.

Key1, key2
A comma means that the keys should be pressed down in succession. Release the first key before pressing down the second.

The names of the keys used in this book have the following meaning:

F1 to F12
These are the function keys which are located above or to the left of the numbers and letters.

Enter
This key is also called the Return key. You will find the Enter key next to the letters at the right-hand side.

Esc
The Esc key is located at the upper left-hand corner of the keyboard. This is a kind of emergency brake. Using the Esc key, you can discontinue the current function in many programs.

Backspace
Using this key, you can delete the symbol to the left of the cursor.

Del or Delete
Using this key, you can delete the symbol to the right of the cursor.

Ins or Insert
In many word processors, the Insert key is used to switch from the insert mode to the overtype mode, and vice versa.

Home
In many word processors, the Home key is used to move the cursor to the beginning of the line or the screen.

End
In many word processors, the End key is used to move the cursor to the end of the line or the screen.

PgUp or Page Up
This key is often used in order to browse backwards through a text.

PgDn or Page Dn
This key is often used to browse forwards through a text.

Shift
The Shift keys are used for typing capital letters and for calling up additional functions in combination with the function keys. You will find them to the left and right of the letters.

Ctrl
The Ctrl keys have no function of their own, but they alter the function of the key which is simultaneously pressed down.

Tab
Tabstops are entered with the Tab key.

Spacebar
Spaces are entered with the spacebar.

Cursor left, right, up, down
These terms are used for the **cursor keys**, which are also sometimes called the **arrow keys**. Modern keyboards are equipped with a separate cursor area. In older keyboards, the cursor area is integrated in the numeric key pad.

1.2 Starting and quitting Windows

When you have switched on the computer and the operating system has been loaded, give the following command:

```
win
```

After a few seconds the Windows desktop will appear on your screen.

The first window you see is the Program Manager. This window is central in Windows - all other programs are started up and operated from here. The Program Manager is activated automatically when you start Windows. When you close the Program Manager, you end Windows.

The most simple way of closing a window, and, in this case, of ending Windows, is to use the key combination Alt-F4. Hold the Alt key down while pressing F4. You are asked to confirm this. Do this by pressing Enter. Subsequently, start up Windows again.

1.3 Windows

In Windows, the screen is called 'desktop'. You can deposit and arrange objects on this desktop, just as upon a real desktop.

When you start up Windows, you will land in the **application window** of the Program Manager. You can direct everything from this main program window. We are now going to use it to show you how to operate windows. What you learn here applies to all other Windows windows.

As you see, within the Program Manager window there is another window called Main. Leave this window untouched for the time being. We shall deal with the Main window extensively in chapter 2.

The following illustration shows what you will see on your screen when you have started up Windows.

Windows

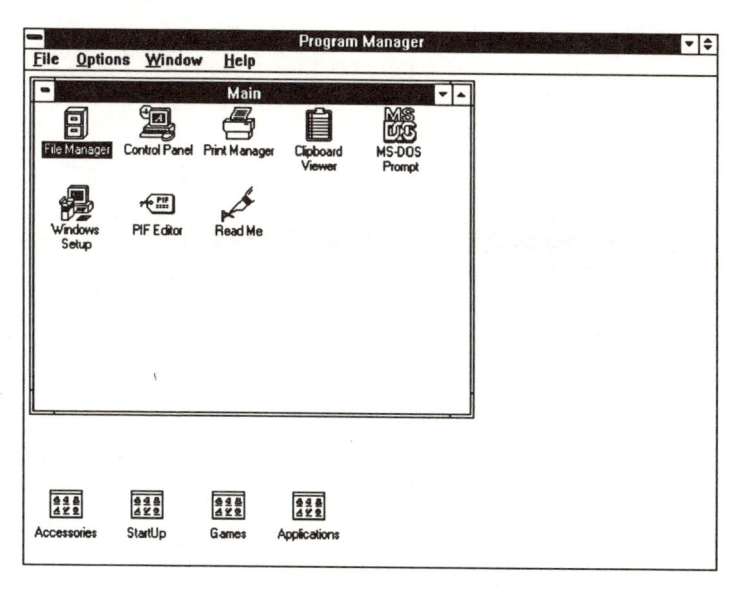

Note: The Program Manager may appear slightly different on your screen; this is due to the fact that the individual elements can be arranged at will. If Windows has just been installed, you will see, in principle, no difference.

In order to refer in the future to the individual elements of a window, we have named them in the following illustration. You will observe that these elements are not always present in each window. You will encounter the basic elements, however, time and again.

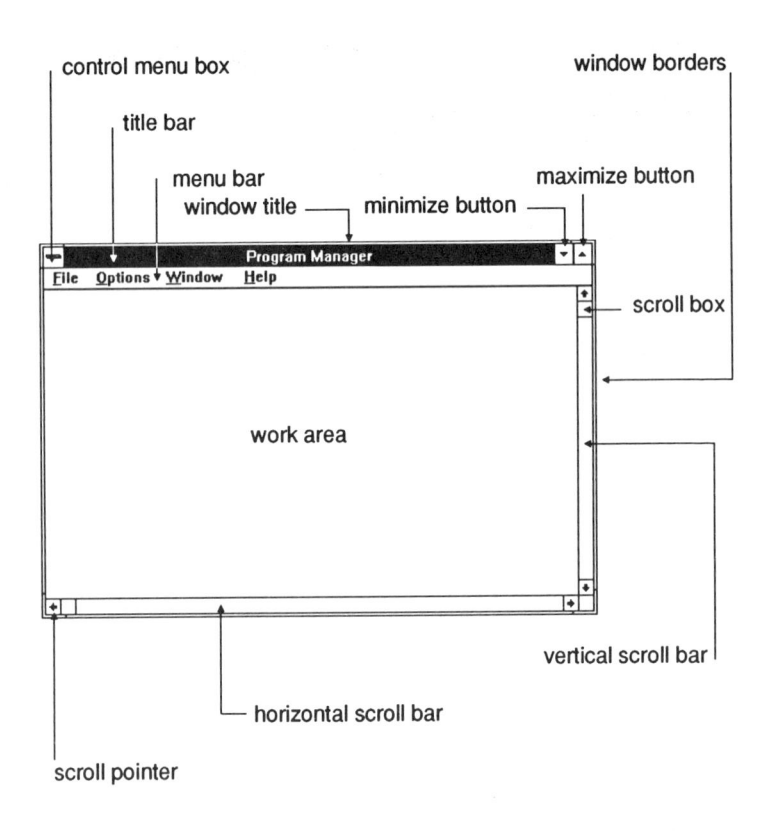

![Diagram of Program Manager window with labels: control menu box, title bar, menu bar, window title, minimize button, maximize button, window borders, scroll box, work area, vertical scroll bar, horizontal scroll bar, scroll pointer]

1.3.1 Moving a window

We shall move the Program Manager window across the desktop. Place the pointer on the bar containing the text 'Program Manager'. Now press the left mouse button, hold it down and move the window using the mouse to the desired position. Now release the left mouse button. This way of working is known as **dragging**.

As you will see, you do not move the contents of the window during this manoeuvre, you only move a frame equal in size to the window. Only when you release the left mouse button do the contents of the window appear in the new frame.

Move the window now to several different spots. You can move the window in such a way that only a small part of it is visible on the desktop. Finally, place the window approximately in the middle of the screen again.

1.3.2 Enlarging and reducing windows

Not only the location but also the size of the window can be changed.

Move the pointer to the outside edge of the window. The form of the pointer now changes from an arrow into an arrow pointing in two directions. Hold down the left mouse button and move the mouse in one of the directions in which the arrow is pointing. The size of the window changes correspondingly.

If you wish to change the size of the window diagonally, set the pointer on one of the corners of the window. By dragging, you can now change the size of two sides simultaneously.

Due to the fact that you can move windows and alter their size, it is possible to display several windows on the screen at the same time.

1.3.3 Reducing windows to icons

Another feature of windows is that you can reduce them to icons.

Whenever you are working with a program in Windows, this takes place within a window. If you wish to interrupt working with a program, you can reduce the window to an icon. Accordingly, it does not occupy unnecessary space on the desktop, and the program itself remains in memory, so that you do not have to quit the program and subsequently start it up again. Thus, you have quick and easy access to a large number of programs without having to load them repeatedly. The maximum number of icons which are simultaneously available is determined by the size of the memory in your computer and the mode in which Windows is being run (more about this later).

To reduce a window to an icon, click on the minimize button. This is the button with the triangular shape pointing downwards, at the right-hand side of the title bar. The following illustration shows the result of this step.

Program
Manager

Windows places the icon at the bottom of the desktop. The icon shows that the corresponding program remains in memory.

1.3.4 Restoring windows

You can restore the icon to the original window using only two keys. Click on the icon. The following menu appears on your screen.

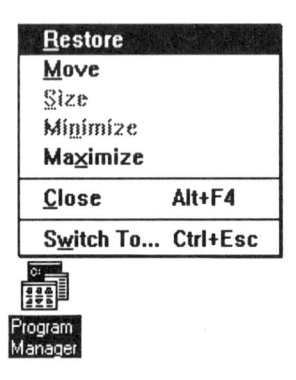

Restore	
Move	
S**i**ze	
Mi**n**imize	
Ma**x**imize	
Close	Alt+F4
S**w**itch To...	Ctrl+Esc

Program
Manager

Choose the *Restore* option by clicking it on. The window returns to its original size and you can continue your work at the same point where you interrupted it previously.

You can also restore a window which has been reduced to an icon by double clicking on the icon in question. In other words, place the pointer on the icon and press the left mouse button twice in rapid succession.

1.3.5 Maximum window

It is also possible to fill the whole screen with just one window. You can do this by clicking the **maximize button**. This is the button with the triangular shape pointing upwards at the right-hand side of the title bar. The window will then occupy the entire desktop. As you will see, the triangle in the maximize button changes into two triangles pointing up and down, symbolising that the button now has the *Restore* function. By clicking on this button you recall the original window.

You are now able to adjust the shapes of the windows on your desktop to your own needs.

1.3.6 Exercises 1 and 2

1) Try to reduce the Program Manager as much as possible without transforming it into an icon. Then restore it to its original size.

2) Change the size of the window in the following order of sequence: maximum window - window - icon - window.

1.3.7 Using Scroll bars

During this reducing process you will have noticed that at the bottom and to the right of the window extra elements have appeared. These are the so-called **scroll**

bars. These appear on the screen whenever the window has become too small to display all the icons which it contains.

Try to reduce the window to the size shown in the following illustration.

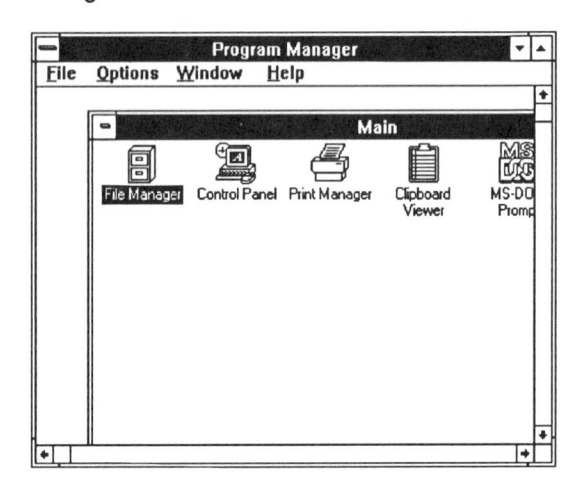

The scroll bars which now appear in the window have two functions. In the first place, they indicate that you are not able to see the entire contents of the window. Secondly, the scroll bars enable you to move the window through the document. You need the scroll bars, for example, if you are processing a text, or making a drawing, which does not quite fit into the window.

You move the window section using the **scroll pointers**, the **scroll box** and the **scroll bar**. Try this out on the horizontal scroll bar at the bottom of the window:

- Place the cursor on the arrow which is pointing to the right and click several times. The contents of the window will be shifted step by step to the right.
- Place the cursor on the arrow which is pointing to the left, click and hold the mouse button down. The contents of the window will move continuously to the left.

The scroll box marks the relative position of the window section. If the cursor is in the upper left-hand corner of the window, the scroll box of the vertical scroll bar will be completely at the top and the scroll box of the horizontal scroll bar completely at the left-hand side.

- Place the cursor on the scroll box of the horizontal scroll bar and drag it from one side of the bar to the other. When you release the mouse button, you will see the contents of the corresponding window section.

You can also move the contents of the window by directly clicking on the scroll bar.

- Place the cursor a little to the right or left of the scroll box and click. With every click you will see the following window section appear, until the right- or left-hand edge has been reached.

1.3.8 Exercise 3

3) Practise working with the arrows and bars until you have mastered these manoeuvres. Then arrange the Program Manager window so that it looks approximately like this:

Program Manager

1.3.9 Closing windows

There are three ways of closing a window:

1) Use the option *Close* from the Control menu (see paragraph 1.4.1),

3) double click on the **Control menu button**.

If you work with a mouse, the third alternative is the most useful.

1.4 Menus

In Windows, you choose options and functions from menus. You will find these menus behind the Control menu button and the menu bar. Each program has its own menus. Many options and functions are alike, however, and can be found at the same place. This makes learning how to operate another program quick and easy.

You open a menu by clicking on its name. You open the Control menu using the Control menu button.

If you are working with the keyboard, you open a menu by holding down the Alt key and simultaneously typing the underlined letter in the name of the desired menu. In this way, you open the *File* menu using Alt-F. The Control menu is an exception to this rule - for this you use the combination Alt-Spacebar.

When you have chosen an option from a menu by clicking on it, the corresponding menu will be closed again automatically. If you wish to close a menu without choosing an option, just click once again on the name of the menu or menu button, or press the Esc key once or twice.

The following table gives a list of all combinations:

	mouse	keyboard
open control menu	click on the control menu button	Alt-Spacebar
close control menu	click on the control menu button	Esc, Esc
open other menus	click on the menu	Alt-letter
close other menus	click on the menu	Esc, Esc

1.4.1 The Control menu

The **Control menu** appears in all applications and always contains, in principle, the same options.

The following illustration shows the Control menu for the Program Manager. Open it by clicking on the button in the upper left-hand corner or by using the key combination Alt-Spacebar.

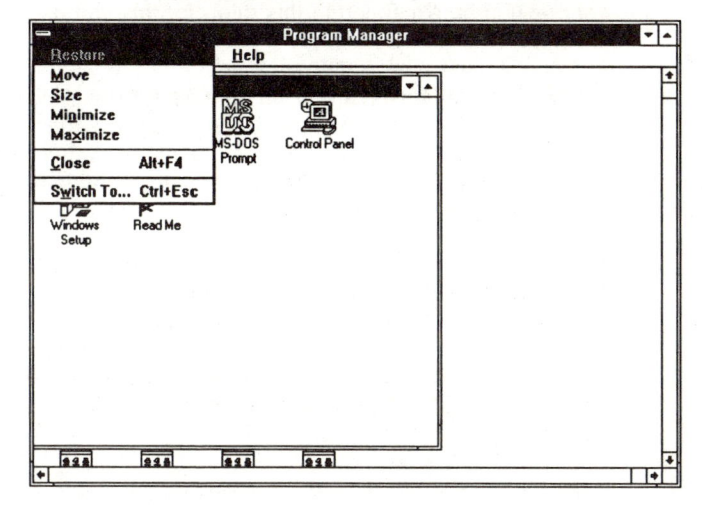

In the upper part of the Control menu you will find the options *Restore Move, Size, Minimize* and *Maximize*. These options are used to alter the size of the window and to move the window if you are working with the keyboard. In this way, you reach the same result as you would do using the mouse in combination with the title bar, the window border etc. Thus, everything which you have done up until now with the mouse to change the form of the desktop, can also be done with options from the Control menu.

In the Control menu, the option *Restore* is grey. This means that this option cannot be used at the moment. In all menus, options which are shown as grey cannot be selected. For instance, in a word processing program the printing option will not be available if no text has been entered as yet. In our example, it is not possible to restore the window to its previous size, because it is neither an icon, nor does it occupy the whole screen.

There are three ways of choosing an option:

1) Click on the option,
2) choose the option using either the up or down arrow key, and confirm this with Enter, or
3) type the underlined letter, for example N for *Minimize*.

Choose now the *Minimize* option. You may personally decide how you wish to do this.

As you know, you can restore an icon to its previous size by giving a double click. Now, however, do that by using the key combination Alt-Spacebar. In the Control menu, the option *Restore* is no longer grey, but the *Size* and *Minimize* options are no longer available. Restore the window to its previous size and reopen the Control menu.

In addition to the five options for operating the window, you will also find the *Close* and *Switch To* options in the

Control menu. By using *Close* you can close the window which is currently active. If, however, you close the Program Manager window, you will quit Windows. Behind the *Close* option you will see the key combination Alt-F4. You can use this as a **shortcut** key combination for this action. Many options have a shortcut like this. In time you will begin to make more use of these in order to increase your working speed with Windows.

Choose the *Close* option. A small window will appear, the so-called dialogue box:

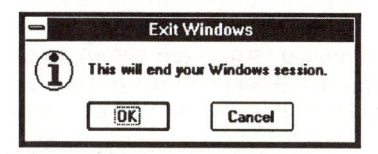

```
┌─────────────────────────────────────┐
│ ─            Exit Windows           │
│ ⓘ  This will end your Windows session.│
│       ┌────┐   ┌──────────┐         │
│       │ OK │   │  Cancel  │         │
│       └────┘   └──────────┘         │
└─────────────────────────────────────┘
```

Here you determine whether or not you really want to end the program. The dialogue box contains several elements, one of which is the **command buttons**, called here *OK* and *Cancel*. A command button works as a switch. You can click on it using the mouse. *OK* means that the command should be carried out. *Cancel* offers the possibility of breaking off an option which has been chosen by accident, so that the option will not be implemented.

You now wish to proceed further, so click on the Cancel button. All programs work with dialogue boxes like these in order to help prevent loss of information due to accidental manoeuvres.

Here are several *remarks* for those who wish to use the keyboard now and again:

In all dialogue boxes with several elements, you use the Tab key to move from one element to the other. The active element is always enclosed by a dotted line. Use the Spacebar to place a cross in a check box and the Enter key or the Spacebar to confirm a command button. Try operating the keyboard in the 'Exit Windows' dialogue box. By the way, comparable key functions are available in earlier Microsoft programs.

The *Switch To* option enables you to transfer to another active program. We shall deal with this option more extensively in section 5.1. The **three dots,** so-called ellipsis, indicates that a dialogue box will appear on the screen whenever this option is selected. In this case, you have to specify the command further.

1.4.2 Other menus

In terms of operation, there is no difference between the Control menu and the other menus. The two following diagrams illustrate this.

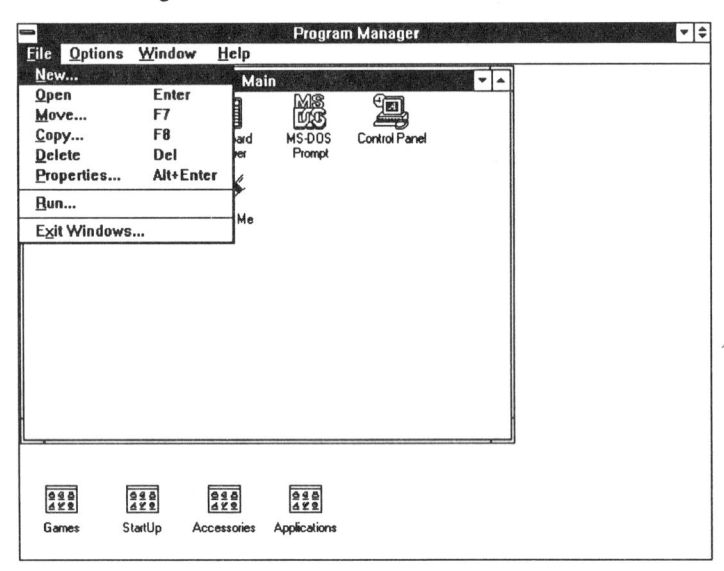

Do not choose an option from the menu. In the following chapter we shall deal extensively with the menus and options of the Program Manager.

When you have opened a menu, you can use the left

and right arrow keys to open up the other menus. Try this out. Then press the Esc key twice to close the current window again.

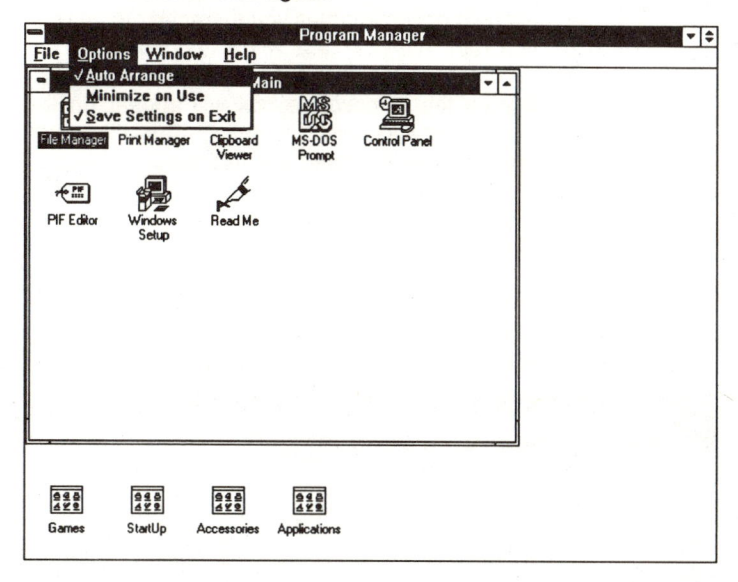

1.4.3 Exercises 4 to 7

4) Restore the desktop to the form which it had when you started up Windows (no scroll bars, the window approximately in the middle of the screen).

5) Open the *Help* menu. Which keys can you now use to open up the other menus? Close the menus once more without choosing an option.

6) Minimize the Program Manager window so that scroll bars appear at the right-hand side and at the bottom of the window. How can the screen section now be moved in a continuous way?

7) In which ways can you close a window?

If you have worked through this chapter thoroughly, you are ready to work with Windows.

2 The Program Manager

The **Program Manager** is the central program in Windows. From this point you start up other programs, adjust Windows to your personal taste or compose program groups. In this way, the Program Manager is there to organize your work.

2.1 Groups

Group is the most important term within the Program Manager. All programs are gathered in groups. You can think of a group as being a folder in which you can keep up to 40 programs. In addition, it is possible to associate a file, which will be loaded automatically at the start of the program, to each of these programs. Thus, it is useful, for instance, to attach a text upon which you are working for a relatively long period of time, to a word processor. Each time you call up the word processor your text will be automatically loaded.

Groups have their own icons. The upper diagram on the next page shows the icons of the Main group, the Start-Up group, the Accessories group, the Games group and the Applications group.

When you first start up Windows, only one group is opened in the Program Manager, that is Main (see the lower diagram on the next page).

This is one of the five groups which are automatically set up at the installation of Windows (depending upon the options chosen). Windows shows, as windows, the groups which have been opened. These windows differ in one aspect from **application windows**. Here we are dealing with **group windows**. In these windows, programs are displayed using program icons which are provided with a subtitle.

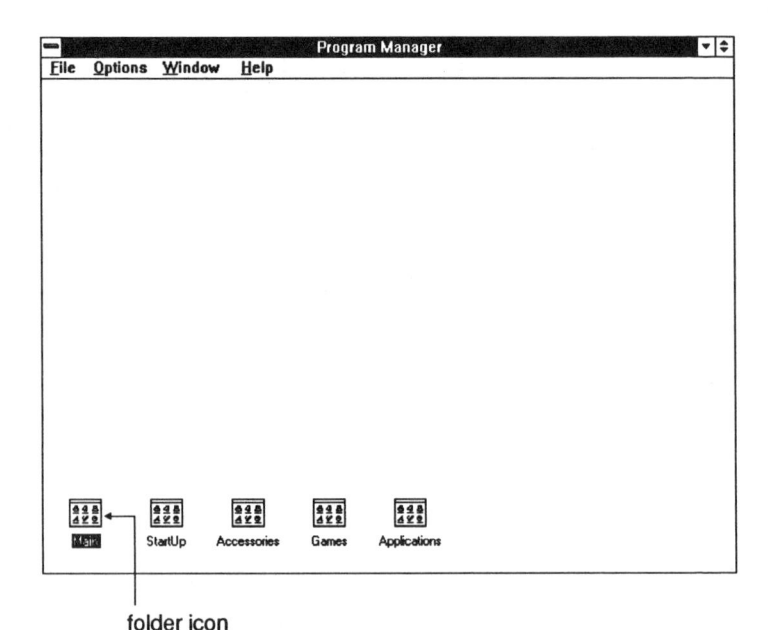

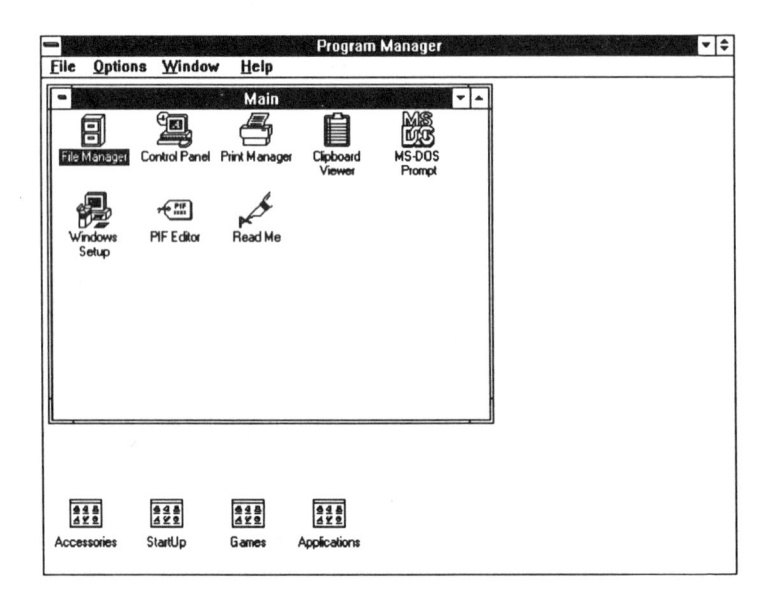

36 *The Program Manager*

folder icon

The most prominent difference with an application window is the absence of a menu bar. In addition, group windows cannot be relocated outside the application window. Try to drag the Main window outside the Program Manager window. You will see that this is impossible. Restore the window to its original place.

The icons in a group window represent programs which can be started with a double click. You can only start a program if the window in which that program is located has been opened.

2.1.1 Opening and closing group windows

You open a group window by double clicking on the group icon. You close it again by clicking on the **minimize button**. This works just as with application windows. You will probably observe a small difference with normal windows: in a document window which is not active, i.e. one in which you are not currently working, the **control menu button**, the **maximize button** and the **minimize button** are not available. These buttons appear in the window bar only when you click on a random spot in the window, thus activating it.

Now open the Accessories, Games and StartUp groups. Then close the four group windows and move the icons in the Program Manager window. To move an icon, place the tip of the mouse pointer on it and drag it to the desired spot. Finally, open the four group windows once more.

2.1.2 Arranging group windows

The Program Manager desktop can give a rather disorganized impression depending upon the way you have moved the icons or the Main window. In order to make the document windows more orderly, you could try to make optimal use of the available space by relocating, maximizing and minimizing. However, due to the fact that the components of the group windows frequently change, this is a tiresome chore. That is why the Program Manager is equipped with a menu which contains special options for arranging windows. The *Window* menu options are shown in the following diagram:

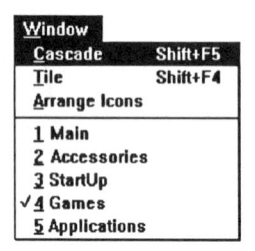

```
Window
 Cascade      Shift+F5
 Tile         Shift+F4
 Arrange Icons
 1 Main
 2 Accessories
 3 StartUp
√4 Games
 5 Applications
```

Choose from the *Window* menu the option *Cascade*. Your screen now looks like this:

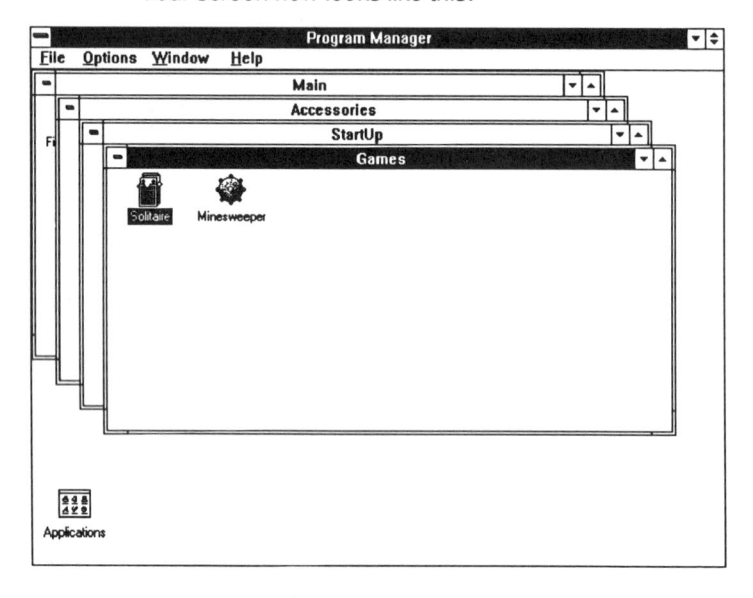

The four open windows are now stacked upon one another and occupy almost the entire application window. The order of sequence of the windows may be a little different on your screen. This depends upon the order

Groups

in which you opened the windows. This is not important for the following exercise. This arrangement has the advantage that within the group windows there is a great deal of space for the program icons. There is often sufficient room for the display of all the program icons without having to make use of the scroll bars. However, one disadvantage is that you can only choose programs in the top window, that is, the window in the foreground. Nevertheless, it is possible to call up other document windows in a reasonably easy way: click once on a random spot in the window which you wish to call up. Place all the windows in the foreground one by one in this way. Then try to restore the original order of sequence.

The second option in the *Window* menu is *Tile*. Activate this option. You see the result in the following diagram:

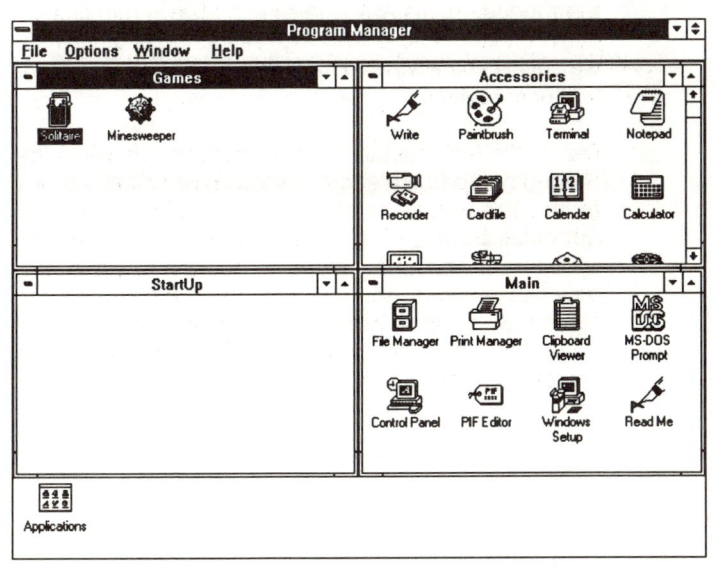

Windows has used the total available Program Manager desktop to equally divide the opened windows. This arrangement is handy if you need several groups at the same time. In this way you can get them all onto your screen. One disadvantage is, however, that the document windows are relatively small and that not all program icons are visible. For this reason, the Accessories window is now equipped with a scroll bar.

2.1.3 Arranging icons

You have probably noticed that the program icons remain at the same place in the group window when you relocate the window or alter its size. You could also arrange the icons manually, but that is laborious and time consuming. That is why we choose the *Auto arrange* option from the *Options* menu.

As soon as this option has been activated, all icons in all group windows, whether reduced to icons or not, will be rearranged. In this way, the screen always remains orderly. If there is no convincing reason to act otherwise, we advise you always to have this option activated as a matter of routine.

Due to the fact that there are no programs as yet in the Startup group (more about this later), you might as well reduce this window to an icon. To do this, click on the **minimize button** of this group or select the *Minimize* option from the Control menu of the Startup group window. An empty space has now been created on the screen. By again selecting the *Tile* option from the *Window* menu, the group windows will appear on the screen as follows:

Groups 41

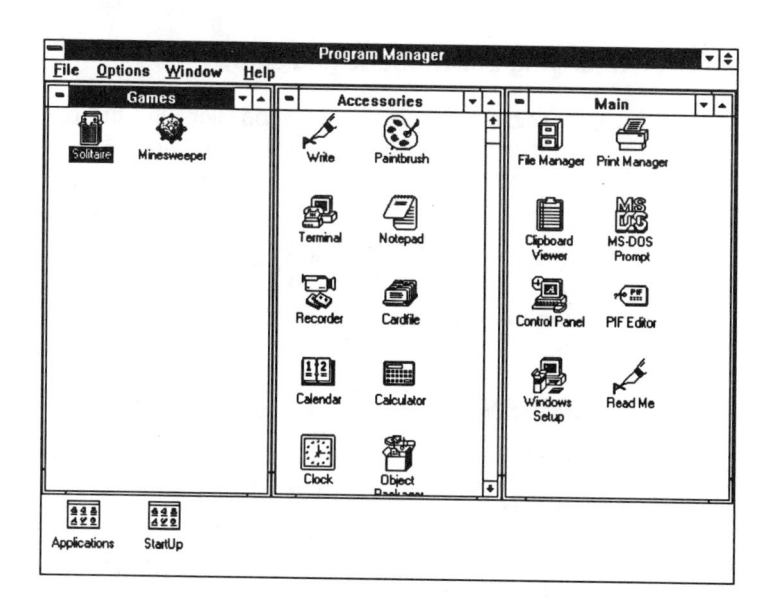

2.1.4 Exercises 8 and 9

8) Close the Games group window and place the other windows next to each other.

9) Open the Games group again. Reduce the window as shown in the following diagram and move it to the lower right-hand corner.

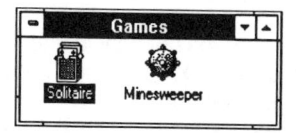

If you are really in a hurry, you may skip the following subsections (2.1.5 to 2.1.10) for the moment and proceed immediately to section 2.2.

2.1.5 Changing descriptions and setup

It is possible to change the composition and the descriptions of the groups to your own requirements. First we shall change the name of the Control panel in Main. This is done as follows:

1) Choose the Control panel by clicking on the icon once.
2) Open the *File* menu and choose the *Properties* option.

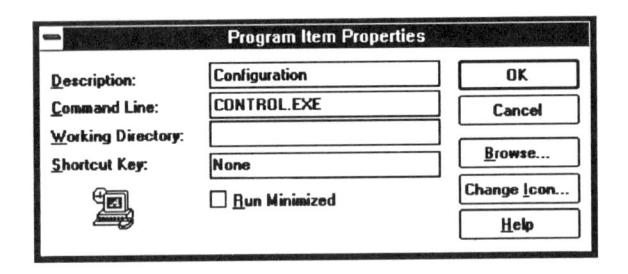

Program Item Properties		
Description:	Configuration	OK
Command Line:	CONTROL.EXE	Cancel
Working Directory:		
Shortcut Key:	None	Browse...
	☐ Run Minimized	Change Icon...
		Help

Type the word 'Configuration' in the textbox and then click on the *OK* button. The new name subsequently appears under the icon on the screen. If the cursor is not in the *Description* textbox, click somewhere in that box to activate it.

We shall deal with the other fields in the following subsections.

The *Properties* option serves not only to alter the names of programs, it also allows you to change group names. However, this can only take place if you reduce to an icon the group whose name you wish to change, or if you activate the group icon in question.

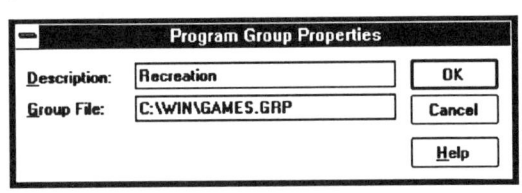

Program Group Properties		
Description:	Recreation	OK
Group File:	C:\WIN\GAMES.GRP	Cancel
		Help

The title of the dialogue box is no longer *Program Item Properties*, it is now *Program Group Properties*. The box now has less buttons. Now change the name of the Games group to, for instance, 'Recreation'. When you have done this, restore the original name.

You can also change the contents of a group very easily. Open the Main group and the Games group and place them adjacent to each other on the screen. You can now move a program by clicking on it and dragging it from one group to the other using the mouse. When you have finished practising, restore the original setup.

2.1.6 Creating and deleting groups

One of the most important features of the Program Manager is the possibility of creating new groups. During the installation of Windows, five groups are created for the most important programs.

By composing groups personally, you can gather all the programs you need for a certain task.

Creating new groups
To make a new group, open the *File* menu and choose the *New* option. The following dialogue box will appear on your screen:

```
┌─────────────────────────────────────┐
│ ▬    New Program Object             │
├─────────────────────────────────────┤
│ ┌─New──────────────┐  ┌─────────┐   │
│ │ ◉ Program Group  │  │   OK    │   │
│ │ ○ Program Item   │  ├─────────┤   │
│ │                  │  │ Cancel  │   │
│ │                  │  ├─────────┤   │
│ │                  │  │  Help   │   │
│ └──────────────────┘  └─────────┘   │
└─────────────────────────────────────┘
```

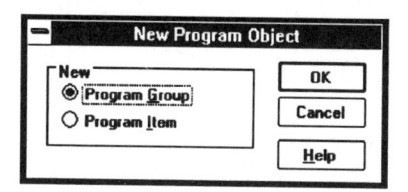

Select the *Program Group* option using the mouse and click on the *OK* button. Another dialogue box will then appear. Enter the name of the group in the *Description* box. Do not enter any name in the Group File box; Windows does this automatically. As description, type in

'Project 1'. When you have clicked on *OK*, Windows will make a new group under the heading 'Project 1'.

Placing programs in a group

You still have to put programs into this new group. Open the *File* menu again and select the *New* option. Select *Program Item* and click on the *OK* button. The dialogue box *Program Item Properties* appears on the screen (see section 2.1.5). The cursor is located in the *Description* box. By pressing the Tab key, you can move from one text box to the other. In the *Description* box you should enter the text which should appear under the icon. Behind *Command Line* type the name of the program which you wish to start up. To include the Clock program, for example, in the new group, type 'clock.exe'. Normally you should enter the complete path name, in this case, 'c:\win\clock.exe'.

Searching for programs

Windows is also very helpful here if you do not know the file name or if you wish to select a path name from a list of choices. Click on the *Browse* button. In the dialogue box which appears on your screen, you can look through the entire disk using the mouse and introduce the desired program into the group.

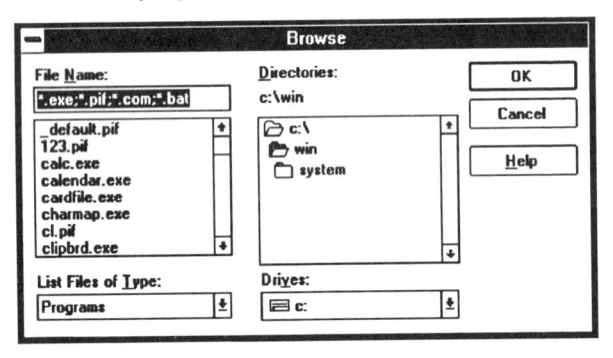

From the *Directories* list, choose the directory or drive through which you wish to search by double clicking on its name. Under *File Name* you will see all the files with the extensions EXE, PIF, COM and BAT in the chosen directory. Use the scroll bar if more files are present than fit into the list of choices. It is, of course, also possible to change the standard code for the file name or to restrict it to one of the possibilities provided.

When you have found the desired program, double click on it to admit it to the group. We have now reached the stage where we can introduce three new programs into the 'Project 1' group. Close all dialogue boxes which are still open. Activate the 'Project 1' group if it is not yet active and choose the option *New* from the *File* menu. Click on *Program Item* and then *Browse*.

CALC.EXE
You will find the CALC.EXE program in the Windows directory. Double click on its name and confirm this using the *OK* button in the *Program Item Properties* dialogue box. If you wish, you may enter a name, but that is not necessary. Windows will automatically register the file name without extension under the icon, in this case, 'Calc'.

SYSEDIT.EXE
Now do the same with regard to the SYSEDIT.EXE program from the subdirectory SYSTEM. This program allows you to examine and alter, quickly and easily, the configuration data in the files CONFIG.SYS, AUTOEXEC.BAT, WIN.INI and SYSTEM.INI.

Copying a program from another group
Finally, Notepad should be admitted as the last program into the new group. Just as with both other programs, you can do this using the *New* option from the *File* menu, but this manoeuvre can also be performed more simply. As you know, it is possible to drag an icon to another group. However, in doing so, the corresponding icon will be removed from its original group. If you hold down the Ctrl key while dragging, you make a **copy** of the program in the new group. The program itself remains in the other group. The new group now appears as follows:

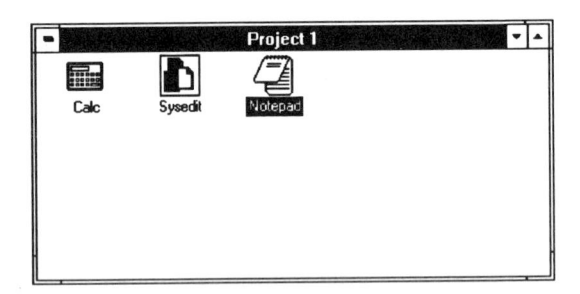

Choosing another icon

When you place programs in a group, you do not have to worry about the icons which represent the programs. Each Windows program has one or more icons.

If, however, you wish to have a different icon than the one in standard usage, click on the *Change Icon* button in the *Program Item Properties* dialogue box. The following dialogue box appears on your screen:

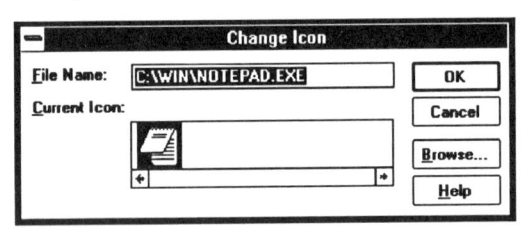

Using the *Browse* button, you can load another file containing icons. The two most important files dealing with this are PROGMAN.EXE and MORICONS.DLL. We wish to attempt to give Notepad the icon which is shown in the following diagram. First activate the Notepad icon by clicking on it and select the *Properties* option from the *File* menu. Then click on *Change Icon*. Subsequently, in the *Change Icon* dialogue box, click on *Browse* and select PROGMAN.EXE. Then click on *OK* and move to the desired icon using the scroll bar.

When you have found the icon of your choice, you only have to double click on *OK* and the Notepad will receive a new icon. In this way you can furnish a program with the icon of your choice. It is worth the effort to see if you can find interesting icons.

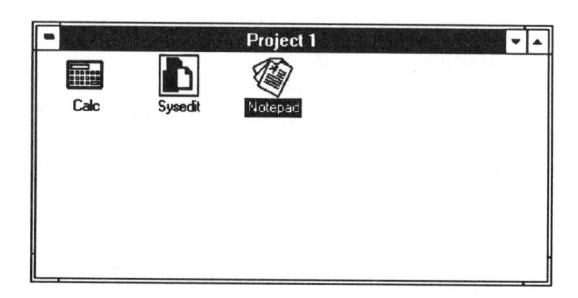

Deleting programs

You are now able to discover on your own how to remove a program from a group. The individual steps can be found in the following summary.

2.1.7 Summary

Creating Program Groups

1. Select the *New* option from the *File* menu,
2. select the *Program Group* option,
3. register the group name in the *Description* box.

Putting programs into a group

1. Select the *New* option from the *File* menu,
2. select the *Program Item* option,
3. register the icon description in the *Description* box and the name of the program (the entire path name if required) in the *Command Line* box.

Deleting programs

1. Mark the program which is to be deleted,

2. select the *Delete* option from the *File* menu. The program will only be removed from the group and not from the disk.

Deleting a group

1. Reduce the group which is to be deleted to an icon and mark it,
2. select the *Delete* option from the *File* menu.

Copying a program from another group

Hold down the Ctrl key while dragging the icon from one group to the other.

Registering a text for an icon

1. Choose the *Properties* option from the *File* menu (Alt-Enter is the shortcut key combination),
2. register the text in the *Description* box.

Choosing another icon

1. Select the *Properties* option from the *File* menu,
2. click on the button *Change icon*,
3. state the file name (PROGMAN.EXE),
4. search for a suitable icon using the scroll bar,
5. double click on *OK*.

2.1.8 Associating documents with programs

In the groups which are set up during the installation, you will find programs which can be started up by clicking on them. In these programs, files can be opened and edited. If you wish, for instance, to work on a letter using Write, then you should first start up that program and then use one of the Write options to load the letter.

If you are frequently working on the same document for a period of time, you can use the possibility of attaching the document to the program which you are using. This is reasonably simple. Select *Properties* from the *File* menu. Behind the file name in the *Command line* box, specify the name of the document which is to be loaded automatically when you start up the program. As you know, you can click on this box using the mouse and move the cursor to the end of the line using the cursor keys. Make sure there is a space between the file name and the document name.

If you have associated a document to a program, you can alter the text under an icon in order to indicate that a document will be automatically loaded when the program is started up.

Now attach the text file README.WRI to the Notepad in the 'Project 1' group.

2.1.9 Other program properties

In the Working Directory text box in the *Program Item Properties* dialogue box, you can specify the directory in which a certain program should be automatically started up. This option is recommended in order to achieve a good, orderly overall view of the files on the hard disk. If you have, for example, a separate subdirectory for draft letters which you write using Notepad, state the subdirectory in the Working Directory box:

```
c:\text\drft_let
```

Notepad will now be started up from the specified directory. Files will also be saved in this directory by default.

We shall now give an indication of how to use this possibility of quickly starting up a program. More information concerning this is available in section 2.2.

You will find the Shortcut key option in the *Program Item*

Properties dialogue box. If you enter one letter here, Windows will make this into a shortcut key which you can use to start up the program. In the case of Notepad, this could be the letter N, for example.

Go to the Shortcut key option using the Tab key or by clicking on the text box and type the letter N. As you see, Windows adds the Ctrl and the Alt key to this letter. From now onwards you can start up the Notepad program *at any time* in the Program Manager by using Ctrl-Alt-N, even if the group window in which the program is located is not active.

Finally, we would like to mention the possibility of starting up the program as an icon instead of as a window or full-screen. This can be particularly advantageous in the case of automatic starting using the Startup group window (more about this later), or when using programs such as Calendar or Calculator which generally fulfil their functions in the background and which you may only wish to employ now and again. If you would like to use this possibility, click on the *Run Minimized* option in the *Program Item Properties* dialogue box.

2.1.10 Other options for operating groups

The *File* menu also contains the following options:

Open	Starts up the chosen program.
Move	Moves an icon from one group to the other. This gives the same result as dragging an icon to another group.
Copy	Copies a program to another group. The program does not disappear from the original group. This has the same effect as holding down the Ctrl key while dragging an icon.
Delete	Deletes individual programs or complete groups of programs.

To delete a program group, reduce it to an icon, mark the icon and select the *Delete* option. If you delete a program, it will be removed merely from the group and not from the disk.

Run — Starts up the program which you request in the dialogue box on your screen.

In the *Options* menu you will encounter three possibilities:

Auto Arrange — The icons will be rearranged every time the size of the window is altered.

Minimize on Use — When a program has been started up, the Program Manager is reduced to an icon.

Save Settings on Exit — Activate this option if you wish to preserve the organization of the desktop as it was during your last session. Turn this option off if you wish to preserve a certain layout for a longer period of time.

With this information you are now equipped to execute all daily tasks using the Program Manager. Here, we would also like to make you aware of the extensive Help function which is available for most Windows programs. If you meet the *Help* option or *?* in the menu bar, you can ask for detailed information about the corresponding program. The operation of the Help function is self-evident.

2.2 Starting up programs

To start up a program, first open the group window in which you have placed that program. Subsequently, double click on the corresponding icon. The application window will be opened and you can get to work.

If you wish to use the keyboard as an alternative to the mouse, move the cursor using the arrow keys to the program of your choice and confirm the selection using Enter.

The quickest method of starting up programs works independently of whichever window is active. We have already mentioned this previously. In the *Shortcut key* box in the *Program Item Properties* dialogue box, allocate a letter which will be used to call up a specific program from the entire Program Manager. However, this method which makes use of the fixed combinations of Ctrl and Alt, should remain restricted to a few well-used programs.

The Startup group window

One of the new features of Windows 3.1 is the possibility of activating one or more programs automatically by placing them in a window when Windows is started up. The previous version also contained the possibility of automatically activating a program at the outset. However, this had to be separately entered in a line specially reserved for this purpose in the file WIN.INI.

Due to the fact that Windows was not only developed for ease of operation but also for the execution of tasks (more or less) simultaneously, it is very feasible that you would wish to run several programs at the same time when carrying out certain jobs in Windows. If you are working on a certain project using various programs during a lengthy period of time, place these programs together in the Startup group window. Every time you start up Windows, the selected programs will be automatically activated, with the accompanying documents if required.

You can relocate the selected programs using the mouse. If you wish to remove them from the original windows, just drag them to the new window; if you also wish to retain them in the original windows, hold down the Ctrl key while dragging.

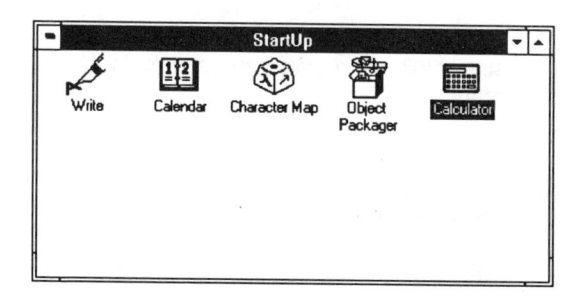

2.3 Exiting the Program Manager

As you know, exiting the Program Manager also means exiting Windows.

There are three ways to exit the Program Manager:

1. Select the *Close* option from the *Control* menu,
2. select the *Exit Windows* option from the *File* menu, or
3. double click on the Control menu button.

In all these three cases, a small dialogue box will appear on your screen. You must confirm in this box that you really wish to quit the program. If you wish to preserve the current layout of the Program Manager and the document windows for the next time you start up Windows, select the option *Save Settings on Exit* from the *Options* menu.

If you accidentally give the command to close the window, click on *Cancel*. Otherwise you should confirm using *OK*. In this way, you exit the Program Manager and Windows.

After working through both these introductory chapters you now command Windows to the extent that you can begin more complicated tasks. In the following chapters we shall deal with other components of Windows. We shall display, in particular, the possibilities which arise from the interaction of individual programs. The first result of this procedure can be seen in the following diagram.

Lindberg & Partners Ltd.
Parachute Makers to the Queen.

Our Motto is:
Gravity can kill

9 Rooftop Boulevard,
Madeira

Mr. N. Armstrong,
1 Apollo Rise,
Cape Canaveral.

Dear Sir,
With regard to your recent order, we wish to state the following amounts:

Art.Nr.	Article	Quantity	Price £	Total £
1.	Silk	50 sq.m	25.00 p/sq.m	1250
26.	Cord	65 m.	1.25 p/m.	81.25
33.	Thread	5 km.	8 p.p/m	400.00
42.	Bag	1	104.48	104.48
51.	Cushions	2	75.00	150.00
			subtotal	1985.73
			VAT 17.5%	347.50
			Total	2333.23

Please pay within 30 days

In order to construct this document, we have used mainly two programs which are part of the Windows package. One of these is the Windows graphical program Paintbrush and the other is the word processing program Write. We shall deal with these programs extensively in both the following chapters.

3 Paintbrush

Paintbrush is a graphical program. It belongs to the Accessories group. Thus, in order to start up this program, you first need to open this program group. If the icon is not visible in the document window which appears on your screen, run through the contents of the window using the scroll bars. As soon as Paintbrush becomes visible, you can start it up with a double click.

Paintbrush offers the possibility of drawing in colour. Of course, you can only make use of this option if you have a colour monitor and colour display adapter. If your computer is equipped with a monochrome adapter, the colours will be reproduced in differing patterns. When we speak of colours in this chapter, we also mean patterns in the case of a monochrome adapter.

Note: If you reproduce your drawing on a black-and-white printer, it is better to reject the colour option. This is particularly applicable when you use grey tints. You can discover how to switch the colour option on and off in section 3.13.3.

In contrast to the other Windows programs, Paintbrush makes use of both mouse buttons. Unless otherwise stated, in using the term 'mouse button' we always refer to the left button. In addition to the right mouse button, the keyboard is also necessary for many functions.

3.1 The window

After starting up Paintbrush the following window appears.

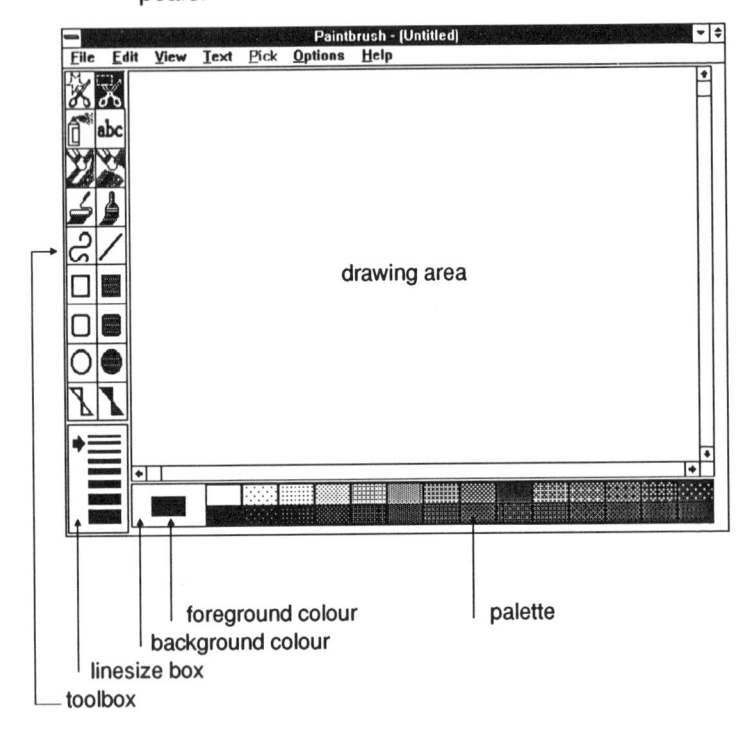

foreground colour
background colour
palette
linesize box
toolbox

In order to have the largest possible area available for the following jobs, enlarge the window to *Maximum window*. This is done by clicking on the maximize button which is located in the upper right-hand corner of the window bar.

We shall first examine the individual elements in Paintbrush.

Toolbox
The toolbox enables you to choose tools to design your drawing. In this way, for example, you can cut out

The window 57

pieces of a drawing, spray a surface in colour or draw rectangles and circles. The following diagram shows the individual tools:

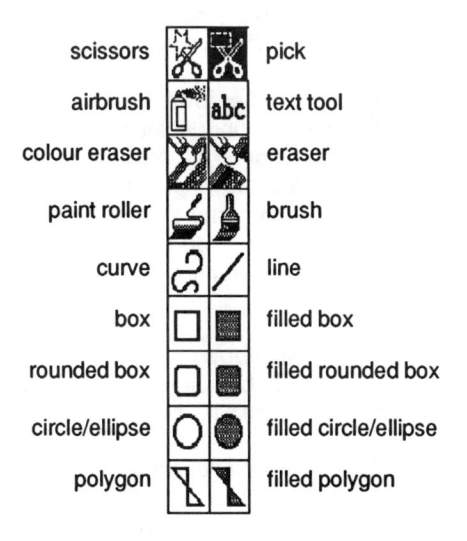

scissors	pick
airbrush	text tool
colour eraser	eraser
paint roller	brush
curve	line
box	filled box
rounded box	filled rounded box
circle/ellipse	filled circle/ellipse
polygon	filled polygon

Drawing area
You make your drawings in the drawing area. The maximum size of the drawing area depends upon your computer's display adapter card and the size of your computer's memory.

The cursor
The cursor marks the position where a line or other object will appear. The form of the cursor depends upon the tool which you have chosen. The cursor becomes an arrow outside the drawing area.

The palette
The palette offers you the possibility of choosing different colours for the drawing. If you have a monochrome display adapter, you will see differing patterns instead of colours. You choose the foreground and background colours from the palette.

Foreground colour
The foreground colour is the colour you use to draw. To choose a foreground colour, place the cursor on the palette and click on the desired colour using the **left** mouse button. The foreground colour can always be altered.

Background colour
The background colour is chosen using the **right** mouse button. This colour can be defined only at the start of the drawing. This is done by clicking on the desired colour and then selecting the *New* option from the *File* menu. You can change the background while drawing by, for instance, making a shadow effect for a caption.

The linesize box
The linesize box allows you to determine the thickness of the line you will use to draw.

Note: It may occur that the thinnest linewidth is not visible. This depends upon the size of the window. Nevertheless, you can choose this linesize and use it without any hindrance.

3.2 The first drawing

The first selections to be made at the beginning of your work with Paintbrush are those concerning the foreground and background colours.

The default setting has the brush as the active tool when Paintbrush has been opened. The icon of the active tool is always displayed in negative contrast.

To make the following small drawing of a house, we shall use the rectangle, line, gum, paint roller and airbrush.

Drawing a rectangle
Using the box tool, you are able to draw rectangles with a chosen size and linesize. We use these in our drawing to make the outline of the house, the window frames, the door and the chimney.

Click on the thinnest linewidth in the linesize box if this is not yet active, and then on the box tool. As you see, the cursor changes into a cross in the drawing area. Ensure that the foreground colour is black and the background colour is white.

You may begin the rectangle at any chosen corner. Press down the mouse button and hold it down while dragging the mouse to the opposite corner. There, release the mouse button. Now draw all the components of the house which you can make using this box tool.

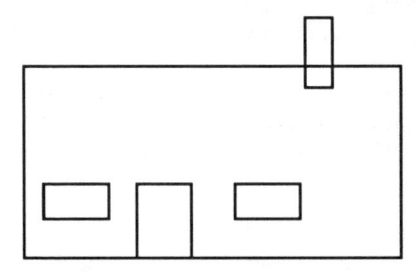

Drawing lines
The line tool is for drawing lines of a chosen length and thickness. In our drawing, we shall use this to make the dividing line between roof and walls.

Click on the line tool and place the cursor in the drawing area. The cursor changes into a cross. Move this cross to the beginning of the line. Now press the mouse button down and drag the mouse to the end of the line. There, release the mouse button. While drawing, the line follows the movements of the mouse, so that you can see exactly how the line will finally appear in the drawing. To draw the dividing line, set the cursor precisely on the upper left-hand corner of the rectangle and press down the mouse button. Subsequently, drag the mouse to the opposite side. You have reached precisely the correct position when the the vertical line of the cross exactly coincides with the vertical line of the rectangle and, in doing so, is no longer visible. Ensure that the line is horizontal.

Erasing
The eraser tools enable you to correct undesired changes in the drawing. Here, we shall use an eraser to rub out the line which runs through the chimney.

Click on the right eraser. The cursor changes into a small rectangle. Move it to the spot where you wish to begin erasing and click. Everything inside the rectangle, including the border of the rectangle, will be rubbed out. In fact, not everything is erased, but everything under the eraser takes on the colour of the background. The result is, however, the same.

A small tip: the size of the eraser depends upon the linesize. In order to erase a sizable area in one go, select a greater linesize. Now erase carefully the line from the chimney.

Colouring in enclosed areas.
You can colour in a enclosed area using the paint roller. Here we use this tool for the patterns of the bricks and roof slates.

Select the colour which you wish to use to colour in the enclosed area. Then click on the paint roller. The cursor changes into a paint roller. The lower left-hand corner of the cursor has a point. This is the so-called **hot spot** of the icon, in other words, this point must be placed upon the area which is to be filled in.

Be careful! If you click outside the enclosed area or if the area is not completely enclosed, the colour will flow out of the area and the entire drawing area will be filled in.

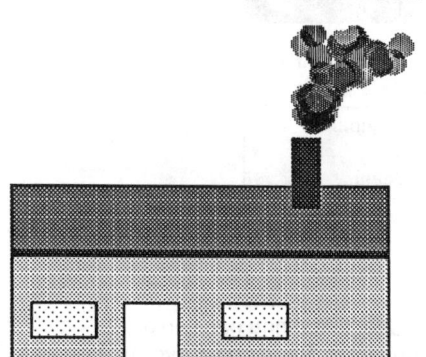

Choose a different colour for each area.

Spraying paint

To complete this masterpiece, we now wish to have a puff of smoke coming out of the chimney. The airbrush tool is very suitable for this. We choose the colour black for the smoke. Place the airbrush above the chimney, press and hold down the mouse button and drag the mouse to the right. The slower you drag, the more dense the spray of colour. Only a few points of colour appear if you use rapid movements. Continue spraying until the column of smoke has acquired the desired form.

Your first drawing using Paintbrush is now complete. If your drawing resembles the drawing in the previous diagram, you may be pleased with yourself. But probably something will have gone wrong here and there. You can read in section 3.4 how to correct an effort which has ended in an unsatisfactory result.

3.3 Saving and opening

If your drawing is successful, you can, of course, preserve it. Just as in all Windows programs, you will find the options for saving and opening files in the *File* menu.

```
File
  New
  Open...
  Save          Ctrl+S
  Save As...
  Page Setup...
  Print...
  Print Setup...
  Exit
```

Save

As you see, this menu has two options available for saving. These are *Save* and *Save As*. You use *Save As* in order to save a drawing for the first time or to save a drawing under another name. A new drawing has no name until it is saved for the first time. You see this on the title bar: 'Paintbrush - (Untitled)'. If you now choose *Save As*, you will see the following dialogue box:

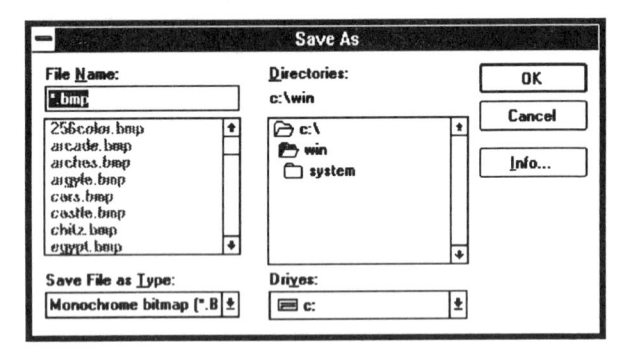

```
Save As
File Name:               Directories:           [ OK ]
[*.bmp]                  c:\win                 [ Cancel ]
256color.bmp             c:\
arcade.bmp               win                    [ Info... ]
arches.bmp               system
argyle.bmp
cars.bmp
castle.bmp
chitz.bmp
egypt.bmp
Save File as Type:       Drives:
[Monochrome bitmap (*.B)] [c:]
```

Type in, for example 'house' and press Enter. If you make a typing error, you can remove it using Backspace. The drawing will now be saved as HOUSE.BMP. The extension .BMP is default for Paintbrush drawings. Leave this unchanged for the time being. You can load the file again later using the name which has been registered. The directories on your screen may have different names than those in the diagram.

Saving and opening

When the drawing has been saved, the registered file name will be placed in the title bar instead of *('untitled')*.

Use the *Save* option (Ctrl-S is the shortcut key) to save a drawing while you are working on it. Acquire the habit of regularly saving your work between times in all programs in which you are working, to prevent a document or the most recent alterations to a document being lost due to a calamity like a power cut.

If you do not wish to save a drawing in the Paintbrush standard format, open the drop-down list at the bottom of the *Save File as Type* box to choose the PCX format or a BMP format with different colour relationships.

Open
If you wish later to load this drawing again, select the *Open* option. The following dialogue box appears on your screen:

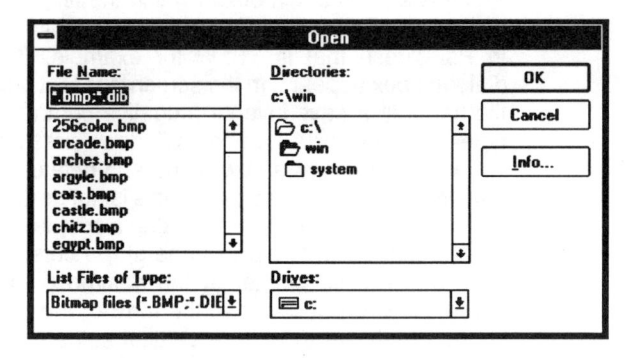

You only need to type the name 'house' and press Enter. After a moment the drawing will be loaded and you can work on it further. The contents of the *Directories* and *File Name* windows are probably different on your screen.

The *Save File as Type* box offers the choice out of the Paintbrush formats BMP and PCX. You can save files in these two formats but you can load another format:

MSP. MSP is the format used in Paint, the graphical program which was supplied with Windows before the 3.0 version. During the loading process, these files are converted into the Paintbrush format. This allows you to work on older drawings in the newer versions of Windows without any problem.

If you wish to save a drawing at a specific place or load it from there, there are a couple of extra procedures.

Operating the dialogue boxes
The *Open* and *Save* dialogue boxes can be almost entirely operated using the mouse. The only exception is the registration of a file name when saving.

These dialogue boxes resemble each other in all Windows programs. In some programs you will encounter options which are specific to that program.

There is always a text box in which the file name must be registered. This box always has a default extension. In Paintbrush that is *.BMP for example. When the dialogue box appears on the screen, the text box for the file name is always inverse (negative contrast). If you type in a letter or a number, Windows presumes that you wish to register a new name and deletes the contents of the box. In many cases, this is not desirable, because you often merely wish to alter a couple of characters. In that case, first press one of the cursor keys or place the mouse pointer at the desired place in the name. As you will observe, the form of the cursor will change from an arrow to a vertical stripe. If you now press the mouse button, you can add or delete a character at this spot.

Another box within the dialogue box shows the subdirectories in your computer. If there are more directories than fit into the window, a scroll bar will appear. Another box within the dialogue box shows the directories in your computer. If there are more directories than fit into the window, a scroll bar will appear.

If you wish to switch to another directory, double click on its name. In this way, you can move quickly and easily through the directory structure of a disk. You can always see which directory you are in by looking at *Directories*.

If you wish to switch to another drive, you can do so in yet another box. In this box, there is a drop-down list showing the available drives. You can open the window by clicking on the arrow and you may select a different drive if you wish.

To open a file, double click on its name in the list under *File Name*. All the files which have been saved in the current directory and which conform to the file pattern can be found in the window under the *File Name* text box. If, for instance, the file pattern *BMP is shown in the text box, you will only be able to see all the files which conform to this pattern. In other words, all the files with the extension BMP.

You place a file in the *File Name* box by clicking on its name. You can then load the file by clicking on *OK*. By double clicking you can load the file in a single action.

Other options which you may see in the dialogue box depend upon the program you are using.

3.4 Correcting mistakes

The mouse is not really ideal as a drawing instrument, due to the fact that, in many applications, it cannot be positioned precisely enough. The chance of ending up with a different result than the one imagined is reasonably large. That is why Paintbrush contains a whole series of functions to undo changes in the drawing.

3.4.1 Erase

You have already been introduced to the most important tool for correcting mistakes, the eraser. There is a normal eraser (right) and a colour eraser (left).

The normal eraser changes the colour of all objects with which it comes in contact into the background colour. The eraser works in the same way as an eraser which rubs out a pencil line from a sheet of paper.

The colour eraser has two functions:

1) It can give another colour to all objects with a certain colour. This is done by making the colour which is to be replaced the foreground colour, and the new colour the background colour. Now double click on the colour gum and the colours will be automatically changed.

2) It can change the current foreground colour into the current background colour. This allows you to remove certain colours specifically, without wiping out other colours in the area in question. If you have made the outline of the house black and you would now like to remove it, choose black as foreground colour and, for example, white as background colour and click on the colour eraser. If you then drag the eraser over the drawing, you will only rub out the black lines, the other colours remain intact.

Note: If you are working without colour, the colour eraser works just as the normal eraser.

Tips:

1) The size of the eraser depends upon the current linesize. If you wish to erase large areas in one go, choose a large linesize. For more detailed erasure, choose a thinner linesize.

2) If you wish to erase in a horizontal or vertical direc-

tion only, hold down the Shift key while dragging the eraser.

3.4.2 Undo

The second possibility of correcting mistakes in a drawing is by using the *Undo* option from the *Edit* menu. In order to give a further explanation of this option we have to examine Paintbrush a little more closely.

In principle, there are two possibilities of saving drawings and reproducing them on the screen. One possibility consists of saving each individual picture element and reproducing it on the screen. If you consider that a VGA screen card has a resolution of 640 x 480 = 307,200 picture elements, you can imagine how much memory a drawing occupies when it is stored on the disk. In addition, the size of the file increases with every extra colour which can be reproduced. An image like this is called a **pixel-oriented** image ('pixel' - picture element).

The other method works in a **vector-oriented** way. To draw a circle, for example, the only information necessary is the position of the centre and the radius. The amount of information which has to be saved is thus considerably less than when using the pixel-oriented method. In addition, the drawing is dealt with in such a way that each element (line, curve, surface etc.) can be addressed separately. Accordingly, each element can be enlarged, reduced, relocated or deleted retrospectively. This is by definition impossible when dealing with pixel-oriented drawings since no circles or lines, but picture elements have been saved.

It is not possible to ascertain which method is better - that depends upon the application. The vector-oriented *drawing* program may be preferred in the case of technical drawings due to the fact that all details can be described using vectors. Other applications lend themselves better to a pixel-oriented drawing method (*paint* program) like Paintbrush. Think of drawing a landscape or a face, subjects which are more difficult to draw using only lines and circles.

In contrast to the case of vector-oriented drawings, problems do arise when elements have to be removed from pixel-oriented drawings. The reasons for this have been mentioned above. Nevertheless, Paintbrush does offer the possibility of correcting undesired changes. The *Undo* option can eliminate everything which has been drawn since the choice of the current tool. If you accidentally press the mouse button outside the enclosed area when you are colouring in, the entire surrounding area will be filled up with the colour in use. This also happens if the area is not completely enclosed. By using *Undo*, you can remove the consequences of this accident. However, this only works as long as the object has not been anchored in the drawing. You anchor an object in the drawing by:

1) choosing another tool,
2) clicking on the scroll bar, or
3) changing the size of the window.

Thus, if you make a mistake, correct it immediately. Otherwise you run the risk that the mistake will be anchored in the drawing and can only be corrected with great difficulty.

3.4.3 Using Backspace

The Backspace key provides a third possibility of correcting a mistake in a drawing. If, for example, you think that you have applied too much paint when using the airbrush, you do not have to remove the whole painted surface with *Undo*. Backspace is handy in this case.

When you press Backspace, the cursor changes into a rectangle with a diagonal cross. You can now erase if you hold down the mouse button. However, there is a difference with normal erasure; only those elements

Correcting mistakes 69

which have been drawn since the choice of the current tool will be removed. If, in our example, you have sprayed the column of smoke over the whole house, you can remove this by using Backspace without erasing other parts of the drawing at the same time.

Backspace has the same effect with all tools. However, both erasers form an exception to this rule. In this case, the effects are precisely the other way around. Everything that you have removed can be restored. If you have accidentally erased too much, you can restore these components by using the Backspace key.

3.4.4 Enlarging screen sections

Although the *Zoom In* option is generally not used for correction, it is nevertheless often used for working on faulty details. You will find the option *Zoom In* under the *View* menu. When you have activated this option, a rectangle will appear in the drawing area. Use this rectangle to select the fragment you wish to enlarge, and click. The fragment under the rectangle will now occupy the entire drawing area. You can now work on the individual picture elements. You will see, in the upper left-hand corner, the influence of the applied changes on the drawing in real size. Choose the brush to work on a screen section.

Click using the left mouse button to establish a picture element. Use the right mouse button to remove a picture element. In fact, you give a picture element the foreground colour using the left mouse button and the background colour using the right button.

When you are satisfied with the result, you can zoom out again. You will find the *Zoom Out* option in the *View* menu. Thus, you will return to the real size drawing again.

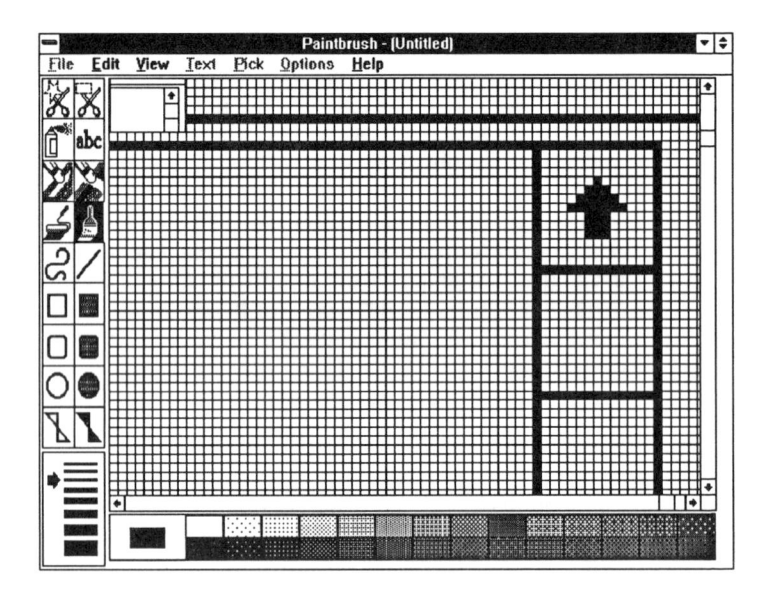

3.4.5 Summary

Paintbrush provides four methods of correcting mistakes in a drawing:

1) You can rub out a chosen part of the drawing using the erasers.
2) The *Undo* option deletes all the changes you have made since choosing the current tool.
3) Using Backspace you remove only those parts of the drawing made since the choosing the current tool.
4) The *Zoom In* option enables you to work on your drawing at pixel level.

In order to deal with not only the theory but also the practice, it is advisable to carry out the following exercises. If you still have the former drawing on your screen, choose the eraser tool in combination with the largest possible linesize, and rub it out.

3.5 Exercises 10 to 12

10) Draw three rectangles stacked upon each other. Fill them in, each with a different colour. Remove the colour using a single option.

11) Choose black as the foreground colour and white as background colour. Again fill the rectangles in using different colours. Remove the black lines without changing the coloured surfaces. Then erase the complete drawing.

Note: You can only do the following exercise if your computer has a colour display adapter.

12) Choose the brush and draw a horizontal line. Use the *Zoom in* option to make it a dotted line. Then erase the line.

3.6 Scissors, pick, brush, line and box

The **scissors** are among the most important tools for working on your drawing. The scissors allow you to cut out irregular shapes. The **pick** allows you to cut out rectangular shapes. The **brush** is for free-form drawing with lines of varying thickness. **Line** is for drawing straight lines. **Box** allows you to make squares and rectangles.

3.6.1 Drawing a window

The following image has been made using the five tools mentioned above.

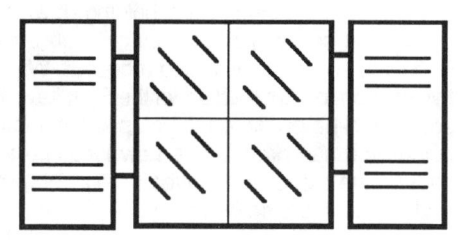

We have done this as follows:

Drawing the frame
1. Select the fourth linesize from the top and a black foreground.
2. Click on the empty rectangle and draw the frame.

Drawing the lattices
1. Select the brush and the thinnest linesize. The brush is really meant for free-hand drawing but with a little help it can also be used for drawing straight lines.
2. To draw a horizontal line, first place the cursor in the middle of the left-hand side of the window. Now hold down the Shift key and draw a line to the right-hand side of the frame.
3. Draw the vertical line in the same way.

Drawing diagonal lines
1. Choose the line tool and the thinnest linesize.
2. This handy option enables you to draw an exact diagonal line. Place the cursor in the window pane in the upper left-hand corner where the first diagonal line should begin. Now hold down the Shift key and draw the line downwards to the right. As you see, the line remains straight and at a constant angle, even when the cursor deviates from the ideal line.
3. Draw both other lines in this way.

Copying lines
1. We shall now copy the lines on the one window pane to the other three. Select the pick. Using this tool we drag a defining rectangle around the diagonal lines.
2. Move the cursor to the upper left-hand corner of the section you wish to define. If you now drag the mouse to the opposite corner while holding down the mouse button, the section will be marked with a dotted line. This marked section is called a **cutout**. When defining this section, do not hold down the Shift key otherwise a square will be produced. If you place the cursor in the cutout you can drag it to a new location. In this procedure, the cutout is removed from its original position and placed in the new position.

Scissors, pick, brush, line and box

3. Hold down the Ctrl key while dragging. This means that you copy the cutout instead of merely relocating it. The Ctrl key ensures that the original contents of the screen remain intact. Place the cursor in the cutout, hold down the Ctrl key and drag the cutout to the next pane.
4. Do this with the remaining window panes.

Note: When you release the mouse button, the cursor changes back from an arrow into a cross. If you move the mouse, you will notice that the form of the cursor changes as soon as you enter the cutout.

The window is completed. Now we only need to draw the shutters.

Drawing the shutters
1. Select the third linesize from the top and the box tool.
2. Draw the outline of the shutter as near to the window as possible.
3. Select a thin linesize and the brush or the line, and draw the top three horizontal lines. Remember that you can also use the Shift key to draw straight horizontal and vertical lines. If the lines are not equal in length, you can use the *Zoom in* option from the *View* menu to correct the length.
4. Copy these three lines to the lower part. Use the pick once more to mark the three lines. Then place the cursor in the cutout and drag in downwards while holding down the Ctrl key.
5. Now mark the whole shutter and place it in the proper position (without holding down the Ctrl key).
6. Then immediately press down the Ctrl key again and copy the complete shutter to the other side of the window.
7. If you now join the window and shutters using the brush or line, the drawing is complete.

3.6.2 Summary

Combined with brush and line, the Shift key allows you to draw straight horizontal and vertical lines. At the same time, the line tool combined with the Shift key allows you to draw straight diagonal lines.

The Shift key also has a special function in combination with the box tool. If you hold this key down while moving the mouse, Paintbrush will draw a square.

The scissors and pick allow you to relocate parts of the drawing or to copy them in combination with the Ctrl key.

You may use another key in combination with the scissors and pick: the Shift key. This ensures that the cutout leaves a trail behind it during dragging. This style is useful, for instance, to suggest movement within a drawing.

Up until now we have always used cutouts in the 'transparent' mode. This means that the previous contents of the screen remain visible and the cutout is laid on top of them. If the cutout should cover or blanket over the the new area, use the right mouse button while dragging, instead of the left one.

The left mouse button is used for transparent relocation and the right button for opaque relocation.

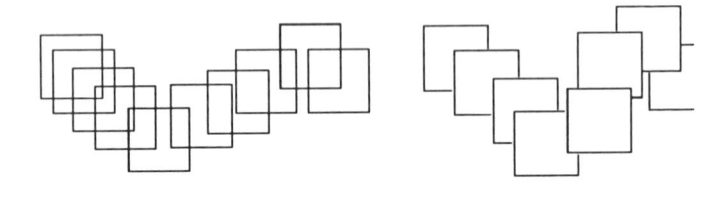

transparant relocation   opaque relocation

Thus, there are six possible combinations for use of the scissors and pick. The following table gives a list of the combinations and their effects:

	left mouse button	right mouse button
no key	transparent relocation	opaque relocation
Ctrl	transparent copying	opaque copying
Shift	transparent trail	opaque trail

3.7 Showing the cursor position

It is sometimes necessary to work more precisely than is possible without optical assistance. In a case like this, select the *Cursor Position* option from the *View* menu. A small window will appear in the upper right-hand corner. This displays the current cursor position in picture elements. The first number represents the X value (horizontal) and the second number represents the Y value (vertical). The counting begins in the upper left-hand corner with the co-ordinates 0,0. The maximum value depends upon your computer's display adapter card.

If you now move the cursor, you will observe that the values in this small window continually change. This provides you with the possibility to draw with the precision of one pixel.

3.8 Making a map

In the following paragraphs we shall draw a map using measurements which we have already determined.

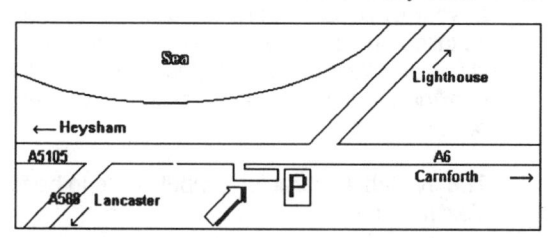

This will later be included in the Cardfile program. For this reason, the map may not be larger than 300 points horizontally and 100 points vertically. We wish to define this drawing area using a rectangle with these measurements. Select the thinnest linesize and the box tool. Switch on the cursor position display. Move the cursor to the position 100,100. Press down the mouse button. Drag the rectangle to the co-ordinates 400, 200 and release the mouse button.

If you want to switch the cursor position display off, select the *Cursor Position* option from the *View* menu again.

Complete the map. Use the brush, line, paint roller and box. Do not add any text as yet. We shall do that in the following section.

3.9 The text tool

It is necessary to be able to introduce text into many application areas of a graphical program. That is why you will find a *Text* menu in the menu bar, with various options for designing letters and texts. A check mark in front of the option's name indicates that the option is activated.

The *Font* dialogue box (see next page) shows which fonts (letter types) are available. The amount depends upon which printer you have installed. You always have at your disposal, regardless of which printer has been installed, the so-called *True Type Fonts* which are provided as standard with Windows 3.1. These fonts appear on the screen exactly as they later appear on the printer.

The available character attributes are to be found in the *Text* menu.

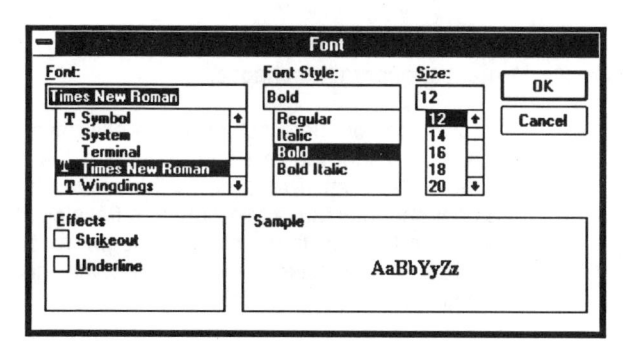

The text tool

In the *Font* dialogue box, there is a box which deals with the possible point sizes of the different characters. The TrueType font (recognizable by the T before the name) contains the greatest number of possibilities; these characters can be scaled, in other words, you can personally determine the desired size on a scale ranging between 8 and 72. One point reflects 1/72 of an inch, meaning that the size of a character can vary from 1/9 of an inch to a whole inch, or 0.3 mm to approximately 2.5 cm.

In addition, the dialogue box provides the possibility of reproducing the characters in bold and/or italics. These attributes can also be allocated to a text using the corresponding options from the *Text* menu.

There are no strict rules for choosing a font and its size. Experiment with the different combinations and observe what comes out of the printer. One rule of thumb is, perhaps, that use of more than three fonts, probably combined with various attributes, tends to make your document appear rather chaotic.

In order to complete our map, we still have to include the text. Select the text tool and place the cursor just outside the map. Press down the mouse button. The cursor changes into a text-cursor, a flashing stripe. This is an indication that you can begin to type. Type 'A5105'. If you make a mistake in doing this, you can delete it using Backspace.

When you have typed this letter, open the *Fonts* option from the *Text* menu. Because the text has not yet been anchored in the drawing, it can still be altered. As you know, choosing another tool or clicking on a scroll bar means that the changes you have just implemented become permanent. Choose different fonts consecutively. The alterations are immediately visible on the screen. We have chosen the Arial TrueType font with point size 10 and the feature Bold for the notation on the map.

Now press Enter. The cursor moves to the next line. Type consecutively, 'A588', 'A6', 'Heysham', 'Lancaster', 'Lighthouse' and 'Carnforth'. If there is no more room on the map, place the text-cursor somewhere else on the screen. Remember that, in doing this, you will anchor all the text which you have introduced up until this moment. Alterations in fonts, attributes and size will no longer have any effect. The P (Parking) is size 18.

All the text has been introduced with the exception of 'Sea'. Now you can cut out these captions using the scissors and put them at the correct place.

Select the *Outline* option from the *Text* menu. In order to make the effects of this option visible, other colours must be chosen for the foreground and background. You gain the best results by exchanging foreground and background colours. This can be done by clicking on white in the palette using the left mouse button, and black using the right mouse button. Then type the word

'Sea' somewhere in the drawing area. Select these words using the scissors or pick and move them to the sea on the map. You use exactly the same procedure with the *Shadow* option.

Set the adapted text at the proper place and save the map under the name ROADMAP.

3.10 Using Circle/Ellipse and Curve

Circles and ellipses can be drawn using the circle/ellipse tool. Curve allows you to make curved lines.

The following drawing is made using only the circle/ellipse and curve tools. With the skills you have acquired by now, it should be no problem to draw this clown.

Nevertheless, we shall outline several little tricks which allow you to reach your objective quickly and easily.

Circle/ellipse
Choose the circle/ellipse tool. Move the cursor to the upper left-hand corner where the ellipse will begin. Give the ellipse the desired form by dragging. To make a circle which is perfectly round, hold down the Shift key

while dragging. We have used this means of working to draw the clown's eyes.

Curve
The clown's bow tie has been drawn using the curve. This tool works as follows: choose the tool, now draw a straight line. In the following two stages, you can change this line into a curve with the form of your choice. Do this by bringing the cursor near to the line and drag it in the desired direction. The form of the line changes. Do this once more; the curve is then complete.

- If you are not satisfied with the result, press the right mouse button to begin all over again. This can only be done provided you have not pressed the left mouse button twice.
- If you wish to bend the line in one direction only, click on the end of the line.

3.11 Special functions

The *Pick* menu is mostly shown as grey, indicating that it cannot be opened. It is only possible to open the *Pick* menu when a part of the drawing has been cut out using the scissors or the pick tool. The following diagram displays the contents of this menu:

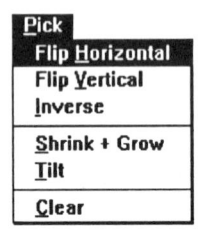

Pick
Flip Horizontal
Flip Vertical
Inverse
Shrink + Grow
Tilt
Clear

Flip Horizontal turns the drawing 180° on its own vertical axis.

Flip Vertical turns the drawing 180° on its own horizontal axis.

Special functions

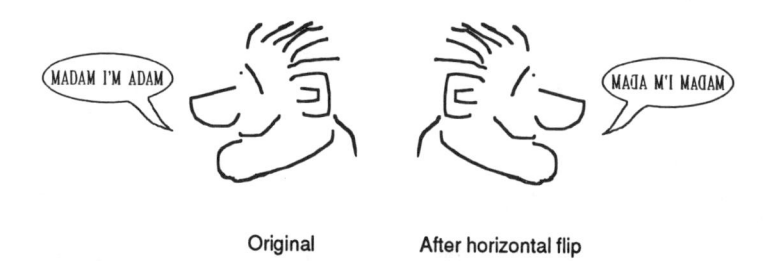

Original   After horizontal flip

Inverse changes all colours into their opposites. Black becomes white, blue becomes yellow etc.

Using *Shrink and Grow* you are able to enlarge and reduce the marked area. Define the area of the drawing which you wish to enlarge or reduce, and select the *Grow and Shrink* option. Place the cursor in a free spot in the drawing area, click on and create a frame by dragging. The defined area will appear in this frame, enlarged or reduced, depending upon the size of the frame you have created. In this way, you can not only change the size but also the proportions. However, due to the fact that the latter is often unwanted, you can ensure that the proportions remain constant by using the Shift key.

Tilt allows you to place parts of a drawing at another angle. Mark the part of the drawing you wish to tilt, and select the *Tilt* option. Place the cursor at a free spot in the drawing area, press the mouse button and drag the cursor to the left or to the right. A dotted line will show how steep the tilt is.

Use the *Clear* option in combination with the *Shrink and Grow* and *Tilt* options. If the *Clear* option is activated, the area marked originally will be automatically cleared after being enlarged, reduced or tilted. A check mark in front of the name will indicate whether or not this option is active.

These extra options can considerably simplify your

work of drawing the clown. Accordingly, you only have to draw the eye once. Copy it using the scissors and then flip it horizontally. A single curve is enough for the bow tie. Copy this curve and then flip it. The bow tie is complete.

3.12 Printing

The drawings which you have made up until now can be saved and loaded again. The only thing we have not yet done is printing these drawings.

The print options in almost all Windows programs can be found in the *File* menu. In addition to the *Print* option you will often find the *Print Setup* option. These options allow you to choose the desired printer and the parameters which are applicable, such as the orientation, the graphical resolution and the number of copies. You will find more information about these options in chapter 5. Here we shall limit ourselves to the *Print* and *Page Setup* options.

3.12.1 Printing a drawing

When you choose the *Print* option, the following dialogue box will appear on your screen:

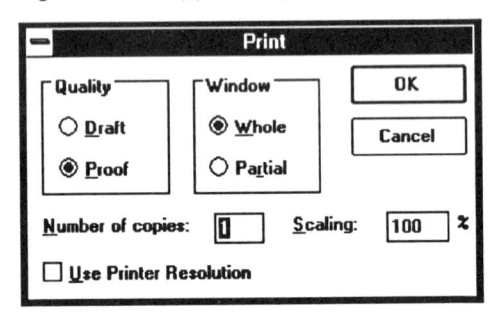

This dialogue box contains an element in Windows with which we are not yet fully acquainted, the **option but-**

tons. These round buttons have the same function as the square check boxes. They are used for switching options on and off. The only difference is that only one option can be chosen using the option buttons, because the alternatives are mutually exclusive.

If you choose *Draft Quality*, the drawing will be printed quicker but will be inferior as regards quality, while *Proof* ensures top quality. Some printers do not allow the printing process to go faster or slower. The draft and proof qualities are identical with these printers.

If you only wish to print a part of your drawing, choose *Partial*. This results in the entire drawing being displayed on the screen before printing begins. Using the mouse, you can determine which part of the drawing should be printed.

You can state the desired number of copies behind *Number of copies*.

Behind *Scaling* you can specify, in the form of a percentage, the scale in which you wish to print the drawing. If you state 100%, the size of the drawing remains unaltered.

If you switch on *Use Printer Resolution*, the drawing will be printed smaller, more detailed and more precise. One disadvantage is that, depending upon the printer, the drawing can end up being very small. Consider that you have made a drawing on the screen with a resolution of 640 by 480 picture elements. No more information is available than can be registered using this number of picture elements. That is why normal drawings are proportionally enlarged during printing to conform to the measurements of the paper. If you switch on *Use Printer Resolution*, the drawing will not be enlarged, and therefore will end up rather small. Using a laser printer with a resolution of 300 by 300 points per inch, the drawing will become a diagram of approximately 5 by 3 cm (approx. 2 by 1½ in.). If you enlarge the drawing area in Paintbrush and your computer has sufficient memory, you will be able to make very detailed drawings.

3.12.2 Specifying the page setup

The *Page Setup* option enables you to determine the position of your drawing upon the paper. At the same time, you can make a header and a footer using this option.

When you have activated this option, the cursor is located in the *Top* box. You can specify the desired sizes of the margins in this and in the other three boxes. Use the mouse to activate the individual boxes directly. Using the Tab key, you can move from one box to the next, step by step.

You can type the text which is to appear above and below the sheet of paper in the *Header* and *Footer* boxes. If the text is lengthier than the notation box, this box will be pushed to the left.

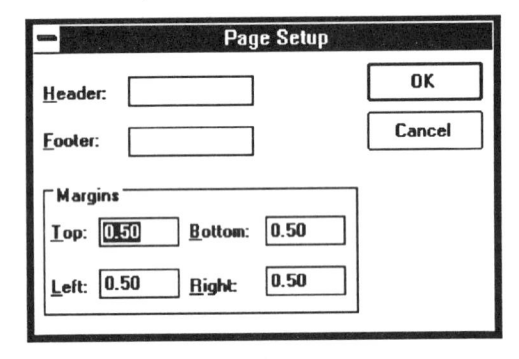

```
┌─────────────── Page Setup ───────────────┐
│                                          │
│  Header: [         ]        ┌────────┐   │
│                             │   OK   │   │
│  Footer: [         ]        └────────┘   │
│                             ┌────────┐   │
│                             │ Cancel │   │
│                             └────────┘   │
│  ┌─ Margins ──────────────────────────┐  │
│  │ Top:  [0.50]   Bottom: [0.50]      │  │
│  │ Left: [0.50]   Right:  [0.50]      │  │
│  └────────────────────────────────────┘  │
└──────────────────────────────────────────┘
```

You can use several special codes in the headers and footers. The following table displays these codes:

&d	current date
&t	current time
&p	page number
&f	file name
&l	left-aligns the header or footer
&r	right-aligns the header or footer
&c	centers the header or footer

3.13 Other tools and options

You have learned a great deal about the options, functions and tools in Paintbrush in the previous sections. However, some parts have not yet been dealt with. We shall give a concise outline of these here.

3.13.1 The polygon

The only tool from the toolbox which we have not yet dealt with is the polygon. This is used to draw closed shapes. Select the polygon and place the cursor in the drawing area. Operation of the polygon is similar to that of the line tool. Draw a line from beginning to end. A special feature of the polygon is that the end point of one line is always the starting point of the following line. This allows you to draw closed shapes quickly. If the polygon is at the stage where you only have to connect the starting point of the first line to the end point of the last line to complete the figure, then give a double click. Paintbrush adds the missing line. It is not necessary to draw the lines by dragging. It is sufficient to move the cursor to the end point and then click.

3.13.2 The filled boxes

The rectangle, the circle/ellipse and the polygon are also available as filled shapes. The drawn shape will be automatically filled up with the foreground colour when you release the mouse button. The outline receives the background colour. If you wish to fill in a shape completely with one colour, choose the same colour for the foreground and the background. The filled tools are used relatively seldom, because similar effects can be gained by using the paint roller.

3.13.3 Image attributes

At the original outset of Paintbrush, the maximum size of your drawings is determined automatically. If you wish to make drawings which are larger or smaller, choose the *Image Attributes* option from the *Options* menu. The boxes within this dialogue box have the following functions:

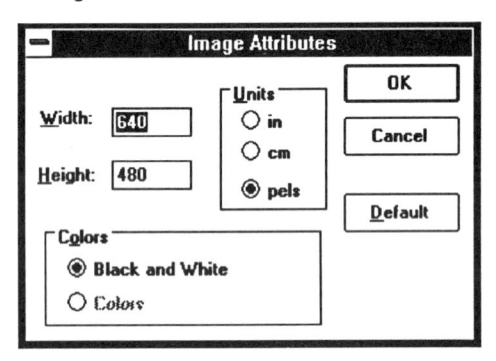

Width   The maximum width of the drawing.
Height   The maximum height of the drawing.

Note: The values which you specify for the width and height of your drawing directly influence the required memory capacity of your computer. Therefore, choose these with care.

Other tools and options

Units — Here you choose the units which refer to the width and height previously chosen. You may choose from inches, centimetres or pixels (picture elements).

Colors — You determine here whether you wish to work in black-and-white or in colour. Keep in mind that working in colour requires more memory and disk capacity. If you merely wish to make a black-and-white sketch, ensure that the proper option has been chosen.

Default — Use this to restore the standard options in the entire dialogue box.

Note: The newly chosen setup only comes into force when you have chosen the *New* option from the *File* menu, or when you start up Paintbrush again.

In addition to using the *Image Attributes* option, the drawing area can be enlarged using two other methods. In the *View* menu, you will find the *Tools and Linesize* and *Palette* options. The default setting has both options active.

By clicking on them, these options are switched off and, accordingly, this ensures that the corresponding components are no longer displayed on the screen. As a result, the drawing area becomes larger. In fact, the real size of the drawing has not been altered but more of the drawing has been made visible.

3.13.4 Determining the shapes and colours

In the *Options* menu, you will also meet the *Brush Shapes* and *Edit Colors* options. The available brush shapes are shown in the following diagram:

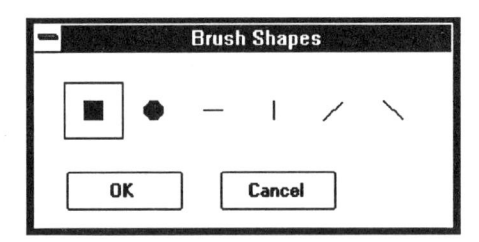

Of the six brush shapes, the default setting has the rectangle active. This is indicated by the frame around this option. You can activate another shape by clicking on it.

It is also possible to call up this dialogue box by double clicking on the brush icon in the toolbox. This is useful when you have to change brush shapes frequently while drawing. In order to try out the effects of working with a different brush shape, select one of the two last shapes (the diagonal stripes) in the dialogue box. Choose an average linesize and try to write your name.

In dealing with the colours, you have much more choice than with the brush shapes, even to the extent that you can mix colours. Call up the dialogue box using the *Edit Colors* option from the *Options* menu, or double click on the desired colour in the palette.

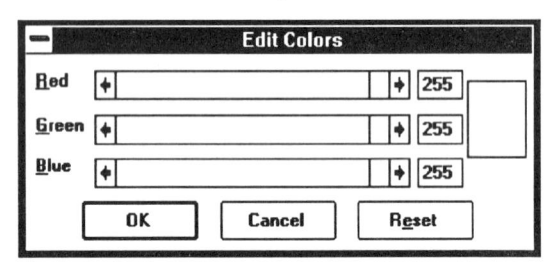

You create a colour by specifying the quantity of each of the three basic colours. In the previous diagram you can see the proportions for white. In this case, the three basic colours all have the maximum value of 255. To make black, you should choose the value 0 for all the

Other tools and options 89

basic colours. In order to avoid having to define your colours time and again, it is possible to save your own colour definitions using the *Save Colours* option, so that you can always load them again using the *Get Colors* option. Both options are to be found in the *Options* menu.

3.13.5 Loading and saving parts of a drawing

It is not always necessary to save an entire drawing. You may also save only a part of it. This can be done by defining the desired fragment using the scissors or the pick. Subsequently, choose the *Copy To* option from the *Edit* menu. In the dialogue box which then appears upon your screen, choose a file name for that fragment and save it.

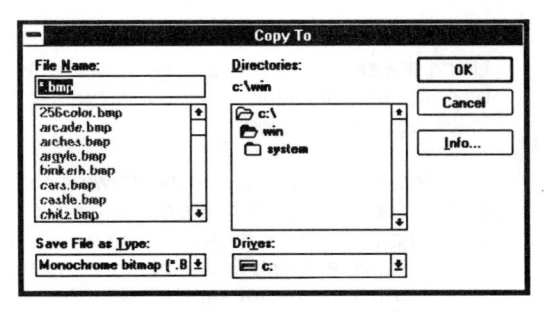

```
-                          Copy To
File Name:              Directories:              OK
[*.bmp]                 c:\win
256color.bmp      ↑     🗁 c:\           ↑        Cancel
arcade.bmp              🗁 win
arches.bmp              🗀 system                 Info...
argyle.bmp
binkerh.bmp
cars.bmp
castle.bmp
chitz.bmp         ↓                      ↓
Save File as Type:      Drives:
Monochrome bitmap [*.B] ±   ▬ c:         ±
```

When the fragment has been saved, you can, of course, open it again. This is useful if you wish to use parts of a drawing in another drawing. It is a good idea, for instance, to build up a library of symbols over a period of time, containing faces, arrows or symbols originating from various technical fields. Libraries like this are also available separately.

Since the appearance of the 3.1 version, Windows has a standard program called *Character Map* in the Accessories group. This provides an abundance of special symbols which can be used in further processing.

In order to load a fragment, select the *Copy From* option from the *Edit* menu. When this has been loaded, it will appear in the upper left-hand corner of the drawing area and you can then move it to the desired spot. If you already have a large series of smaller drawings, you can quickly make a new drawing in this way.

3.14 The letterheading

We showed you a letter at the end of the previous chapter. The letterheading was drawn up in Paintbrush.

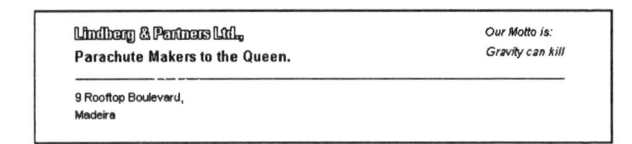

```
Lindberg & Partners Ltd.                    Our Motto is:
Parachute Makers to the Queen.              Gravity can kill
─────────────────────────────────────────────────────────
9 Rooftop Boulevard,
Madeira
```

Using the skills which you have now acquired, it must be possible to draw this letterheading yourself. Keep the following points in mind:

- Select black and white as the drawing colours.
- Use the whole width of the drawing area.
- Your drawing does not have to be a perfect replica of our example. If you find a different font more attractive or if you are not satisfied with the shape of the framework, go to work using your own ideas.
- Save the drawing in the BMP format under the name 'letthead'.

3.15 Summary of all tools

To conclude this chapter dealing with Paintbrush, we shall give a summary of all tools and the keys which you can use in combination with these.

Summary of all tools

	Shift	Ctrl	Backspace	double click
scissors		x	x	
pick	x	x	x	x
airbrush	x		x	
text	x		x	
color eraser	x		x	x
eraser	x		x	x
paint roller			x	
brush	x		x	x
curve			x	
line	x		x	
box	x		x	
rounded box	x		x	
circle/ellipse	x		x	
polygon	x		x	

The table shows the key or mouse click which, when combined with a certain tool, has an extra function. Generally, the guidelines are:

- The Shift key serves to make straight lines, circles and squares. When erasing, only conceptually straight lines will be rubbed out. In combination with the scissors or pick, the Shift key will leave a trail behind the drawing; this is known as 'sweeping'.
- The Ctrl key, in combination with the scissors or pick, is used for copying.
- The Backspace key erases only those elements which have been drawn with the tool which was ultimately chosen and which is still active. An exception is the combination with the eraser - this combination restores the parts have just been erased.

A **double click** works as follows:

- On the pick: the drawing fills the entire screen.
- On the colour eraser: everything which has been drawn in the foreground colour receives the background colour.
- On the eraser: deletes the current drawing. In this case, a dialogue box will appear on the screen enabling you to cancel this deletion or to save the drawing before it is deleted. A double click has the same effect here as the *New* option from the *File* menu.
- On the brush: activates the dialogue box for the brush.

Tip: If you double click on a colour in the palette, you can directly change this colour using the *Edit Colors* dialogue box (see section 3.13.4).

Using the knowledge of the Paintbrush graphical program which you have acquired in this chapter, you can also make more complicated drawings. Owing to the many functions of this program, this work can be easily carried out.

4 Write

Write is a word processing program which can reproduce text and images simultaneously on the screen. What you see upon your screen is reproduced almost identically upon paper; we call this WYSIWYG: *what you see is what you get*. A limited number of easy-reference functions allows the beginner to quickly become familiar with this program.

Before we begin working with Write, we wish to mention a number of ground rules of which you should be aware when working with a word processor and which apply in principle to all word processors:

- The Enter key is only used at the end of a paragraph. You can keep on typing within the paragraph, due to fact that the program ensures that the words at the end of one line neatly move on to the following line. This is called word wrapping.
- If you create long documents, it is advisable to save these regularly in between times. Some programs allow you to do this automatically in intervals which are pre-determined. If this option is not available, as is the case in Write, we advise you to save your file manually every half hour.
- Details concerning the layout, such as determining the end of the page and other breaks, are mostly organized after the contents of the document have been finalized.

4.1 Starting up Write

Start up the program by opening the Accessories group and click on the Write icon.

Write

The program appears showing an empty window. The insertion point, or cursor, is to be found in the upper left-hand corner.

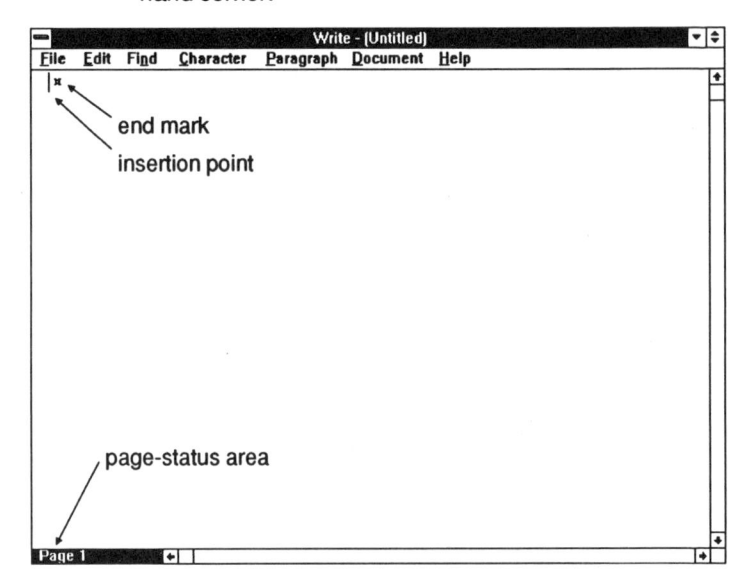

![Write window showing end mark, insertion point, and page-status area]

The end mark indicates the end of the document. The text which you type in appears in front of the insertion point. You can now begin on your first document.

4.2 Compact summary

This section is aimed at those who wish to put their documents on to paper as soon as possible.

Entering text
Type in the text continuously. Only press Enter when you have reached the end of the paragraph.

Moving the cursor
Use the cursor keys to move the cursor through the document. Accordingly, you can reach any desired place in the document. If you alter an existing document, keep in

mind that the new text will be incorporated in the existing document. To correct a mistake, first delete the passage in question and then type in the correct text.

Deleting a character
Backspace removes the character to the left of the cursor and Delete removes the character to the right of the cursor.

Saving a document
Choose the *Save* option from the *File* menu, or *Save As* if you are saving the document for the first time, or if you wish to save an altered document under a different name.

Printing a document
Choose the *Print* option from the *File* menu. Ensure that the printer is connected.

4.3 Moving the cursor

The cursor (the insertion point) can be moved through a document in several ways. The following table displays all the keys and key combinations geared to moving the cursor. In this, the Go To key is the 5 on the numeric keypad.

key or key combination	function
Ctrl-cursor right	to the next word
Ctrl-cursor left	to the previous word
Go To-cursor right	to the next sentence
Go To-cursor left	to the previous sentence
Home	to the beginning of the line
End	to the end of the line
Go To-cursor up	to the previous paragraph

Go To-cursor down	to the next paragraph
Ctrl-PgUp	to beginning of current window
Ctrl-PgDn	to end of current window
Go To-PgUp	to beginning previous page
Go To-PgDn	to beginning next page
Ctrl-Home	to beginning of document
Ctrl-End	to end of document

Mouse
Using the mouse you can place the cursor directly in the position required by moving the mouse pointer to that position and clicking.

The scroll bars
You can move the section of text in the window by using the scroll bars. By clicking on a spot next to the scroll button on the scroll bar, the next piece of text is brought into the window.

4.4 Correcting text

In order to correct typing errors, you can use the following keys:

- Use Backspace to remove the character to the left of the cursor.
- Use Delete to remove the character to the right of the cursor.

4.5 Exercise 13

13) Retype the following text including the mistakes. Within a paragraph, the cursor moves automatically from the end of one line to the beginning of the next. Thus, within a paragraph, it is not necessary

Selecting text 97

to press the Enter key. The ends of the lines are not permanent and change according to the current settings on the computer. Press the Enter key twice between the paragraphs.

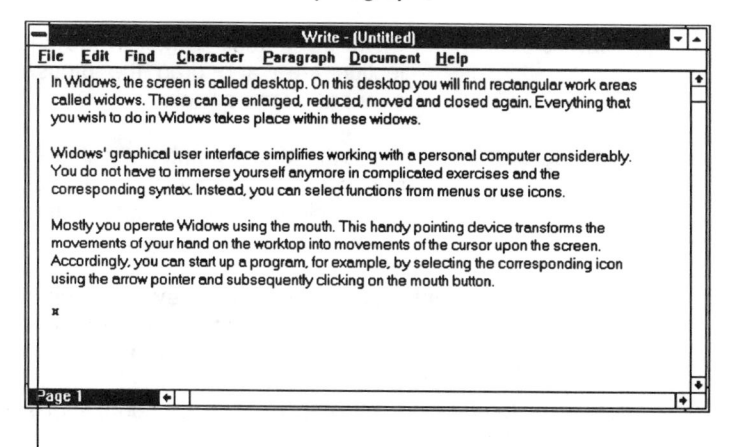

```
┌─────────────────────────── Write - (Untitled) ───────────────────── ▼ ▲ ┐
│ File  Edit  Find  Character  Paragraph  Document  Help                   │
│ In Widows, the screen is called desktop. On this desktop you will find rectangular work areas │
│ called widows. These can be enlarged, reduced, moved and closed again. Everything that │
│ you wish to do in Widows takes place within these widows.                │
│                                                                          │
│ Widows' graphical user interface simplifies working with a personal computer considerably. │
│ You do not have to immerse yourself anymore in complicated exercises and the │
│ corresponding syntax. Instead, you can select functions from menus or use icons. │
│                                                                          │
│ Mostly you operate Widows using the mouth. This handy pointing device transforms the │
│ movements of your hand on the worktop into movements of the cursor upon the screen. │
│ Accordingly, you can start up a program, for example, by selecting the corresponding icon │
│ using the arrow pointer and subsequently clicking on the mouth button.   │
│                                                                          │
│ x                                                                        │
│                                                                          │
│ Page 1    ←                                                              │
└──────────────────────────────────────────────────────────────────────────┘
```
| selection area

4.6 Selecting text

In order to work on sections of text, these have to be selected. The simplest method of doing this is to place the mouse pointer at the beginning of the section which is to be selected, click, and then drag the mouse to the end of the section required. In doing this, you must hold the mouse button down. The selected section will be displayed inversely. Using the keyboard, you select a section of text as follows:

1) Place the cursor at the beginning of the section which is to be selected.
2) Hold down one of the Shift keys and move the cursor, using the cursor keys, to the end of the required section.

In addition to this method, you can also use the selection area to select larger sections. In the previous diagram, you will have noticed that the selection area was located to the left of the text.

Using this area, you can select text as follows:

Lines Place the mouse pointer in the selection area and drag the mouse over one or more lines.

Paragraphs Place the mouse pointer at a chosen position in the selection area. By double clicking you select the entire paragraph.

Whole document Hold down the Ctrl key and click in the selection area. The complete document is now selected.

In order to undo the selection, click on a random spot in the document.

Note: It is not possible to select columns in Write.

4.7 Processing text blocks

Selected texts or sections of text are called blocks. The ability to process text blocks is very important in a word processing program. It is often necessary to relocate, delete or copy individual lines or paragraphs in a document. All this takes place using text blocks. In Windows, this means that the text blocks are placed in the so-called *Clipboard* from where they can be extracted when necessary.

4.7.1 The Clipboard

The Clipboard in Windows is a reserved section of memory where information can be stored temporarily, to be extracted again later.

Caution: Information in the Clipboard is lost as soon as you deposit new information there. If you exit Windows you will also lose the information in the Clipboard.

The most important function of the Clipboard is the exchange of data between Windows programs. Accordingly, it is no problem to copy a Paintbrush drawing to the Clipboard and then to introduce it into a Write document. Exchange of data between normal DOS programs is not possible except in the 386 enhanced mode of Windows. You can make use of the Clipboard in this mode to exchange data between DOS programs, although this has some restrictions.

In chapter 15 at the end of this book, we shall deal further with advanced techniques of data exchange using Object management and OLE operation.

You can examine the current contents of the Clipboard by starting up the program with a double click on the corresponding icon in Main.

Clipboard Viewer

Once the Clipboard is active, it is possible to save the contents.

4.7.2 Cutting, copying and pasting

All Windows programs can make use of the Clipboard. In most applications you will encounter menu options which are linked to the Clipboard. You will almost always find these in the *Edit* menu.

Although the Edit menu is a little different in each program, it almost always contains the options Cut, Copy and Paste.

Edit	
Undo Editing	Ctrl+Z
Cut	Ctrl+X
Copy	Ctrl+C
Paste	Ctrl+V
Paste Special...	
Paste Link	
Links...	
Object	
Insert Object...	
Move Picture	
Size Picture	

The Cut option places the selected section in the Clipboard and removes it from the document. If information was already stored in the Clipboard it will be lost.

The Copy option also places the selected section in the Clipboard but does not remove it from the document. If information was already stored in the Clipboard it will be lost.

The Paste option extracts information from the Clipboard and adds it to the document at the current cursor position. In doing this, the contents of the Clipboard are not lost, so that you are able to extract the information and place it in the document as often as you wish. You only lose the contents of the Clipboard at the moment that you cut or copy a section again.

The other options, some of which are not available as you will observe, will be dealt with at the end of this chapter.

It is not necessary to choose these options from the menu. It is also possible to evoke them using the key combinations which you find behind the names of the options in the Edit menu. In addition, Windows possesses two other keys by which information can be placed in the Clipboard. The first of these is the PrintScreen key. In DOS, you use this key to send the contents of the screen to the printer. In Windows, the contents of the screen are sent to the Clipboard when you press the PrintScreen key. Secondly, there is the combination Alt-PrintScreen. If you press this, only the contents of the active window will be placed in the Clipboard.

To practise, we shall now change the text which you have just typed. We intend to place the second paragraph before the first. To do this, the block must first be selected. Place the cursor at the beginning of the second paragraph and drag the mouse to the end of it. It does not matter if you drag the cursor too far because you can always drag it back again.

When you have selected the paragraph, choose the *Cut* option or use Ctrl-X. Then move the insertion point to the beginning of the document and choose the *Paste* option or use Ctrl-V. The order of sequence of the paragraphs has now been changed.

4.8 Find and Replace

Using the *Find* and *Replace* options from the *Find* menu, you can search for specific pieces of text and change them if necessary.

4.8.1 Finding text

The *Find* option is often used to look for certain pieces of text or to check whether certain terms occur in a document. The *Find* option works, in principle, in the same way as the *Replace* option, so we shall deal with both of these at the same time. In both cases, searching begins from the current cursor position onwards and is automatically continued round again from the beginning of the document until the entire document has been scrutinized.

4.8.2 Replacing text

The *Replace* option is mostly used when a word has been erroneously written throughout the whole document and has to be replaced by the correct word. Another possible application occurs when you type an abbreviated version of a long word and replace it later with the proper word. For example, you type repeatedly 'DNA' and later replace it with 'deoxyribonucleic acid'.

The *Find* menu contains the following options:

```
Find
  Find...
  Repeat Last Find  F3
  Replace...
  Go To Page...     F4
```

Use the *Repeat Last Find* option to continue searching if that has been interrupted.

When you activate the *Replace* option, the following dialogue box will appear on your screen:

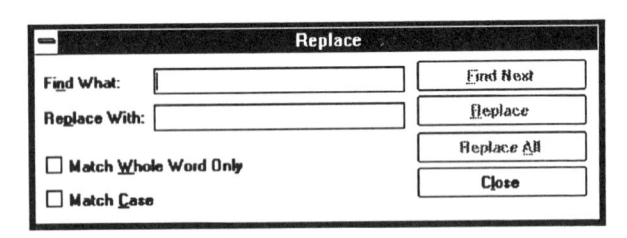

```
┌─────────────────── Replace ───────────────────┐
│ Find What:  [                ]     Find Next  │
│ Replace With: [              ]     Replace    │
│                                    Replace All│
│  ☐ Match Whole Word Only                      │
│  ☐ Match Case                      Close      │
└───────────────────────────────────────────────┘
```

In the *Find What* text box, specify the letter, the word or the group of words which should be found.

You may wish to search for special signs, for instance, tabs, paragraph marks or manual page endings. Due to the fact that you cannot type in these signs, you have to register a code instead. This code is made up of a caret symbol (not the Ctrl key) followed by a letter. The following table provides a summary:

code	meaning
?	random character, for example, 'ban?' for 'band', 'bank' etc.
^w	space
^t	tab
^p	paragraph mark
^d	manual page break

In this way, using '^t' you can search for the next tab.

In *Replace With*, specify the text which should replace the original text. If you wish, for instance, to remove all paragraph marks from a text, specify '^p' in the *Find What* text box and leave the *Replace With* box empty.

In searching, there are two options which help to determine what will be found. If you activate the *Match Whole Word Only* check box, Write will only find the text if it is not part of a longer word. In a case like this, the word 'house' will not be found in 'household'. If you activate *Match Case*, text will only be found if it is written identically to the text being sought. If, for example, you have specified 'Windows', then 'windows' will not be found.

The following list displays the options you will encounter in the *Find* and *Replace* dialogue boxes.

Find Next — Searches further for the specified text.
Replace — Replaces the found text. Write then waits for further instructions.
Replace All — Replaces the specified text throughout the whole document.
Replace Selection — Changes all occurrences of the specified text in a selected section of the document. When you

have selected a section, the *Replace All* button changes automatically into *Replace Selection*.

4.8.3 Exercise 14

14) The text which you typed in previously, contains two mistakes. Correct these using the *Replace* option. Change all occurrences of 'widows' into 'windows' and 'mouth' into 'mouse'.

4.8.4 Possible mistakes using Find and Replace

Use the *Replace All* option with care, because this may have unwelcome side-effects. Take the following example:

In the sentence *Newall laid his wallet next to the wall under the poster of Cornwall.* We wish to replace 'wall' with 'door'. Choose the *Replace* option and specify the word 'wall' in the *Find What* text box. Press Tab to move to the *Replace With* box and type in 'door'. Then click on the *Replace All* button. The result is as follows: *Nedoor laid his dooret next to the door under the poster of Corndoor.*

To correct this mistake you have to undo the replacement. This time, replace 'door' with 'wall'.

In order to prevent mistakes like this, when using *Replace* you should activate the *Match Whole Word Only* option, where possible. Then Write will only find whole words and not also parts of words. In some cases, the *Match Case* option can also be very useful.

4.9 Document layout

Once the text for a document has been finalized, the layout has to be given attention.

4.9.1 The ruler

The ruler is an important aid when dealing with the layout of a document. This displays the horizontal positions of the text and the tabs. In addition, you can determine the line spacing and the alignment by clicking on the corresponding icon in the ruler. You activate the ruler using the *Ruler On* option from the *Document* menu.

Note: Reproduction of a document on paper may differ from the reproduction on the screen because there is not always a corresponding display font for every printer font. As mentioned previously, the WYSIWYG principle (*what you see is what you get*) does apply to the TrueType fonts. The text in the line and the position of the word wrap are correct, even though the lines themselves may vary a little in length.

4.9.2 Character styles

It is possible to accentuate sections of text by giving them a bold or italics format or by underlining them. You will find these options in the *Character* menu.

First select the section of text and then choose *Bold*, *Italics* or *Underline*. You may also choose a combination of these three character styles. If you wish to undo these settings again, choose *Regular*. You can switch off the individual character styles by again selecting the character style in question. The check mark in front of the name of the character style then disappears.

```
Character
Regular      F5
Bold         Ctrl+B
Italic       Ctrl+I
Underline    Ctrl+U
Superscript
Subscript
Reduce Font
Enlarge Font
Fonts...
```

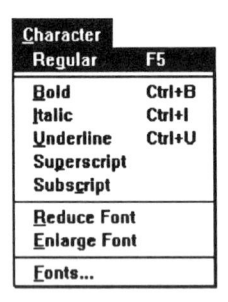

4.9.3 Subscript and superscript

The *Character* menu also contains the *Subscript* and *Superscript* options. To give a section of text one of these styles, select the text and then choose *Subscript* or *Superscript*.

4.9.4 Font and font size

You may choose from a great number of fonts when making your document, dependent upon the sort of printer which you have installed. In any case, the so-called TrueType fonts, supplied as standard with Windows 3.1, are available, regardless of the printer installed. These fonts appear on the screen exactly as they do on the final result from the printer.

Choose the desired font from the *Character* menu. In order to make a choice from all the fonts available, select the *Fonts* option. A dialogue box containing all the available fonts will then appear on the screen (see next page).

Choose here the font and font size. Changes in font, font size, and character style will only come into force in the text which you subsequently type in. If you wish to alter the design of a previously typed section of text, select that first.

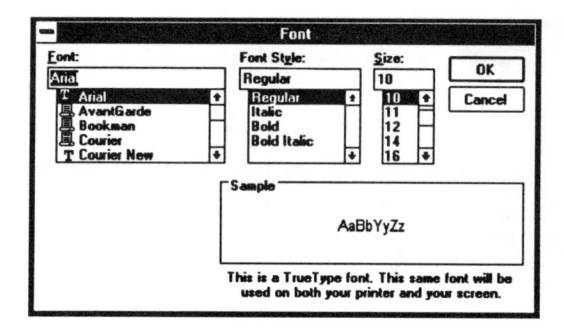

4.9.5 Formatting paragraphs

A paragraph is text up to the next Carriage Return (a Return is made by pressing the Enter key). To align a paragraph you may choose from:

- at the left margin
- centered
- at the right margin
- justified.

Select one or more paragraphs and click in the ruler on the corresponding icon, or choose the required option from the *Paragraph* menu.

The line spacing can also be adjusted:

- single space
- 1 1/2 space
- double space.

The line spacing can be determined using either the ruler or the *Paragraph* menu.

The text which you type will appear between the left and right margins. To change the distance between the margin and the text of one or more paragraphs, choose the *Indents* option.

```
Paragraph
  Normal
√ Left
  Centered
  Right
  Justified
√ Single Space
  1 1/2 Space
  Double Space
  Indents...
```

This text has been left-aligned.

                                    This text has been right-aligned.

                        This text has been centered.

This text has been justified. In order to align a text on both the left and right sides, the distance between the words, and occasionally, the the distance between the letters within a word, is increased.

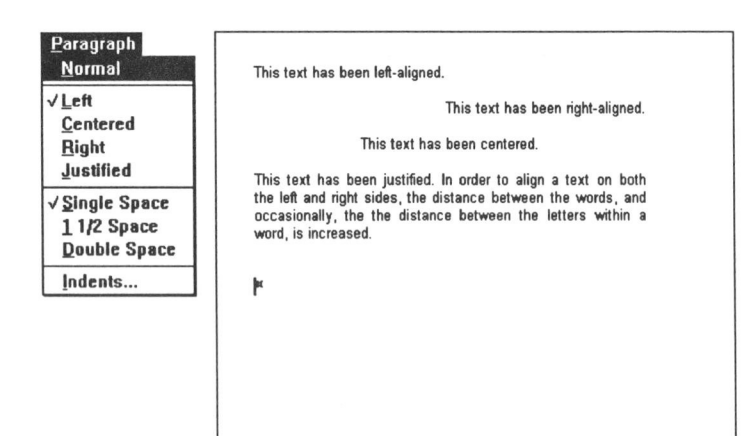

The numbers on the ruler show the width in inches of the indentation when printed. The beginning and end are marked with small triangles. Depending upon what you have selected, you can allow the changes to apply to the whole document or to only a part of it.

Indentations can not only be created using the ruler, they can also be created using the *Indents* option.

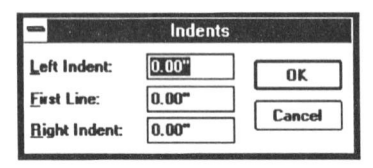

```
            Indents
Left Indent:  [0.00"]    [  OK  ]
First Line:   [0.00"]
Right Indent: [0.00"]    [Cancel]
```

Specify the indentation of the text from the left margin by registering a value in the *Left Indent* box. The value for *Right Indent* determines the indentation from the right margin. The value for *First Line* is only relevant to the indentation of the first line.

The following diagram shows the basic form for indentation.

Document layout

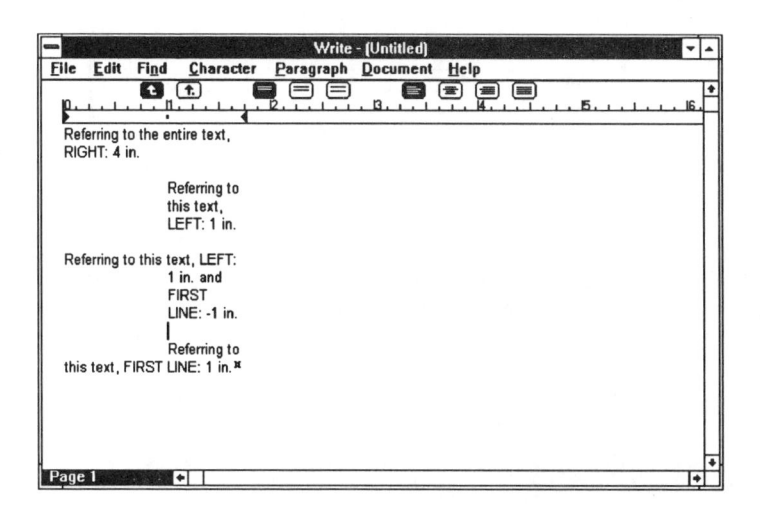

```
Referring to the entire text,
RIGHT: 4 in.

            Referring to
            this text,
            LEFT: 1 in.

Referring to this text, LEFT:
        1 in. and
        FIRST
        LINE: -1 in.

            Referring to
this text, FIRST LINE: 1 in.
```

4.9.6 Using tabs

Using a tab ensures that a text begins exactly in a certain column. Use of tabs is advisable when you have chosen a proportional font for your document. In a font like this, the width of the individual letters differs. For example, much less space is required for an l than for an M. A proportional font is also used for the Windows 3 menus. A disadvantage of a proportional font is shown if you attempt to construct a table using spaces:

one two one two
two six two six
six ten six ten

Each word in this table consists of three letters and the intervening space is three spaces. Nevertheless, the table is not in line. That is why we use tabs in a case like this. A tab marks an absolute position with regard to the left margin. You reach this position by pressing the Tab key. Write provides the possibility of adjusting 12 tabs. The standard distance between the tabs is 0.5 inches. Choose the *Tabs* option from the *Document* menu. The following dialogue box will appear:

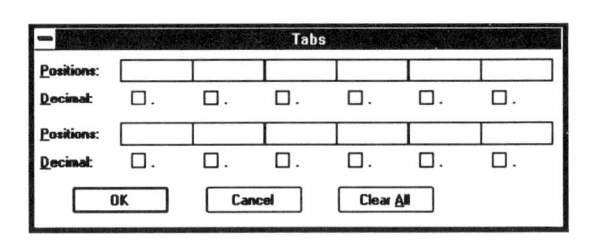

Specify the distances of the tabs from the left margin using the text boxes behind *Positions*. If you wish to use decimal tabs, click on *Decimal*.

The following diagram shows the effects of left-aligned tabs and decimal tabs:

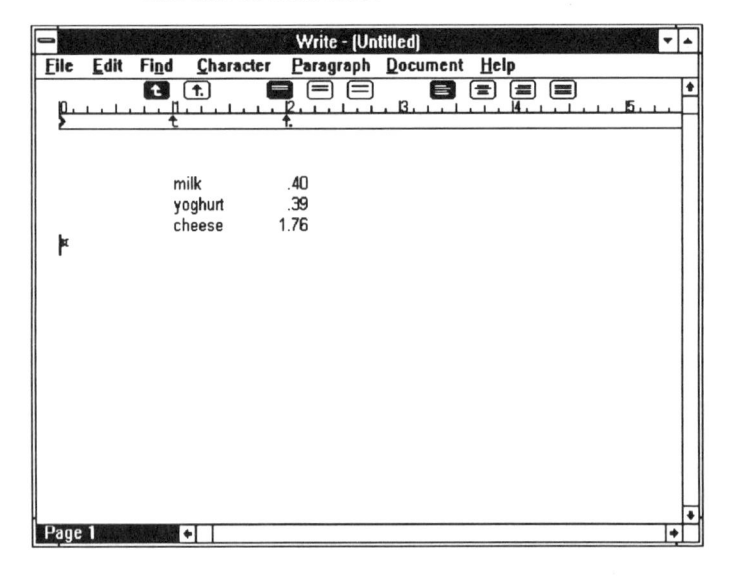

Decimal tabs serve to align numbers according to the decimal point. Whole numbers are right-aligned.

You can either adjust the tabs using the *Tabs* option from the *Document* menu, or using the ruler. In the diagram you see a left-aligning tab (left button) and a decimal tab (right button).

It is very simple to place a tab using the mouse. First choose the sort of tab you wish and then click on the desired position in the ruler. The corresponding tab icon will appear there. To remove a tab, just drag it out of the ruler.

4.9.7 Hyphenation

When you have typed a text, you will observe that the layout of the lines will appear very irregular if you have aligned the text to the left. This is due to the fact that words are not broken off. If a long word extends further than the end of a line, Write will automatically wrap all of it to the following line. This leads to great irregularity. To prevent this, it is better to use optional hyphens in long words. If such a word does appear at the end of a line, Write can break it off at the marked position. If the word fits into the line, the optional hyphen is not visible. You can place an optional hyphen using the key combination **Ctrl-Shift-hyphen**. These optional hyphens are only visible at the end of a line. You can delete them if desired in the same way as all other characters.

4.9.8 Exercise 15

15) After so much theory, it's time for practice again. The aim is to give the exercise text the layout shown on the following page.

If you choose Times New Roman font with font size 12, then the text should appear similar to that in the diagram. When you have altered the order of sequence of the paragraphs and have corrected the mistakes, you can begin on the layout.

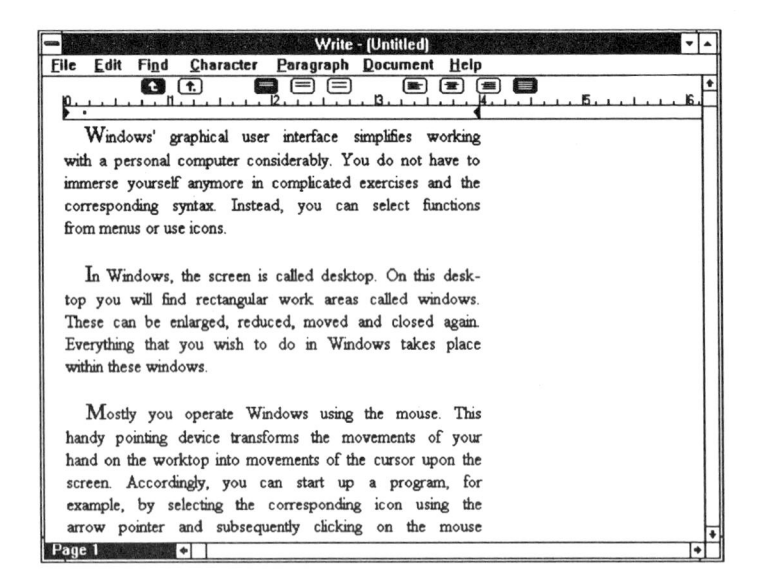

```
─────────────────────────────────────────────
|                  Write - (Untitled)      ▼ ▲|
| File  Edit  Find  Character  Paragraph  Document  Help |
```

Windows' graphical user interface simplifies working with a personal computer considerably. You do not have to immerse yourself anymore in complicated exercises and the corresponding syntax. Instead, you can select functions from menus or use icons.

In Windows, the screen is called desktop. On this desktop you will find rectangular work areas called windows. These can be enlarged, reduced, moved and closed again. Everything that you wish to do in Windows takes place within these windows.

Mostly you operate Windows using the mouse. This handy pointing device transforms the movements of your hand on the worktop into movements of the cursor upon the screen. Accordingly, you can start up a program, for example, by selecting the corresponding icon using the arrow pointer and subsequently clicking on the mouse

1) First determine the indentation of all three paragraphs. Select the whole text by placing the mouse pointer in the selection area, holding down the Ctrl key and clicking. Subsequently, choose the *Indents* option from the *Paragraph* menu and type the value 0.2 in the *First Line* text box.
2) Then make the text 4 in. wide. To do this, activate the ruler, select the entire text again and drag the boundary of the right margin to 4.
3) Now it's time to think about the font. When the entire text has been selected, choose the *Fonts* option from the *Character* menu. In the dialogue box which then appears on the screen, select Times New Roman as the font with a point size of 12. To make the first letter of each paragraph larger, select the letter and enlarge it from 12 to 16 points. You could also make this letter bold as an extra attribute. You have to do this for each first letter individually.
4) Place an optional hyphen in the word 'desktop' in the second paragraph.
5) Finally, justify the text. Select the entire text again and click on the icon for Justified in the ruler (extreme right).

After these implementations, the document should approximately resemble the previous diagram.

4.10 Determining the page layout

The page layout deals with both margins and with headers and footers. The *Page Layout* option in the *Document* menu in Write provides the following possibilities for the layout:

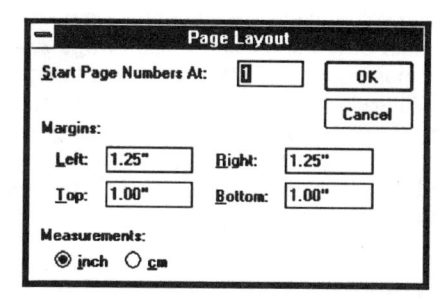

The margins and the headers and footers can be specified in this dialogue box. By specifying a value in the text box *Start Page Numbers At*, you can specify the page where the page numeration should begin.

4.10.1 Entering text in headers and footers

It is also possible to introduce text into the headers and footers, in addition to the regular text on the page. Text in these headers and footers often consists of the page number, the name of the document or the author, or other important information. You must specify the distance of the header or footer to, respectively, the top and bottom edge of the paper. We recommend that the position of the header and footer be adapted to the page layout.

From the *Document* menu choose *Header* or *Footer*. The corresponding dialogue box will appear on the screen. Specify the desired text and its position in this box.

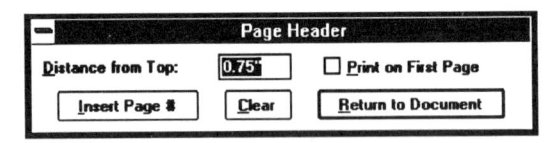

```
┌─────────────────── Page Header ───────────────────┐
│  Distance from Top:  [0.75"]    ☐ Print on First Page │
│     [ Insert Page # ]  [ Clear ]  [ Return to Document ] │
└───────────────────────────────────────────────────┘
```

If you wish to determine the positions of the header and footer, activate the dialogue box and enter the corresponding value. If you wish to enter the page number in the header or footer, click on *Insert Page #*. At the current cursor position in the document '(page)' will appear. Write will substitute the proper page number when printing. This will not work if you type '(page)' yourself in the top line. Page numbering can only be introduced using the corresponding button in the *Header* and *Footer* dialogue boxes.

4.10.2 Page endings

While you type the text, Write displays the current page number at the bottom of the screen. As long as you have not introduced any repagination, this number will remain as 1.

In order to make those points visible where Write will break the document into pages when printing, choose from the *File* menu the *Repaginate* option. Normally, Write will automatically break the document into pages when printing. However, if you wish to influence the position of the page endings personally, activate the *Confirm Page Breaks* option button. Subsequently, the entire document will be reviewed and at the end of every page you will be asked to confirm the page break, or to shift it to another position.

If you wish, you can determine the page endings while typing the text in. You can create a page ending using the key combination Shift-Ctrl-Enter. This page ending is shown as a dotted line.

When Write has carried out the repagination, a double arrow will appear in the selection area at the beginning of every new page.

4.11 Saving and printing documents

Just as in all Windows programs, you will find the *Save* and *Save As* options in the *File* menu. If you save a document for the first time, use the *Save As* option, otherwise choose *Save*.

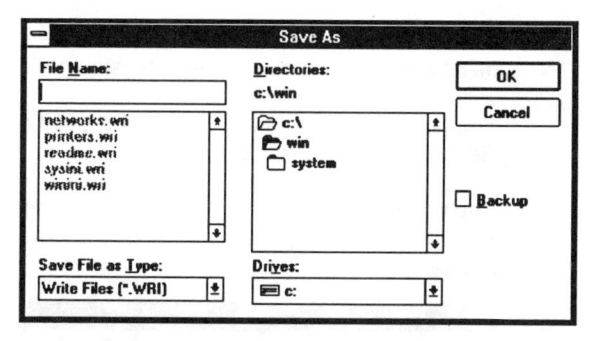

You can activate the *Backup* option in the *Save As* dialogue box; this means that every time the document is saved in the future, Write will make a reserve copy (backup) with the extension BKP.

Further, the dropdown list provides the following possibilities when saving files:

Write Files   Files are saved in the Write format by default.

3.0 Write   This format appears only if you have an embedded or linked object in the file. Use this option when you need the file to be compatible with Windows version 3.0.

Word for DOS   The document is saved in such a way that it can be directly loaded and edited in Microsoft for DOS. If you save a document with images in the Word format, the images will be removed from the document.

Word for DOS/txt only   The document is saved as an unformatted Word file.

Text Files   The document is saved as an ASCII file without further formats.

All Files   This is identical to Write Files.

The document is saved in the Write format by default. In this case, the file receives the extension .WRI.

You will find more information about the *Save* and *Save As* options in section 3.3.

You will also find the *Print* option in the *File* menu. If you activate this option, the dialogue box shown below will appear.

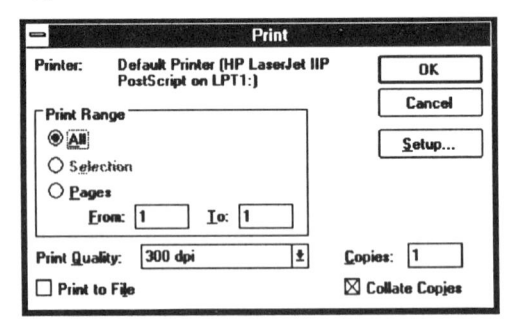

Using the option buttons, specify whether you wish to print the entire file or a part of it. In the latter case, choose *Selection* if a part of the file has been selected. If you choose *Pages*, you can then specify which pages should be printed. State the number of copies in the *Copies* text box. Finally, choose the print quality. If necessary, you may fill in more options using the *Setup* box. It is also possible to print a document to another file.

4.12 Combining text and pictures

One of the most important functions of Write is the ability to combine text and pictures. For a long time Write was one of the few programs which provided this possibility. Nowadays it is becoming more and more common to be able to process text and picture in combination. Advanced programs such as Word for Windows now offer more than Write, in that respect. Nevertheless, Write does contain a large number of possibilities, certainly now that Windows has OLE technology at its disposal since the 3.1 version.

The Clipboard is used in order to introduce a picture into Write. This takes place as follows:

1) Start up the Paintbrush program,
2) create or load a drawing,
3) copy the drawing to the Clipboard. In Paintbrush this entails that the drawing must be cut out.
4) Start up Write,
5) extract the drawing from the Clipboard and add it to the document.

The only restriction is that Write is not able to display text **next** to a picture. Further, you may cut out, copy and delete the picture just as you would text in the document. In addition, it is possible to process pictures using the *Move Picture* and *Size Picture* options from the *Edit* menu. When you have selected the picture, you can move it right or left or alter its size.

At the end of chapter 2 you were presented with a document which we made using Paintbrush and Write. You have drawn the letterheading in the meantime, but the following text is still missing:

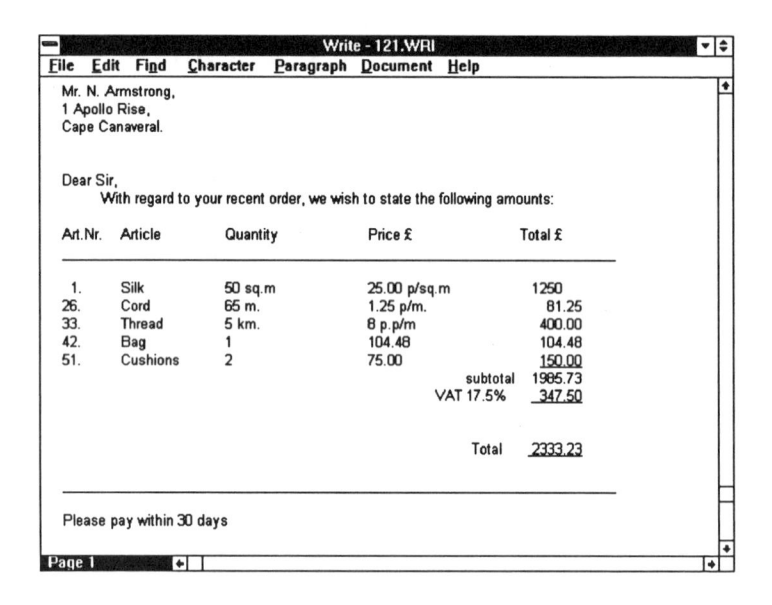

```
-                         Write - 121.WRI                    ▼ ≑
File  Edit  Find  Character  Paragraph  Document  Help
Mr. N. Armstrong,
1 Apollo Rise,
Cape Canaveral.


Dear Sir,
       With regard to your recent order, we wish to state the following amounts:

Art.Nr.  Article      Quantity        Price £              Total £
─────────────────────────────────────────────────────────

  1.    Silk         50 sq.m         25.00 p/sq.m          1250
 26.    Cord         65 m.           1.25 p/m              81.25
 33.    Thread       5 km.           8 p.p/m               400.00
 42.    Bag          1               104.48                104.48
 51.    Cushions     2               75.00                 150.00
                                              subtotal    1985.73
                                              VAT 17.5%    347.50

                                              Total       2333.23
─────────────────────────────────────────────────────────

Please pay within 30 days

Page 1
```

4.13 Exercise 16

16) Retype this text in Write. Format the text and numbers using tabs. Introduce the company emblem using Paintbrush. As you see, Write provides almost everything you might expect from a word processor. By the way, large parts of this book have been constructed using Write.

4.14 OLE technology

At the end of this book, in chapter 15, we shall return to this combination of documents using Write and Paintbrush. In the light of the OLE technology which was introduced as standard in Windows in 1992, we shall outline the interesting constructions which dynamic data exchange programs such as Paintbrush and Write are capable of producing.

5 Operating Windows

The first four chapters have shown that Windows is a very sophisticated system. This system must, of course, be set up and managed. There are four programs available for this:

1) The Task List
The Task List is used to operate the active programs.
2) The Control Panel
The Control Panel is used to adjust Windows to your personal requirements.
3) The Print Manager
The Print Manager takes care of the transport of data to one or more printers.
4) The PIF Editor
Using the PIF Editor, programs which have not been specially developed for Windows can be adapted to the demands and properties of Windows so that they can be used without any problem in Windows.

5.1 The Task List

You can start up the Task List in three ways:

1) Using the *Switch To* option from the Control menu.
2) Using the key combination Ctrl-Esc.
3) Double clicking on an empty spot on the desktop.

The diagram which is shown on the next page illustrates what appears on your screen.

This window shows all the programs which are active at that moment.

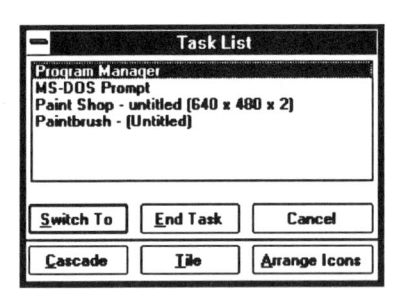

The six buttons have the following functions:

Switch To If you click on this, you will switch over to the program which is selected at that moment. You achieve the same effect by double clicking on the name of the program in the list.

End Task End the selected program using this button. You can also end programs which were not specially developed for Windows by using this button. However, only use this button for DOS programs in an emergency, since there is a risk that information may be lost or that other problems may arise if you do this. You are recommended to quit programs which have not been developed for Windows in the way in which you are accustomed using DOS.

Cancel Using this, you exit the Task List.

Cascade If you click on this, the windows will be stacked upon one another.

Tile If you click on this button, the windows will be placed adjacent to one another.

Arrange Icons Use this option to rearrange the icons on the desktop.

5.2 The Control Panel

The Control Panel allows you to adapt Windows to your own personal demands and desires.

Control Panel

Accordingly, you can determine the appearance of the desktop, the colour of the window borders or the printer to be used by Windows.

The Control Panel is located in Main. Open this group and double click on the Control Panel icon. The following window will appear on your screen.

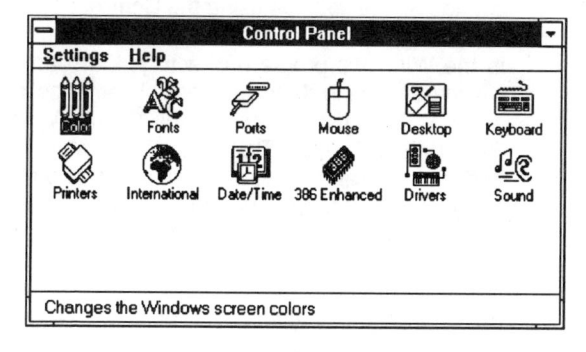

This window may appear a little different on your screen, depending upon the configuration of your computer system. The icon for the 386 enhanced mode will only appear if a 386 computer has been started up in this mode, and the network icon will only appear if the computer is connected to a network.

The settings which are used in the configuration of Windows are mainly stored in the WIN.INI and SYSTEM.INI files. These files are read in every time Windows is started up. Using the Control Panel, it is possible to alter both these files quite easily.

If you have worked with older versions of Windows, you will appreciate the Control Panel. In the older versions, all changes in the WIN.INI file had to be carried out manually using the Notepad. It is still possible to work on the WIN.INI file in Windows 3 versions using the Notepad. However, we do not recommend this, due to the fact that faulty specification may lead to the system not starting up or the production of wrong results. The Control Panel alters the WIN.INI and SYSTEM.INI files for you automatically.

Nevertheless, if you do wish to make direct changes manually, then you should use the Notepad or the system configuration editor to deal with the WIN.INI and SYSTEM.INI files. Some changes can only be implemented in this way, because it is not possible to change all the settings using the Control Panel.

In the Windows program directory, there are text files which describe in detail the possible settings in WIN.INI and SYSTEM.INI. These are the WININI.WRI and the README.WRI files. First read these files thoroughly and, if necessary, make a reserve copy of both configuration files, just to be sure, before you begin to work on them. In addition, only carry out alterations when you fully understand their effects.

In the following sections, all possible settings in the Control Panel will be individually described.

5.2.1 Colour

You can choose the colours or patterns for the display of the following components of the screen.

- Desktop
- Application workspace
- Window background

The Control Panel 123

- Text in window
- Menu bar
- Text in menu
- Title bar (active)
- Title bar (inactive)
- Text in title bar (active)
- Text in title bar (inactive)
- Window border (active)
- Window border (inactive)
- Window frame
- Scroll bars
- Button face
- Button shadowing
- Text in button
- Highlight in button
- Disabled text
- Highlights
- Highlighted text

Double click on the *Color* icon. The following window will appear on your screen:

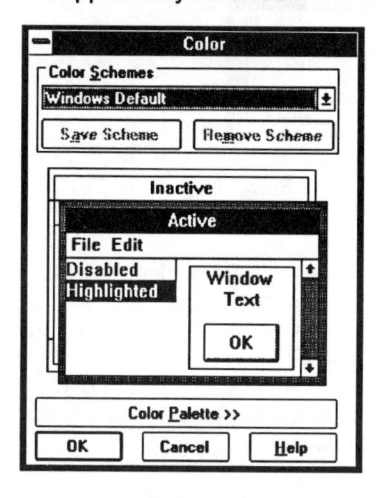

Approximately in the middle of the window you will see an example of the present colour set-up. Above this, you will find a frame with the name *Color Schemes*. You will find a so-called **drop-down list** in this box. You will recognize this by the arrow which points downwards. When you click on this arrow, a list of possibilities will open up. The names you see here refer to varying colour and pattern combinations. If you choose one of these schemes, you will be able to see immediately the results of this in the sample screen. For example, the *Bordeaux* colour scheme produces a combination of dark red and purple colours. When choosing colours it is not necessary to limit yourself to the colour schemes in the list. You can compose personal colour schemes and even develop your own colours. This is done on the *Color Palette*. Activate this by clicking on the button of the same name. The screen now appears as follows:

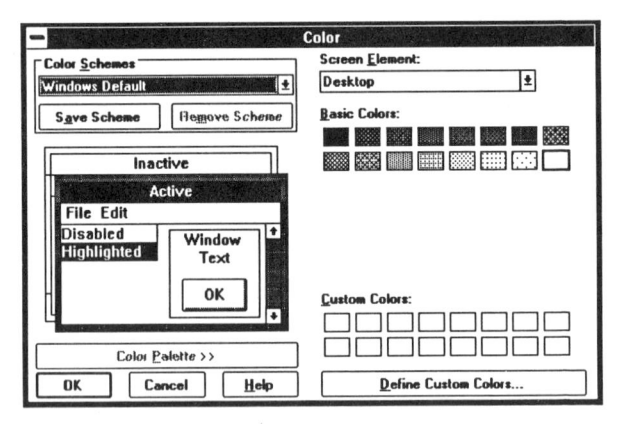

Three elements have been added. The *Screen Element* drop-down list provides the possibility of choosing the part of the screen which is to receive another colour. *Basic Colors* provides the choice from 48 colours. The *Custom Colors* palette allows you to define the colours personally. This takes place by calling up the *Define Custom Colors* window.

You can define a maximum of 16 colours. There are two methods of defining colours. Using the mouse, select the colour you wish directly from the *Color Refiner Box* or specify the *Saturation*, the *Hue* and the *Luminosity* by allocating them values by clicking on the arrows next to the corresponding boxes.

The altered colour is displayed in the left half of the *Color/Solid* box. The solid colour which most closely approaches the mixed colour is shown in the right half of this box. Solid colours can be reproduced directly on the screen, while mixed colours are simulated using a point grid. If you choose the solid colour, click on the right half of the box or use the key combination Alt-E.

If you are satisfied with the colour you have made, choose a box for the new colour in the *Custom Colors* palette. If this box already contains a colour, it will be replaced by the new colour. Click on the *Add Color* button to place the colour on the palette. When you have carried out all the desired alterations, click on *Close*. You may use your own colours in the same way as the standard Windows colours.

In order to allocate a different colour to individual screen elements, choose the required element from the *Screen Element* drop-down list or click on it in the sample screen. Then click on the desired colour in the palette. The result is immediately visible on the sample screen. If you are satisfied with the chosen colour combination, click on *OK*. Windows will use the new colours straight away.

It is also possible to give the chosen scheme a name and to save it under this name. Click on the *Save Scheme* button to use this option and then state a name for the colour scheme. Now you are able to load this scheme just as the standard schemes. If you do not need the scheme any longer, delete it using the *Remove Scheme* button. Return to the Control Panel by clicking on *OK* or *Cancel*.

5.2.2 Fonts

Windows supports the use of *TrueType Fonts*. These are fonts which can be scaled and which appear on the screen just as they do finally on paper. In this case, it does not make any difference which printer has been installed.

In dealing with special specification of fonts, choose the *Fonts* option in the Control Panel.

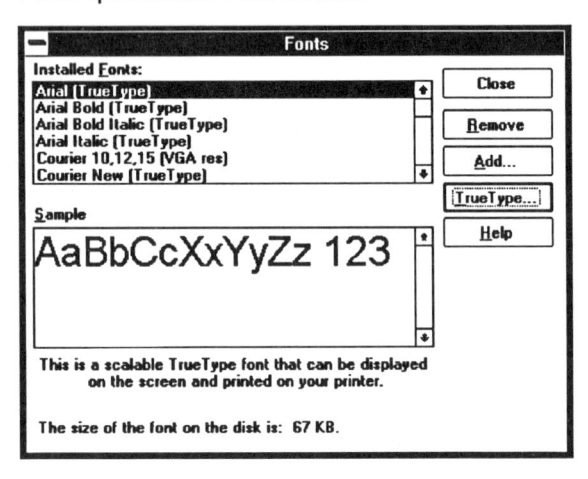

```
┌─────────────────────── Fonts ───────────────────────┐
│ Installed Fonts:                                    │
│ ┌─────────────────────────────┐  ┌──────────┐      │
│ │ Arial (TrueType)            │▲ │  Close   │      │
│ │ Arial Bold (TrueType)       │  └──────────┘      │
│ │ Arial Bold Italic (TrueType)│  ┌──────────┐      │
│ │ Arial Italic (TrueType)     │  │  Remove  │      │
│ │ Courier 10,12,15 (VGA res)  │  └──────────┘      │
│ │ Courier New (TrueType)      │▼ ┌──────────┐      │
│ └─────────────────────────────┘  │   Add... │      │
│                                  └──────────┘      │
│ Sample                           ┌──────────┐      │
│ ┌─────────────────────────────┐  │TrueType..│      │
│ │                            ▲│  └──────────┘      │
│ │ AaBbCcXxYyZz 123            │  ┌──────────┐      │
│ │                             │  │   Help   │      │
│ │                            ▼│  └──────────┘      │
│ └─────────────────────────────┘                    │
│ This is a scalable TrueType font that can be        │
│ displayed on the screen and printed on your printer.│
│                                                     │
│ The size of the font on the disk is: 67 KB.         │
└─────────────────────────────────────────────────────┘
```

In the dialogue box which then appears, you will see a window in the upper left-hand corner indicating the current font. Whether or not it is a TrueType font will be stated between brackets. Supplementary information about the fonts is given in the space below when a certain font has been selected. Click, for example, on the first font. The font will be reproduced in the *Sample* screen. Under this, extra information is given about the font and the size of the file.

The size can be important if memory capacity is restricted. Every font takes up room. That is why the possibility of not working or of working only with *TrueType Fonts* is provided. If you wish to use the latter op-

The Control Panel 127

tion, click on the *TrueType* button. In the subsequent dialogue box, you can select the *Enable TrueType Fonts* options (default) or not, as required. You can also switch off the other fonts by selecting the *Show Only TrueType Fonts in Applications* option.

5.2.3 Ports

Specify the communications settings for the ports using the *Ports* option. This concerns COM1, COM2 etc.

First choose one of the ports from the list and then click on the *Settings* button.

The settings which you choose for Baud Rate, Data Bits, Parity, Stop Bits and Flow Control will be saved for the port in question.

In the *Advanced Settings* dialogue box, you are able to specify or alter a port address and an IRQ line. More information about the configuration of ports can be found in chapter 11.

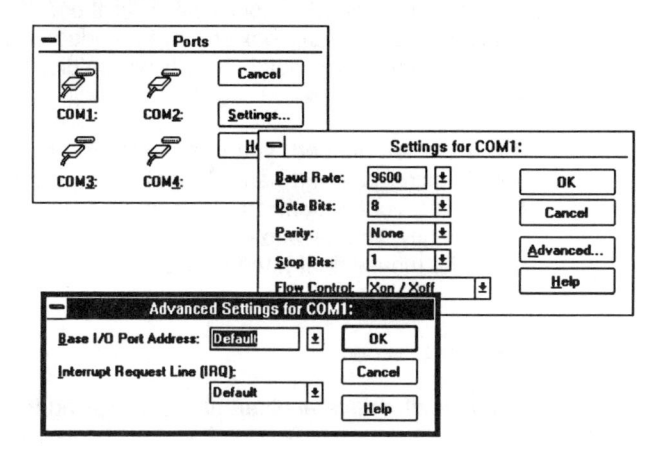

5.2.4 Mouse

You can change three settings regarding the mouse. These are the speed with which the mouse moves over the screen, the interval within the double click and whether you wish to use the left or the right mouse button. If an LCD screen is connected to your computer, a fourth specification possibility is present, namely the *Mouse Trails* check box. This option has been included due to the fact that the mouse sometimes gets lost on an LCD screen. Activate this option if you have an LCD screen.

The *Mouse Tracking Speed* allows you to determine the relation between the movement of the mouse upon the desk and the movement of the mouse on the screen. If you alter the speed of the mouse the new speed is applicable from that moment onwards. If you wish, you can try out the new speed immediately.

Using *Double Click Speed* you can determine the interval within the double click. If the interval is too short, it is very difficult to produce a double click. That is why you are able to try out this specification in the *TEST* box. Place the mouse in this box and try to produce a double click. If you are successful, the box will be displayed inversely.

If you are left-handed, you may prefer to operate the mouse using your left hand. In that case, activate the *Swap Left/Right Buttons* box. Because this option works immediately, you have to use the right mouse button to make the mouse right-handed again.

5.2.5 Desktop

You can alter several different settings using this component:

- Pattern
- Switching between applications

- Screen Saver
- Wallpaper
- Icon Spacing
- Wrap Title
- Granularity
- Border Width
- Cursor Blink Rate

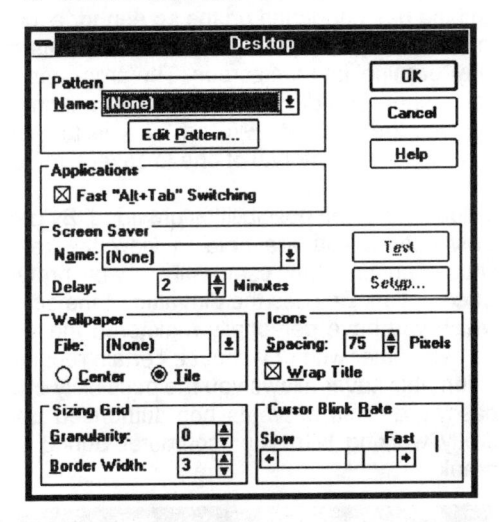

In dealing with the design of the desktop, you are able to choose from three sorts. The first possibility is that of giving the desktop a certain colour. You have already read how that can be done. We shall deal with the other two possibilities here.

Using *Pattern*, you determine which pattern from the drop-down list is to be be used for the background. If the patterns which are supplied are not to your liking, it is possible to develop a pattern personally using *Edit Pattern*.

Using *Applications*, you can determine if you want to switch quickly between applications using Alt-Tab (default specification). By pressing this combination you will see the available applications reproduced consecutively in a frame in the middle of the screen. This combination also works with DOS applications, but then the names of the programs are shown at the top of the screen.

The *Screen Saver* box contains so-called screen savers. These are programs which dim the screen when nothing has happened on the screen for a long time. In this way, you can prevent certain elements of the display 'burning' into the screen. The programs differ from each other regarding extra moving forms on the screen besides the dimness. We advise you to make use of this. Specify an interval of one to several minutes.

Select one of the possibilities provided. By pressing the *Test* button, you are able to view the result of the chosen option. Many users will probably prefer the **Marquee** option. Besides the dimming of the screen, a text which you have personally registered moves over the screen, either with or without a certain regularity. In addition, this saver allows you the possibility of entering a password. This prevents non-authorized persons secretly working with your computer during your lunch break.

Screen Savers do not work if a DOS application is active. Only when you have switched back to the Program Manager or to a Windows application does the Screen Saver come into operation.

Using *Wallpaper*, you are able to choose whether you wish to use one of the standard Paintbrush drawings as background for the desktop or one of your own creations (that can be any pixel file with the BMP appendix). If you *Center* the wallpaper, it will appear in the original size in the middle of the screen. If you choose *Tile*, the wallpaper will cover the entire background. In this case, the wallpaper will be copied a number of times until the entire background is filled in. In this form, the background occupies much more memory space than it would do as a pattern. Therefore, do not use Wallpaper when a great deal of memory is required.

Another way of changing the design is to specify the *Icon Spacing*. Windows makes use of this value in pixels to determine the distance between program and document icons. If you register a value here which is too small, the captions under the icons may overlap each other.

There is also the possibility of breaking off program titles which are rather long and allowing them to proceed further in the next line. This is called *Wrap Title*. Activate this option by clicking on the check box.

Border Width allows you to determine the width of the window borders. The possible values range from 1 to 50.

Using *Granularity*, you determine the distances applied in the relocation of windows and icons on the screen. If you record the value 0, you can relocate these at random. With the grid set to a number greater than 0, all items in your desktop align in an orderly fashion and are pulled to the nearest invisible grid line whenever you move any of them. The greater the value you record, the larger the scale of positioning. You can specify values between 0 and 49.

The final specification possibility allows you to alter the *Cursor Blink Rate*.

5.2.6 Keyboard

This option allows you to determine how quickly the keyboard should react to a keystroke. If you choose a high speed for the keyboard and you hold down a key, the corresponding character will be repeated very quickly. You can test the chosen speed by holding down a key in the test box.

5.2.7 Printers

There are numerous possibilities to specify *Printers*. When you have given a double click on the corresponding icon, the following window will appear:

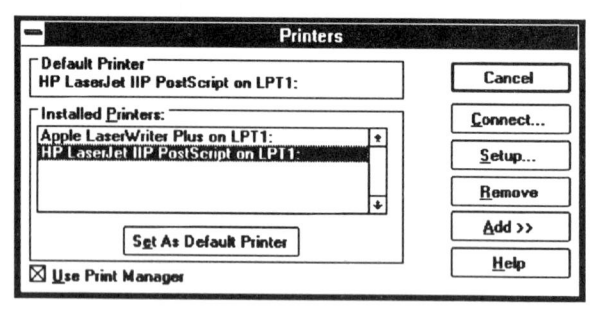

```
┌─────────────────────────────── Printers ───────────────────────────────┐
│ ┌─Default Printer─────────────────────────┐      ┌──────────┐          │
│ │ HP LaserJet IIP PostScript on LPT1:     │      │  Cancel  │          │
│ └─────────────────────────────────────────┘      └──────────┘          │
│ ┌─Installed Printers:─────────────────────┐      ┌──────────┐          │
│ │ Apple LaserWriter Plus on LPT1:       ↑ │      │ Connect..│          │
│ │ HP LaserJet IIP PostScript on LPT1:     │      └──────────┘          │
│ │                                         │      ┌──────────┐          │
│ │                                       ↓ │      │  Setup.. │          │
│ └─────────────────────────────────────────┘      └──────────┘          │
│                                                  ┌──────────┐          │
│           ┌─────────────────────┐                │  Remove  │          │
│           │ Set As Default Printer│              └──────────┘          │
│           └─────────────────────┘                ┌──────────┐          │
│   ☒ Use Print Manager                            │  Add >>  │          │
│                                                  └──────────┘          │
│                                                  ┌──────────┐          │
│                                                  │   Help   │          │
│                                                  └──────────┘          │
└────────────────────────────────────────────────────────────────────────┘
```

Before you install a printer, we wish to deal with several fundamental points.

One of the great advantages of Windows is that all programs can cooperate with the installed printer. Once you have installed a printer, all programs can make use of it. You do not have to adjust the program to suit the printer.

The first step in the installation is to choose the proper driver for your printer. Windows has an abundance of printer drivers available, but it may occur, unfortunately, that it has no driver for your printer. This need not be a problem if your printer can be operated by a driver which is supported by Windows. Most matrix printers, for instance, can be operated as an IBM or an Epson printer. And on almost all laser printers the HP LaserJet emulation can be chosen.

When selecting the proper printer, the possibilty of choosing a so-called emulation for almost all printers is available. And, due to the fact that the IBM, the Epson and the HP emulation are probably available, the choice of printer driver need not be much of a problem.

The supplier of the printer may also have a special driver for Windows in stock.

In principle, the more you know about your printer the less problems you will meet. That is why it is advisable to study carefully the printer instruction manual.

Installing the printer
If, during the installation of Windows, you have not registered which printer you will use, or if you wish to do this later, proceed as follows.

Click on the *Add* button in the *Printers* dialogue box. A list containing all available printer drivers will appear on the screen.

Choose the proper driver for your printer. If you have a driver from a printer manufacturer who does not appear in the list, choose *Install Unlisted or Updated Printer*. Click on *Install*. Windows now asks for the disk with the printer driver, in order to copy it to the hard disk. When this has taken place, the name of the new printer will appear in the list of the installed printers.

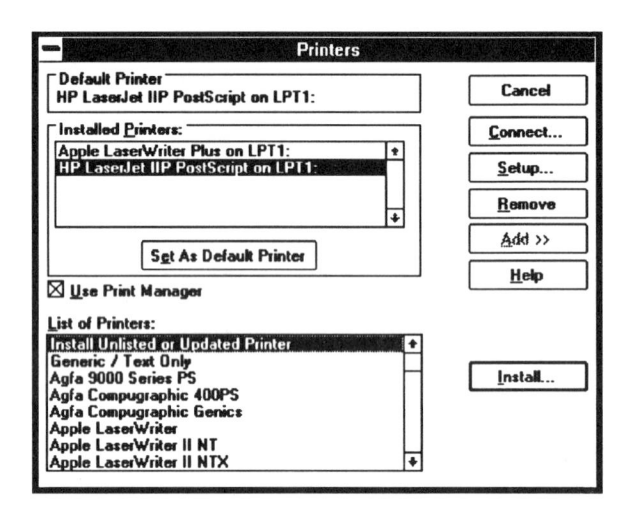

Determining the printer port

Subsequently, you should inform Windows via which port the printer should be addressed. This occurs in the *Connect* dialogue box which is called up by clicking on the *Connect* button. The screen now appears as follows:

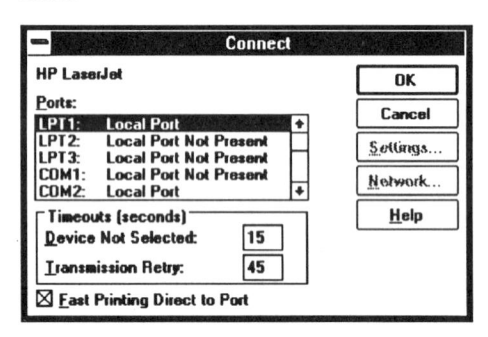

Choose here the port to which the printer is connected. The code LPT1 represents the first parallel port. The printer is connected to this port in most cases. The code COM1 represents the first serial port. This is often used for plotters. The communication settings of this port are specified in the dialogue box which is opened by clicking on *Settings*.

The printer settings

In order to be able to operate a printer properly, Windows has to be familiar with its settings. The window in which you determine the settings can be opened by clicking on the *Setup* button in the *Printers* dialogue box. The exact appearance of this box depends upon the printer you wish to install. That is why we cannot give a valid general description of this box. Instead, we shall take a HP LaserJet as an example in order to show which settings may occur.

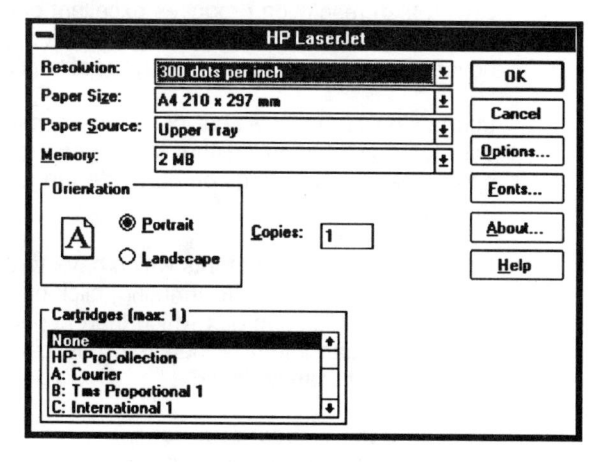

```
┌─────────────────────────────────────────────────┐
│  ─                    HP LaserJet               │
│  Resolution:  300 dots per inch       ±    ┌──────┐ │
│  Paper Size:  A4 210 x 297 mm         ±    │  OK  │ │
│  Paper Source: Upper Tray             ±    ├──────┤ │
│  Memory:      2 MB                    ±    │Cancel│ │
│  ┌ Orientation ──────────────────────┐     ├──────┤ │
│  │       ● Portrait                  │     │Options..│ │
│  │  [A]                  Copies: [1] │     ├──────┤ │
│  │       ○ Landscape                 │     │Fonts...│ │
│  └───────────────────────────────────┘     ├──────┤ │
│  ┌ Cartridges (max: 1) ──────────────┐     │About...│ │
│  │ None                            ↑ │     ├──────┤ │
│  │ HP: ProCollection                 │     │ Help │ │
│  │ A: Courier                        │     └──────┘ │
│  │ B: Tms Proportional 1             │              │
│  │ C: International 1              ↓ │              │
│  └───────────────────────────────────┘              │
└─────────────────────────────────────────────────┘
```

The first setting is *Resolution*. In the drop-down list you can select one of the possibilities.

The *Paper Size* setting is extremely important. Select a size from the list.

In many printers the paper can be loaded in different ways. Determine which way you wish to use under *Paper Source*.

With a laser printer, the quantity of memory available is very important when you wish to print large pictures with high resolution. State the correct size in *Memory*. If you have problems when printing pictures, it may be necessary to equip the printer with some extra memory.

The *Orientation* can be determined in most printers. You may choose between *Portrait* and *Landscape*. *Portrait* is the more suitable for most applications. Spreadsheets form an exception. Here, many columns have to be displayed next to each other. In this case, choose *Landscape*.

If your printer works with different printing resolutions, specify in the *Resolution* box which of these you wish to use. A high resolution produces excellent print quality, but is very time consuming. Low resolution offers the advantage of speed, without exceptional quality.

Information about available cartridges applies mostly only to laser printers. In the *Cartridges* box you can choose which extra fonts on cartridge are available to the printer.

If you wish to use other fonts which have to be loaded into the printer memory for printing, click on the *Fonts* button. In the dialogue box which then appears on the screen, you can inform Windows of the names under which the fonts can be found.

Choosing the standard printer
The standard printer is the printer which many Windows programs automatically choose when the *Print* option is selected. By clicking on the name of the desired printer in the *Installed Printers* box and then on the *Set As Default Printer* button, you can establish this printer as the standard printer.

Using the Print Manager
If you activate the *Use Print Manager* box all transport to the printer will be sent via the Print Manager so that you are able to continue working while printing is going on. In addition, you are able to revise the individual print jobs later, which can be very handy, for example, in a

network. If you switch off this option, you can only continue working when printing has been completed. More information about using the Print Manager can be found in section 5.3.

5.2.8 International

Using the *International* option, you can adapt Windows to the special circumstances of a country, such as the units of currency and quantity. Most options are self-evident. Here is a compact summary of the options:

Country Here you should specify which country you wish to regard as base. When a choice has been made for a certain country, all other options are provided with the standard settings for that country.

Language In Windows applications, this option deals with, for instance, the regulation of sorting according to order of sequence, or use of capitals and small letters.

Keyboard Layout This defines the effects of certain keystrokes with regard to the specified country (concerning special characters mostly). It may happen that you will discover, when a new Windows version has been installed, that some keys react rather strangely. In a case like this, perhaps a wrong keyboard has been specified. Try *US International*.

List Separator In English, a comma is often used to separate the different elements in a list. In other lan-

	guages this is often a semi-colon.
Date Format	By clicking on the *Change* button, you can alter the notation of the date, within certain limits. This deals with the order of sequence of the components and the length.
Time Format	By clicking on the *Change* button, you can alter the notation of the time, within certain limits. This deals with the separation symbol between the different components, and the form.
Currency Format	By clicking on the *Change* button, you can alter the notation of currency, within certain limits. This deals with the symbols and the numbers behind the point.
Number Format	By clicking on the *Change* button, you can alter the notation of the numbers, within certain limits. This deals with the separation symbols and the numbers behind the point.

5.2.9 Date/Time

This option allows you to specify the date and time. This function replaces the DOS commands DATE and TIME. Using the mouse, mark the value you wish to change. As you know, this is done by dragging the mouse pointer over the box. The marked value will increase or decrease by clicking on the arrows. Confirm this using *OK* or correct this using *Cancel*.

5.2.10 Network

The Network icon only appears in the Control Panel if your computer is connected to a network. The contents of the dialogue box depend upon the sort of network.

Network

Several possibilities are:

- sign on and off the network
- change user identification and password
- send messages to other network users.

5.2.11 386 Enhanced

If you have a 386 machine with a minimum of 2 Mb memory, Windows will start up in the 386 enhanced mode. The following icon will then appear in the Control Panel:

386 Enhanced

In the 386 processor extended mode there is the possibility of using the so-called 'virtual memory'. This means that you can make use of more memory than is in fact present (see below). In addition, in this mode, multitasking is possible with programs which were not specially developed for Windows. **Multitasking** means that several programs can be more or less run simultaneously.

In which mode Windows is being run in your case (the 386 enhanced mode or the standard mode) is shown in the *Help* menu of the Program Manager under the *About Program Manager* option.

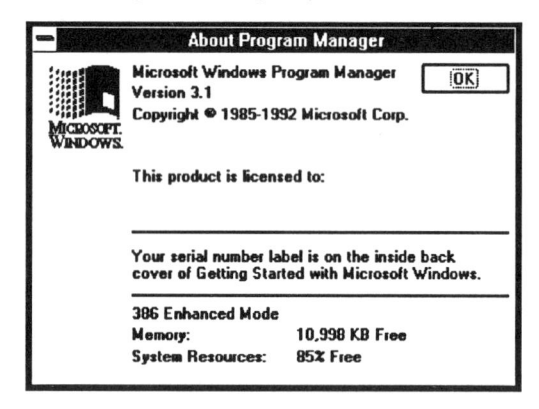

```
┌─────────────────────────────────────────────────┐
│                About Program Manager            │
├─────────────────────────────────────────────────┤
│         Microsoft Windows Program Manager  ┌──┐ │
│         Version 3.1                        │OK│ │
│ MICROSOFT Copyright © 1985-1992 Microsoft Corp.└──┘│
│ WINDOWS.                                        │
│                                                 │
│         This product is licensed to:            │
│                                                 │
│         ─────────────────────────────────────   │
│         Your serial number label is on the inside back │
│         cover of Getting Started with Microsoft Windows. │
│         ─────────────────────────────────────   │
│         386 Enhanced Mode                       │
│         Memory:              10,998 KB Free     │
│         System Resources:    85% Free           │
└─────────────────────────────────────────────────┘
```

In this example, Windows is being run in the enhanced 386 mode and has an available memory of 10,998 Kb, while this computer has only a 4 Mb memory. Windows obtains the extra memory by using a section of the disk to save parts of programs which are not required at present.

A couple of extra pieces of information are needed in order to be able to work optimally in the 386 mode. Due to the fact that, in this mode, different programs can run practically simultaneously, it is possible that two or more programs will require a printer or a modem at the same time. By using the *Device Contention* option you can specify how Windows should handle those requests.

Always Warn   Use this option to ensure that a warning is always given if a program requires a certain device which is already in use. The question as to which program should receive preference comes along with the warning.

The Control Panel 141

Never Warn This setting should be used with great care. With this option, it is possible for two programs to use a device simultaneously. However, this double usage may lead to erroneous results.

Idle Use this option to determine how many seconds should elapse before the second program may make use of the device.

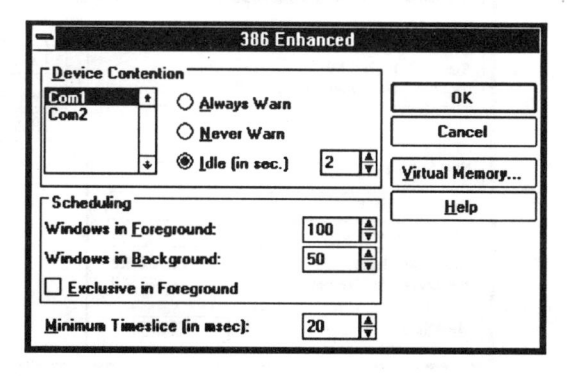

The following options deal with multitasking.

Using the *Windows in Foreground* and *Windows in Background* boxes, it is possible to specify the relative proportions of processing time which the programs have to share. 'Foreground' refers to the active window - all other programs run in the background. The absolute values which you specify have no real meaning. What is important is the relation between the two numbers. More about this in section 5.4. *Exclusive in Foreground* means that when a Windows program is in the foreground, all Windows applications can be run, but programs which have not been developed for Windows are excluded.

Virtual Memory By clicking on the *Virtual Memory* button, you can open an extra dialogue box in which you can change the settings for the use of the exchange files. These settings determine the use of the virtual memory. The program calculates the maximum free space usable. You should make use of the possibility of 32 bits disk access when you have a computer with at least a 386 DX.

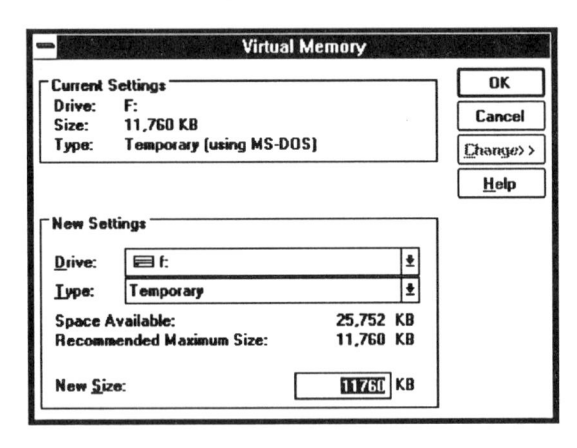

```
┌─────────────────── Virtual Memory ───────────────────┐
│ ┌─ Current Settings ──────────────────┐   ┌────────┐ │
│ │ Drive:   F:                         │   │   OK   │ │
│ │ Size:    11,760 KB                  │   ├────────┤ │
│ │ Type:    Temporary (using MS-DOS)   │   │ Cancel │ │
│ └─────────────────────────────────────┘   ├────────┤ │
│                                           │Change>>│ │
│                                           ├────────┤ │
│                                           │  Help  │ │
│                                           └────────┘ │
│ ┌─ New Settings ──────────────────────────────────┐  │
│ │ Drive:  [≣ f:                              ][±] │  │
│ │ Type:   [Temporary                         ][±] │  │
│ │                                                 │  │
│ │ Space Available:           25,752 KB            │  │
│ │ Recommended Maximum Size:  11,760 KB            │  │
│ │                                                 │  │
│ │ New Size:                  [  11760 ] KB        │  │
│ └─────────────────────────────────────────────────┘  │
└──────────────────────────────────────────────────────┘
```

5.2.12 Drivers

To connect extra peripheral devices such as video recorders and sound cards, separate drivers have to be installed.

In the window below *Installed Drivers*, it is possible to select a program in order to remove it or to change its settings. A number of drivers have been included here, being standard with the installation. The *Add* command button opens a dialogue box in which a new driver can be specified for installation.

The *Remove* command button allows you to remove programs which have become surplus. Do not, however, remove the drivers which were supplied as standard with the installation. These are extremely important for the optimal working of the system. The *SetUp* button can only be activated if settings have to be specified in a certain driver.

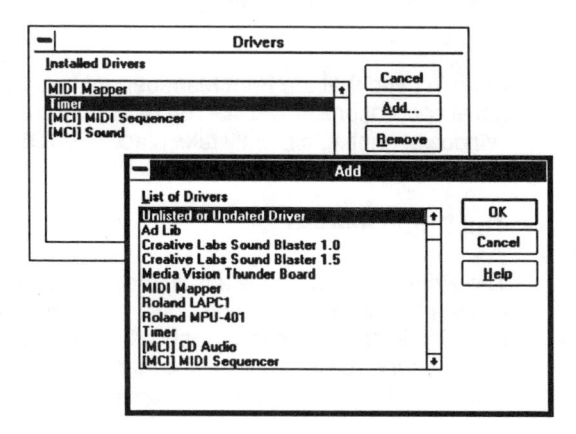

5.2.13 Sound

Here you can specify whether or not the computer should warn you with a sound signal if a mistake is made. This is done by activating the corresponding check box. If a sound card is installed in your computer, the use of recorded files enables you to allocate certain sounds to system procedures and exceptional events in applications.

5.3 The Print Manager

At the beginning of this chapter you have seen how printers are installed and how you can specify whether the Print Manager should be used or not.

Print Manager

If you have opted for this possibility, all Windows applications will send their data for the printer to the Print Manager which then takes care of the actual printing. This takes place in the background so that you can get on with your work.

Keep in mind that the Print Manager only works in Windows applications. If you start up DOS applications from Windows, printing can only take place via DOS.

5.3.1 The Print Queue

The Print Manager is always started up automatically when a Windows application prints something. All print commands are collected in a list called the **print queue**. If you double click on the Print Manager, the window shown on the following page will open.

You will observe that, in this example, two files are waiting in the queue. The upper file is first in line. This is indicated by a small drawing of a printer in front of it. Other files receive consecutive numbers. What is further visible depends on the settings specified in the *View* option. Here you can specify whether the time and date of the print command and the size of the file to be printed should be registered.

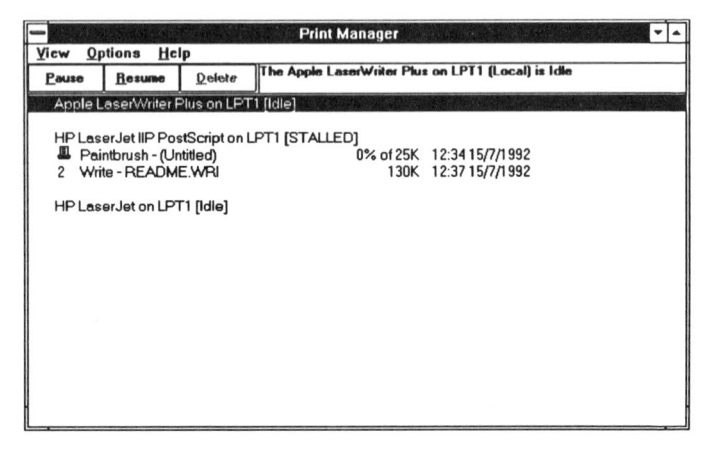

```
─                              Print Manager                          ▼ ▲
View  Options  Help
 Pause   Resume   Delete  The Apple LaserWriter Plus on LPT1 (Local) is Idle
 Apple LaserWriter Plus on LPT1 [Idle]

 HP LaserJet IIP PostScript on LPT1 [STALLED]
 🖨 Paintbrush - (Untitled)              0% of 25K  12:34 15/7/1992
 2  Write - README.WRI                         130K  12:37 15/7/1992

 HP LaserJet on LPT1 [Idle]
```

We shall not elaborate further here on the commands which deal with working with networks. That is beyond the scope of this introduction.

5.3.2 Processing the print queue

Using the *Pause* and *Resume* command buttons it is possible to, respectively, break off and resume the print commands. Keep in mind that the printer will continue printing for a short time after the *Pause* button has been pressed, due to the fact that in the buffer (printer memory) there will be a residue of text or picture.

If the print queue contains various files which have not yet been printed, you can drag them using the mouse to another position in the queue to have them printed earlier or later. You can also remove a file by marking it and then activating the *Delete* command button. If you wish to delete all print commands in one go, close the Print Manager. As a safeguard you will be asked if you really wish to delete all files. If you confirm this, all files will be removed from the print queue.

5.3.3 Commands from the Print Manager

The commands in the *Options* menu refer to the following:

Low Priority Printing in the background is allocated less time so that the program in the foreground can continue working almost without interruption.

Medium Priority The processing time is divided as evenly as possible.

High Priority Print Manager is allocated relatively more time and therefore is able to to process the print command as quickly as possible. The current application in the foreground runs slower because of this.

The following commands in the *Options* menu deal with messages which Print Manager gives from time to time to remind the user, for example, to refill the paper tray etc.

Alert Always A message is given when a condition occurs which requires user interaction.

Flash if Inactive The Print Manager flashes on and off and emits a sound signal to let the user know that it has a message. This message will appear when the Print Manager is made active. This is the default setting.

Ignore if Inactive If the Print Manager window is inactive the message will be ignored. This setting does not influence messages about inadequacies or defects such as 'Printer not ready'.

5.3.4 Printing to a file

Now and again it may be necessary to transmit the contents of a program to a file instead of directly to the printer. This may be the case, for example, if information has to be added to another program or if a file is to be printed at a later date. If you have worked with DOS a lot, you will have frequently made use of this possibility. While in DOS, however, a file often had to be saved temporarily, in Windows this work is largely performed by the Clipboard. Nevertheless, if you wish to print to another file, proceed as follows:

1) From the *Options* menu, choose *Printer Setup*.
2) In the *Installed Printers* box, select the printer you wish to use. It is often sensible to select the driver for *Generic/Text only* which may have to be installed first. This driver has the advantage that no operating symbols are included in the text, which may be important in certain tasks.
3) Choose the *Connect* button.
4) Choose the *FILE* option in the *Ports* box.
5) Confirm using *OK*.
6) Specify the corresponding printer in the *Printers* dialogue box as default printer, and click on the *Close* button.

If you now wish to print from an application, you will repeatedly be asked the question to which file the document should be transmitted. Of course, you can also specify here a drive and path.

5.4 The PIF Editor

If Windows has to start up an application which has not been specially developed for Windows, such as WordStar or dBase, extra information is required. This information concerns the treatment of the programs and how these make use of the various parts of the computer such as memory, screen and printer port. This information is relayed or altered via the PIF Editor. The letters PIF stand for **Program Information File**. The PIF Editor is to be found in the *Main* window (previously in *Accessories*).

Starting up and running a program is a rather technological happening. When describing the PIF Editor we shall have to immerse ourselves a little deeper in the Windows technology and also in that of computers where necessary. The reader who is not planning to use DOS applications may skip the rest of this section. If, however, you do think you will run DOS programs in Windows - and this can be meaningful especially if you have a 386 machine - the following information is essential.

The PIF Editor is represented by the following icon. It resembles a label with information, such as is used with suitcases or freight.

PIF Editor

Start up the PIF Editor by double clicking on the icon. The window which is then opened differs according to the type of computer and depends upon the operating mode of Windows. Here is a diagram of the PIF Editor in the Windows 386 enhanced mode.

PIF files

The PIF Editor saves information in files with the extension PIF, if you do not specify otherwise. This concerns files which contain program information from a certain program. These files are created automatically if you use *Windows Setup* from *Main* to search the hard disk for applications for installation. A precondition is that Windows is familiar with the application.

Each program may only have one single PIF file. Assignment takes place using the program name. For instance, the PIF file of the QBASIC program is called QBASIC.PIF. When a program is started up, Windows automatically looks for a PIF file of the same name. It is, however, also possible to 'start up' a PIF file instead of a program. Windows will in fact start up the corresponding program. In this way, you can attach various PIF files to one program in order to allow that program to run in different configurations.

5.4.1 Specifying operating modes

Windows can run in two different ways: the standard mode (s) or the 386 enhanced mode (3). Using the starting up command WIN, Windows is automatically started up in the optimal mode for the computer in question. The standard mode is usually set up in the case of a minimum configuration for Windows; that is, a 80286 processor and a memory expanded to 2 Mb. The enhanced mode only works with a 386 processor or more advanced processors, with a minimum of 2 Mb memory. Optimal operation is obtained from 4 Mb upwards.

Standard mode
Windows is started up in this mode with the command:

```
WIN/S
```

A precondition is that the computer satisfies the minimum demands outlined above.

If you activate the PIF Editor in this mode, the windows will appear differently than in the above diagram. The transfer option *Advanced* is absent. The result can be seen on the following page.

![PIF Editor window screenshot showing fields for Program Filename, Window Title, Optional Parameters, Start-up Directory, Video Mode (Text selected), Memory Requirements KB Required 128, XMS Memory KB Required 0 KB Limit 0, Directly Modifies checkboxes (COM1-COM4, Keyboard), No Screen Exchange, Close Window on Exit (checked), Prevent Program Switch, No Save Screen, Reserve Shortcut Keys (Alt+Tab, Alt+Esc, Ctrl+Esc, PrtSc, Alt+PrtSc). Status bar: "Press F1 for Help on Program Filename."]

The 386 enhanced mode

Start up the Windows 386 enhanced mode using the following command:

```
WIN/3
```

A precondition is that you have a computer with the necessary 80386 or 80486 processor and a minimum of 2 Mb memory.

Note: According to Microsoft, the 386 enhanced mode is only quicker than the standard mode if the computer has a memory of more than 2 Mb.

5.4.2 Entering program information

In each PIF file, program information is stored in two groups, one for the standard mode and the other for the 386 enhanced mode. The PIF Editor can be switched over to the group in question to register or alter the corresponding data. To do this, click on *Mode* and then on either *Standard* or *Enhanced*.

To gain information about the various import, operation and options boxes, click on *Help*. Operation of this special help function for the PIF Editor is similar to the normal help functions for Windows. Thus, you can just press F1 to ask for context-oriented help.

General information
General information includes information such as the name of the program, the directory in which it can be found and the way in which can be started up.

Behind *Program Filename* you should always specify the drive, the directory and the complete name of the program file. Behind *Window Title* you can specify a text of your choice which will be placed under the icon.

Optional Parameters deals with the information which you would place behind the program name in the case of calling up the program from MS-DOS. Thus, in a program request such as FORMAT A:/4 you should specify here A:/4.

The *Start-up Directory* is the directory to which the computer should switch before the start of the program.

Method of working
The other options in the PIF Editor determine the working methods of the program which is to be started up. This concerns the memory required, usage of the screen etc. In this, the data for the standard mode and the enhanced mode differ from one another. We shall outline the various possibilities within both modes.

Use *Video Mode* to determine the way the program should make use of the screen. With a program which uses exclusively ASCII characters, click on *Text*. When dealing with programs which deal with more than one screen page and where you are not sure how the program will make use of the screen, select the *Graphics/Multiple Text* option. This option demands more memory, but makes it easier to switch between programs.

Under *Memory Requirements* you can fill in two options, depending upon the mode in which Windows is running. In any case, you must specify how many Kb are **minimally required** to run the program. This value does not limit the memory but allows Windows to work faster. If less memory is available, for instance, Windows will not even try to start up the program, but will immediately state that the operation is impossible. In addition in the 386 enhanced mode, you should specify how much memory is **desired** for an optimal way of working. In this way it is possible to limit the space for a program, since Windows will not make more space available than is specified here. If you specify -1 here, Windows will reserve as much space as possible but maximally 640 Kb.

Display Usage deals with display in either a window or full-screen. More memory is needed for the *Windowed* option. A chosen option can be switched to the other option using Alt-Enter. Using the *Windowed* option, it is also possible to exchange data between programs quickly.

In addition, it is also possible to guide the *Execution* of the program in question. If a program has to continue to run while you switch over to another application, click on *Background*. This can be useful with printing and copying programs. If you click on *Exclusive*, all other programs will be halted, regardless of whether the background execution has been activated or not.

In standard mode, the *Directly Modifies* options are used to indicate that the application uses certain resources in a way which prevents sharing those resources with other applications. For example, some communications applications take control of the communications ports they are using, to the exclusion of other applications. This may also happen with the keyboard. This means that, for example, the shortcut keys are out of use in Windows. It is important to specify those components which will be directly modified, otherwise unpredictable things may happen, such as in the case of two applications using the same communications port at the same time, which can result in garbled or lost data.

The *No Screen Exchange* option allows you to switch off the PrintScreen key and the Alt-PrintScreen key combination. If you select this option, you cannot copy information from the application window to the Clipboard using these keys.

If an application which was not specially developed for Windows is ended, Windows usually has a pause to allow you to view the most recent data of the application. You can then mark the information or, by pressing a key, further process this information in Windows. Using *Close Window on Exit*, you ensure that Windows proceeds further when you close an application.

If you have activated the *Prevent Program Switch* you are not able to switch to another program when you have started up a program.

If you activate the *No Save Screen* option, Windows assigns the operation of the screen display of the corresponding application in the standard mode to the application itself. This is occasionally necessary to free *screen memory* for use elsewhere. The application in question should be equipped with a display memory otherwise you will encounter a ragged and deformed screen when you return to the application.

In the standard mode, you can also fill in specifications concerning the XMS memory and the reservation of shortcut keys.

5.4.3 Advanced options

In the PIF Editor window in the 386 enhanced mode, you will find a box called *Advanced*. By clicking on this box, you will open a window with detailed information about the execution and operation of the program. These options only need be changed occasionally.

```
┌─────────────────────────────────────────────────────────┐
│  —              Advanced Options                        │
│ ┌Multitasking Options──────────────────────────┐ ┌────┐ │
│ │Background Priority: [50]  Foreground Priority: [100]│ │ OK │ │
│ │           ☒ Detect Idle Time                 │ ├────┤ │
│ └──────────────────────────────────────────────┘ │Cancel│ │
│ ┌Memory Options──────────────────────────────────┐ └────┘ │
│ │   ☐ EMS Memory Locked    ☐ XMS Memory Locked  │        │
│ │   ☒ Uses High Memory Area ☐ Lock Application Memory│   │
│ └────────────────────────────────────────────────┘        │
│ ┌Display Options─────────────────────────────────┐        │
│ │Monitor Ports:  ☐ Text  ☐ Low Graphics  ☐ High Graphics│ │
│ │        ☒ Emulate Text Mode  ☐ Retain Video Memory│     │
│ └────────────────────────────────────────────────┘        │
│ ┌Other Options───────────────────────────────────┐        │
│ │☒ Allow Fast Paste         ☐ Allow Close When Active│   │
│ │Reserve Shortcut Keys: ☐ Alt+Tab ☐ Alt+Esc ☐ Ctrl+Esc│  │
│ │                       ☐ PrtSc  ☐ Alt+PrtSc ☐ Alt+Space│ │
│ │                       ☐ Alt+Enter                   │  │
│ │Application Shortcut Key: [None              ]       │  │
│ └─────────────────────────────────────────────────┘       │
│ Press F1 for Help on Priority.                            │
└───────────────────────────────────────────────────────────┘
```

Multitasking

The method which Windows uses to run different programs practically simultaneously is called **multitasking**. In this context, each program which runs in Windows is called a **task**.

If a non-Windows application is being run, only one of the specified values for *Background Priority* and *Foreground Priority* will be recognized, depending on whether you have switched over to the program (foreground) or not (background). Values between 0 and 10,000 can be used to specify priority. In this way, you can determine how much time the program should allocate to the program in question. The actual priority, however, depends upon the relationship between all the programs running.

$$\text{percentage processor time} = \frac{\text{program priority}}{\text{total of all priorities}}$$

Example

Two background programs are running in addition to the program in the foreground. All applications have a background priority of 50 and a foreground priority of 100. The sum of all priorities is 50 + 50 + 100 = 200. The program in the foreground receives 100/200 = 50% of the time, the background programs each get 50/200 = 25%.

By clicking on *Detect Idle Time*, you can instruct Windows to take into consideration the time consumed in waiting for information. This increases the effectiveness. You should avoid this option if the application runs very slowly even in Windows.

Memory options

With reference to *Expanded Memory* (EMS) and *Extended Memory* (XMS) individually, it is possible to prevent Windows from parking parts of the corresponding memory on the hard disk, by using the *Lock* memory options. In this way, you can increase the effectiveness of the program in question, but, of course, only at the cost of the rest of the system.

By activating the *Uses High Memory Area* you can determine that the application is able to address the first 64 Kb of the extended memory.

Using *Lock Application Memory* you are able to prevent the conventional memory used by the program being temporarily placed on the hard disk. This allows the program to work faster.

Display options

The *Display Options* determine how much memory Windows has to deploy as screen memory in order to have enough reserve (buffer) for display. At the same time, you should determine here in which mode the monitor lines should be controlled in order to inform Windows when the program has switched the screen over to a certain mode.

There are three different modes: *Text*, *Low Graphics* and *High Graphics*. By using *Emulate Text Mode* it is possible to increase the speed of many programs.

There is no transfer to the text mode of the graphic card, this is merely simulated.

Normally, when memory is made free by transferring the screen from a higher to a lower resolution or to text, this memory is made available to other Windows programs. Because of this, it may be impossible to switch back if there is not sufficient memory left over. You can prevent this by activating the *Retain Video Memory* option.

Operating keys
The last group, *Other Options* deals mainly with the operation of the keys.

If you select a certain shortcut key (combination) in the *Reserve Shortcut Keys* option, it is no longer possible to use this shortcut key in Windows. This is necessary if the program itself uses one of more of these key combinations.

Finally, it is possible to assign a shortcut key to an application. If you specify Ctrl-Alt-F8 here, for example, you can always call up the application with this key combination. You may not use the Esc, PrintScreen, Enter, Backspace and Tab keys here. On the other hand, you are obliged to use either the Alt or the Ctrl key in the combination. However, it is probably more efficient to fill in this combination in the corresponding program in the Program Manager by making use of the *Program Item Properties* dialogue box. In fact, this option in the advanced frame of the PIF Editor seems to be superfluous.

Allow Fast Paste is geared to working with the Clipboard. If you have no success in extracting text from the Clipboard, switch this option off.

The *Allow Close When Active* option closes the active application when you exit Windows. If this option is selected you can quit Windows without having to quit every application separately.

Caution: Selecting this option could result in loss or damage to your files because Windows discontinues the program without further warning.

5.4.4 Exercise 17

17) When Windows Setup automatically installs applications, PIF files are made in the Windows directory for each of these applications. Open these files using the PIF Editor and describe which specifications have been made.

6 File Manager

The File Manager provides the possibility of bringing some order into the great number of files which land on the hard disk with the passage of time. This arranging takes place with the assistence of the directory structure as available in DOS.

File Manager

The function of directories is to gather files into logical groups so that they can be found more easily. In this way, a directory can contain all texts which have been produced by a certain word processor. And, for example, all files which belong to a certain project can also be placed in one directory. Or, in the same way, it is possible to imagine a directory which bundles together all files which have been made in a certain month. As you see, there are many possibilities to organize information. You may personally choose the method which most closely fits your own requirements. The Windows File Manager is there to assist you.

6.1 Working with directory windows

Start up the File Manager by double clicking on the icon. Activate the *Indicate Expandable Branches* option in the *Tree* menu. The diagram on the following page shows what then appears on your screen.

When working with the File Manager, you are dealing, in the first place, with a window which shows on the left-hand side of the screen the directory structure of the hard disk or floppy. On the right-hand side of the screen, the files contained in the specified directory are shown. An unlimited number of this sort of directory windows can be displayed.

Working with directory windows 159

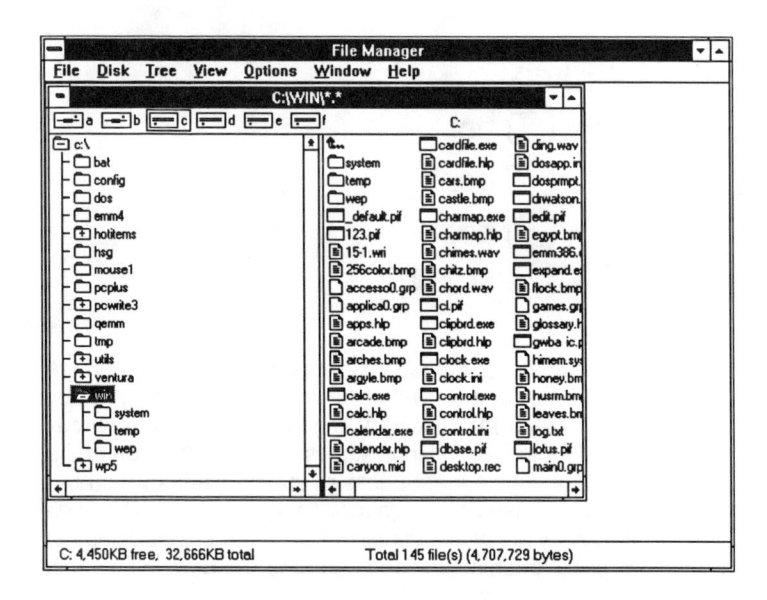

In the top line, station icons represent the available drives with the corresponding drive letters. To switch from one drive to the other, click on the icon required. The current drive is shown, together with the current directory, in the title bar.

Most space in the window is occupied by the directories. The structure of the directories is probably different on your screen to the one shown here. Only the Windows directories will resemble each other a little. Because of this, we shall limit ourselves to this directory for our exercise material. We shall first examine the icons for the directories. If drive C is the current drive, the icon in the upper left-hand corner will appear as follows:

```
🗁 c:\
├─ 🗀 bat
├─ 🗀 config
├─ 🗀 dos
├─ 🗀 emm4
```

As mentioned, the letter C represents the drive and the backslash is the symbol for the **root directory**. Each drive has a root directory which is divided into various subdirectories. A minus sign is shown in the icon of the C drive, which means that all subdirectories which belong to this directory are now being displayed. These directories are also symbolized by a folder icon. Using the mouse, double click on C and the Window will contain only the following icon:

You will now see a plus sign in the icon. It is obvious what this means: this directory contains more subdirectories.

To try this out, look through the entire directory structure of your hard disk. Double click on every folder which has a plus sign. When you have done this, the complete structure should be evident. It is probably sensible to enlarge the window containing the directory, in order to see as much as possible of the structure. Parts which are not yet visible can be brought into view using the scroll bars.

What you have just done in the window using the mouse, can also be done using the *Tree* option from the menu bar.

Working with directory windows

Tree	
Expand One Level	+
Expand Branch	*
Expand All	Ctrl+*
Collapse Branch	-
√ Indicate Expandable Branches	

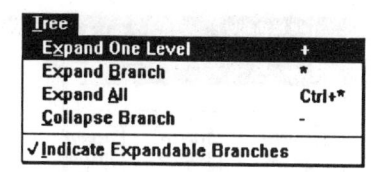

The *Expand One Level* command has the same effect as clicking on a folder which contains a plus sign. The *Expand Branch* command can lighten the work a little since all the subdirectories will be opened in one go, and not just the first subdirectory as in the first option.

By activating the *Expand All* option, the complete directory structure of the disk will be presented concisely. The *Collapse Branch* option removes all subdirectories of the selected directory from the window.

If you neutralize the last option, *Indicate Expandable Branches*, no plus or minus signs will be shown in the icons.

These options will probably be seldom used, because the commands can be implemented more quickly using the mouse.

To summarize, behind a folder with a plus sign there are more directories. A minus sign means that it is possible to remove one level from the window.

We have now learned how to approach directory structures. We shall now deal with the contents of directories. Call up the Windows directory structure (WIN). In this you will undoubtedly find the SYSTEM subdirectory. We shall examine the contents of this subdirectory further. Click on the icon of the WIN\SYSTEM subdirectory. The right-hand side of the screen now appears as shown in the diagram on the following page.

The contents of the windows and the names may be a little different on your screen. This is not important.

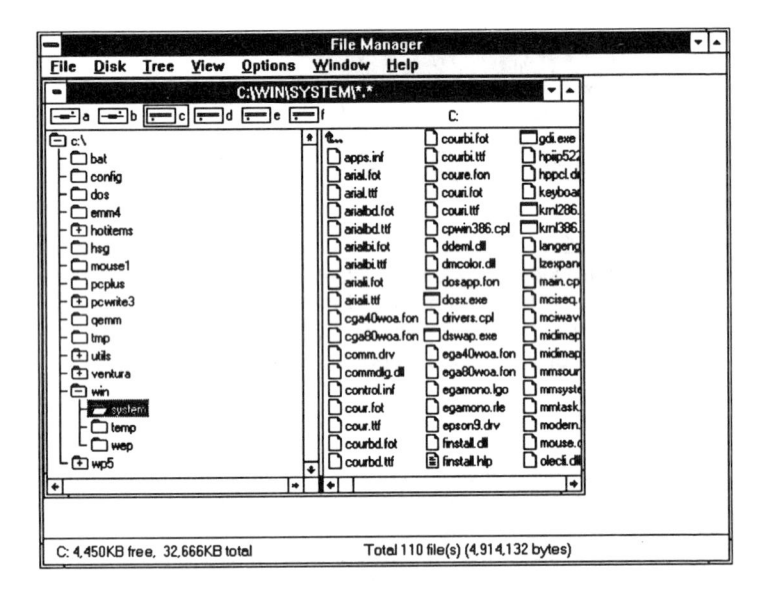

Open a new window by selecting the *New Window* option from the *Window* menu. Then click on another directory icon, for instance the \WIN\WEP icon, although you may choose another. There are now two windows in the File Manager. One window contains the directory structure on the left and the files from the SYSTEM directory on the right. The other window contains the directory structure on the left and the files in WEP on the right. In order to see both, we now give the *Tile* command from the *Window* menu. This is the same command as in Program Manager. The composition of the screen is approximately as follows (see next page).

The layout of the windows is determined under the *View* menu. The commands in this menu are subdivided into various groups.

Working with directory windows 163

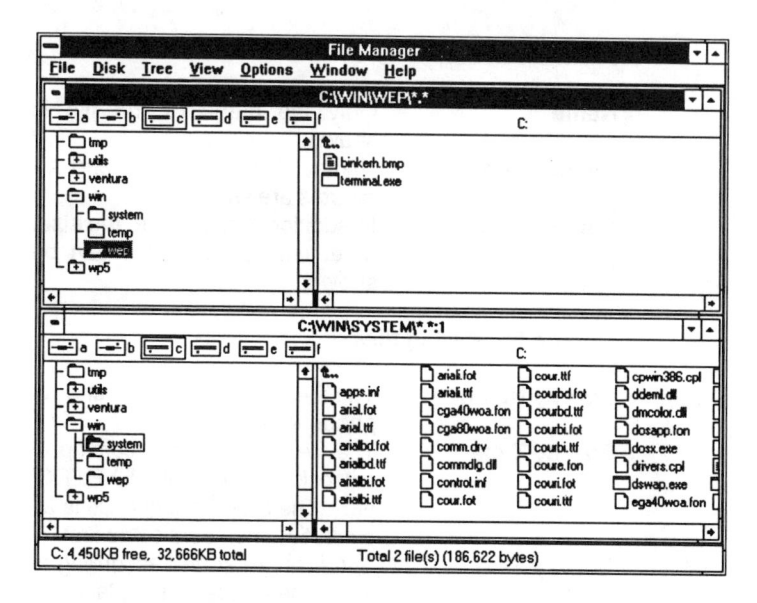

Window layout

The first three options in this menu deal with the layout of the windows.

Tree and Directory If you activate this option, the windows will appear on the screen in the same way as we have described above: the directory structure on the left and the files of the selected directory on the right.

Tree Only When this option is activated, only the directories are displayed, on the left-hand side. The right side remains empty.

Directory Only In this case, only the files in the selected directory are shown in the entire window. Practice will teach you which is the most useful method for your own work.

Split Split allows you to divide the screen into two sections according to your own requirements.

File Information

Name	Only the name of the file is shown.
All File Details	Name, size, date, time and attributes are shown.
Partial Details	In addition to the name, the size, date, time or attributes can be shown.

Criteria for sorting files

Sort by Name	The files are sorted by name alphabetically
Sort by Type	The files are sorted according to extension (BAT, COM, EXE, TXT etc.). The order of sequence is alphabetical; numbers come first.
Sort by Size	The files are sorted according to size. The largest file is placed at the top.
Sort by Date	The files are sorted according to the date of the most recent alteration. The file with the most recent changes is placed at the top.

File types

Name	This conforms to the MS-DOS rules. For example, A*.TXT means that all files which begin with the letter A and have TXT as extension, will be shown in the window.
Directories	The subdirectories are shown.
Programs	Programs are shown; in other words, files with the extensions EXE, COM, BAT and PIF.
Documents	Files which are attached to programs.
Other Files	All other types of file.

Working with directory windows

Show Hidden/ System Files — Shows those files which have the Hidden or System attribute.

```
View
√ Tree and Directory
  Tree Only
  Directory Only
  Split
√ Name
  All File Details
  Partial Details...
√ Sort by Name
  Sort by Type
  Sort by Size
  Sort by Date
  By File Type...
```

Using these options, it is possible, to a large extent, to display files in a window in a way which suits you. In this context, one point should be made concerning file attributes. MS-DOS has four attributes which assign certain properties to files:

attribute	property
R (Read only)	file is safeguarded against alteration
A (Archive)	file to be placed in archive
H (Hidden)	hidden file
S (System)	system file

A file which is safeguarded against alteration cannot be deleted or changed. An archive file has been created or altered since the most recent backup on the hard disk and therefore will be processed in the following backup. A hidden file is not normally shown; especially under MS-DOS, a hidden file cannot be shown without special tools or options. System files are those files which are part of the operating system. All file attributes can be altered using the *Properties* option from the *File* menu (Alt-Enter).

In the window, you will observe four different icons in addition to the file names, size etc. These represent:

Directories. Are always placed in front in alphabetical order.

Programs and batch files. Files with the extensions COM, EXE, BAT and PIF.

Document files. These files are attached to programs. When a file like this is selected, the corresponding program is also started up.

All other files.

6.2 Copying, moving and deleting files

Most people use the File Manager to copy, delete or move files. We shall perform a couple of exercises in this area. You should have an empty, formatted floppy for this. If you do not have a formatted disk available, look up how you can format a floppy using the File Manager in section 6.6. You can also use a test directory instead of a floppy. Section 6.4 describes how to create this.

If you have not yet already done so, divide the screen as described previously, i.e. activate the *Tree and Directory* option from the *View* menu. The directory structure is displayed on the left and the files of the WIN directory on the right. Using this, we shall practise copying and moving files.

Copying
In copying, the original file is retained at its original position and a copy is made at the desired position. To copy a file, hold down the Ctrl key and drag the file in ques-

Copying, moving and deleting files 167

tion to the desired drive or directory. Then release the
Ctrl key.

Moving

In moving, a copy is made at the desired position and
the original file is deleted. Here you should hold down
the Shift key, drag the file to the desired drive or directory. Then release the Shift key.

First *copy* the CLIPBRD.EXE file to the floppy or to the
test directory. Then *move* the file to the floppy. By this
action you have removed the CLIPBRD.EXE file from
the WIN directory. In order to restore it to the original directory, proceed as follows:

Click on the icon of the drive in which the file is now located. A window will appear on your screen. The drive
in question will be shown on the left, with subdirectories
if any. On the right, you will see the files including the
file you have just placed there.

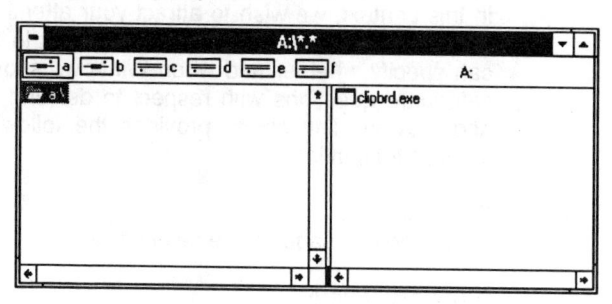

Then select the *Tile* option from the *Window* menu. The
windows will be placed neatly next to one another on
the screen. Now you only need to copy the file to the directory or to move it in order to restore the original situation. One important rule to be kept in mind when copying or moving files is that source and destination
directories should both always be visible when working
with the mouse. Working with the mouse can also be
easier. If you wish to drag files to another drive, Windows presumes that you wish to copy. If you drag within

the same drive, however, Windows presumes that you wish to move the file. In these cases, it is not necessary to use the Ctrl and Shift keys.

Deleting
It is very easy to delete files and directories in Windows. Select the file or directory required and press the Delete key. When you have confirmed that you wish to do this, the file or directory will be deleted.

Notes:
- If you do not have a special Help program, deleted files are lost forever, unless you run Windows under DOS 5.0. Under DOS you can recall deleted files using the UNDELETE command.
- When a directory is deleted, **all files and subdirectories** which are part of the deleted directory will also be deleted. Therefore, use this option only with great care.

In this context, we wish to attract your attention to the *Confirmation* option in the *Options* menu. In this, you can specify whether and when Windows should pose safeguard questions with respect to deleting, copying and moving. The option provides the following possibilities for confirmation:

File Delete
A warning message before deleting files.

Directory Delete
A warning message before deleting directories.

File Replace
A warning message before writing over existing files of the same name.

Mouse Action
A warning message before moving or copying when you drag files using the mouse.

Disk Commands
A warning message before formatting or copying a disk.

Note: You can also copy, move and delete files using commands from the *File* menu. Shortcut keys are also available, including F7 for moving and F8 for copying.

We have not yet touched on the possibility of processing several files simultaneously when dealing with copying, deleting and moving. To do this, a number of files must be selected. This is called **extending a selection**. In this, you are able to select a block of consecutive files by clicking on the first file and then moving to the last file and clicking while holding down the Shift key. It is also possible to make a selection of files by clicking on a number of dispersed files while holding down the Ctrl key.

Subsequently, the Copy, Delete and Move commands refer to all the selected files. Care must be taken especially with the *Delete* command, since a large number of files can be deleted with a single command.

The entire selection can be undone by clicking on a random file. A specific file can be removed from the selection by holding down the Ctrl key while clicking on the file in question.

6.3 Exercise 18

18) Select five files of your own choice and copy them to the floppy in one go.

6.4 Editing directories

When working with directories, three activities are important. Firstly, you should be able to create directories; secondly, you should be able to delete them, and thirdly, you should be able to switch from one directory to another.

Switching is very simple in Windows. You only have to click on a directory using the mouse. **Deleting** also poses few problems. Select the directory in question in the directory window and press the Delete key. If you confirm the safeguard question, the directory will be deleted.

Before creating a new directory, first select the directory under which the new directory should be placed. If, for instance, you wish to add a subdirectory to the WIN directory, select this directory first. Then, give the command *Create Directory* from the *File* menu. The name of the directory may contain up to eight characters, based on the normal DOS conventions, and it may also be followed by a period and an extension containing three characters.

Using these newly acquired skills, you can create a directory structure conforming to your requirements.

Directories are extremely important in the organization of data. Nevertheless, they do have one small disadvantage. Imagine that you are looking for a file of which you can only remember the first letter and the extension, but you cannot remember in which directory the file has been placed. Then there is no other alternative to searching through each individual directory for the file. This is a rather laborious task. Windows, however, has a suitable option for a job like this: *Search* from the *File* menu. Specify the name, with or without wild cards, and Windows will search through the entire disk if necessary to find this file or files.

Example
You are looking for the text of a letter, but you have forgotten the name of the file. You know that the extension must be TXT. In the dialogue box of the *Search* option, specify *.TXT behind *Search For*. Behind *Start From*, specify the drive supplemented by a directory to begin, if required. Finally, click on the *Search All Subdirectories* check box. A list containing all text files will appear on the screen a few seconds later.

6.5 Exercises 19 to 21

19) Create the subdirectory TEST under the WINDOWS directory.

20) Copy all files from the practice floppy to this directory.

21) Delete the directory again.

6.6 Editing disks

The *Disk* menu contains the options which enable you to format and copy disks. In addition, it is possible to give the disks a name. The individual options can be seen in the following diagram.

```
Disk
Copy Disk...
Label Disk...
Format Disk...
Make System Disk...
Select Drive...
```

Copy Disk This option is used to make backup copies. Source and destination disks must have the same capacity for storage. The hard disk cannot be edited using this option. When dealing with disks of differing formats, the files should be selected and copied manually.

Label Disk Each disk may receive a name for identification purposes. This process of naming is only useful when, for example, an archiving program can make use of this name.

Format Disk This option allows you to prepare disks in drive A or B to receive information. The *Capacity* drop-down list is used to specify the capacity of the

	disk in the drive in question. In addition there are options enabling you to specify a lable, to create a system disk and to implement rapid formatting.
Creating a system disk	This is similar to the formatting option, but in this case the operating system is also copied on to the disk.

6.7 Associating documents and programs

By using the *Associate* option from the *File* menu you will get to know an interesting feature of Windows. We have already encountered the four icons which can occur in a directory window. One of these is the so-called **document** icon. If you give a double click on this icon, a program will start up which loads the corresponding document into the memory. If you, for example, double click on a file with the extension BMP, Paintbrush will be automatically loaded. This, in turn, loads the selected file. This is possible due to the fact that a whole series of attachments has been made during the installation of Windows. These are all located in the WIN.INI file under the heading [Extensions]:

```
cal=calendar.exe ^.cal
crd=cardfile ^.crd
trm=terminal.exe ^.trm
txt=notepad.exe ^.txt
ini=notepad.exe ^.ini
pcx=pbrush.exe ^.pcx
bmp=pbrush.exe ^.bmp
wri=write.exe ^.wri
rec=recorder.exe ^.rec
hlp=winhelp.exe ^.hlp
```

Here, certain programs have been attached to the extensions of the files. If you wish to implement a new association, first select a file with the corresponding extension in the directory window, for example, TEST.DOC, and then select the *Association* option. In the dialogue box which then appears you will be asked to which program the files with the DOC extension should be attached. In this case, this could be Word for Windows.

Thus, in principle, you are able to associate almost all files. This means that you are immediately able to start up all files which appear in the directory window, whether they are files which can be executed (COM, EXE, BAT, PIF) or associated documents. In both cases, a double click is sufficient to start up a program.

6.8 File Manager settings

In addition to the *Confirmation* option which we have already dealt with, the *Options* menu contains other interesting options which influence the appearance of the File Manager on the screen.

Font The *Font* dialogue box enables you to choose a font for the directories and files in the various windows. It is also possible to choose a different font size. A larger font will probably make reading in the windows less strenuous on the eyes. You can specify in the check box whether characters should be shown in capitals or small letters.

Status Bar If this option is activated, a bar containing information about the current selections will be displayed at the bottom of the screen.

Minimize on Use If this option is activated, the File Manager will be shown as an icon when an application is started up from the File Manager.

Save Settings on Exit Using this option, you are able to specify whether or not alterations should be saved when you quit the File Manager. This concerns settings in the menu which regulate whether the display should be in small or capital letters, or whether the status bar should be shown etc. If you have activated this option, the same settings will appear the next time you start up the File Manager. The settings are saved in the WINFILE.INI file.

6.9 Summary

To conclude this chapter we have summarized the main functions of the File Manager in the following table:

task	execution
copy file	Ctrl-drag
move file	Alt-drag
delete file	Delete
selecting consecutive files	Shift-click
selecting at random	Ctrl-click
Starting up program	double click on file name

Application and appearance

7 Clock

7.1 Application and appearance

On almost every desk there is a clock. That is also the case with Windows. In Accessories there is a simple but useful program which displays the time on the screen.

7.1.1 Icon

The following icon represents the Clock in the Accessories group.

Clock

As you see, the hands are not moving.

7.1.2 Window

To start up the Clock program, double click on the icon. The following standard window containing an analogue clock will appear on the screen.

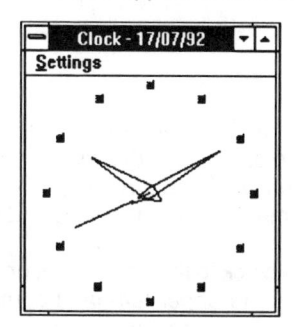

The menu bar contains only one menu: *Settings*. This menu provides the choice between several options.

Analog or Digital
Here, you are able to choose between an analogue clock or a digital clock. You only need to click on the desired option.

Set Font
If you have opted for a digital display, you may then select a font of your choice using the *Set Font* option. It is not possible to adjust the size.

No Title
The title bar will be switched off if you activate this option. You can restore it by double clicking on the top edge of the clock.

Seconds/Date
These options deal with the seconds and the date. In the case of a digital clock the date is shown in the window, and with an analogue clock the date is shown in the title bar.

Note: If a digital clock is displayed in the window, this means that the clock has been set previously and specified as digital. The Clock is displayed in the form in which it was set on the previous occasion.

7.1.3 Analogue

The *Analog* option is the default option in the Clock program. If you enlarge or contract the window, Clock will adjust the display in a way that a round clock is always visible, even if you make the window long and narrow.

We shall reduce the clock to the size of an icon. Click on the Control menu in the upper left-hand corner of the window and then on *Minimize*. The clock now displays only the hour and minute hands. But check this for a

Setting the Clock 177

couple of minutes. You will see that the clock keeps on ticking even though it resembles an icon.

7.1.4 Digital

Digital is the other method of expression. You can switch to this by activating the *Digital* option in the *Settings* menu. The window with the digital settings appears as follows.

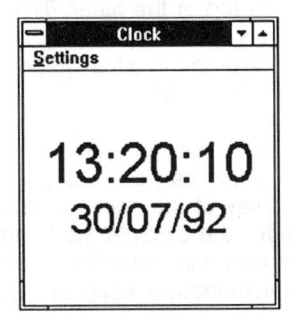

```
┌─────────────────┐
│ ▬    Clock  ▼ ▲ │
│ Settings        │
│                 │
│   13:20:10      │
│   30/07/92      │
│                 │
└─────────────────┘
```

This setting remains - even if you have quit Clock or Windows - until you switch over to the analogue method of display using the *Analog* option.

If you reduce the Clock to the size of an icon in this form, you will see only the hours and minutes, just as in the analogue version. The clock keeps on ticking here as well.

7.2 Setting the Clock

The Clock displays the time according to the computer. If this time has been specified correctly, there will be no need to alter it. But it will have to be altered in the case of moving from summer to winter time and vice versa.

To do this, go to the Control Panel in Main. Click on the *Date/Time* option. In the dialogue box which then appears, you can alter the time using the increase/decrease buttons next to the text boxes, or by directly specifying the correct time behind *Date* and *Time*.

7.3 Exercises 22 and 23

22) Start up Clock and another application consecutively, Write for example, without closing Clock. Reduce both windows so that they appear next to one another or one on top of the other. Then activate the window of the second application, in this case Write. Does the clock in the other window keep on ticking?

23) Reduce the clock as analogue clock and then as digital clock, as much as possible, but in such a way that the display of the seconds remains just visible. Then move the clock to the bottom of the screen. You are now able to work with other applications and simultaneously keep an eye on the time.

8 Calendar

8.1 Application and appearance

Windows was designed as a user interface with the intention of providing the user with facilities for carrying out clerical tasks, both professional and private. A calendar is indispensable in a system like this. The Calendar program in the Accessories group is able to process a number of different calendars. Accordingly, it is possible for various people to have their own personal calendars or appointment books, while a calendar can also be reserved for business use only. Each of these calendars is saved as an individual file and is recognizable by the CAL extension.

8.1.1 Icon

The Calendar program in the Accessories group window is represented by the following icon:

Calendar

You can open this Windows program by double clicking on the icon.

8.1.2 Window

When the program has been opened the window appears as shown on the following page.

Firstly, you will see a list of appointments for the day in question. Based on its own system time, the computer is able to display the present day and date. Modern computers can now display this each time they are started up. With older computers, it is sometimes necessary to enter or correct the date using the DATE instruction in DOS. The window may be larger or smaller on your computer. This may result in a difference in the day layout.

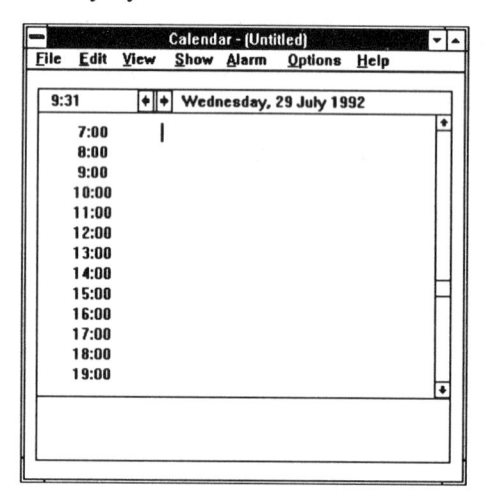

8.1.3 Calendar with daily schedule

At the top of the work area, the current time, day of the week and the date are displayed. Under this, there is a list of times with an interval of a half hour between each time. This schedule is standard at first. The time which is shown at the top of the list (here 7.00 AM) is called the **starting time**. You may determine this starting time personally. Thus, you can arrange this to coincide with the beginning of your day. If it should occur that you have an appointment before the normal starting time, you can shift to an earlier hour using the scroll bars or the PgUp key. This also applies to the times at the end of the day. In the Calendar, the day extends from 0.00 to 23.00 hours. Due to this, you are only able to see a part of the daily schedule when the program is started up.

Application and appearance

In the lower part of the screen, space has been reserved for setting down notes. Here in this scratch pad, you can jot down reminders and notes about matters which are not directly linked to a fixed time, such as making telephone calls, birthdays etc.

The two boxes with scroll arrows, between the time and date information, enable you to browse through the previous day (left box) or through the following day (right box), by clicking on the corresponding box. The daily schedule, beginning at the starting time, is displayed together with the notes.

8.1.4 Calendar with Month view

If you click on the *View* menu, the *Day* and *Month* options will appear. You will see by the check mark that the calendar is currently set to the Day schedule. Now select *Month* by clicking on it or by using the F9 key. If you prefer to work with the mouse, the quickest way of switching over from Day to Month view is to double click on the date, thus on the text to the right of the scroll arrows.

The Month view provides a list of all the days in the month. The day in which the cursor is located is displayed inversely. This is the current day and this is also indicated by a 'greater than' and a 'smaller than' sign. Using the cursor keys and the PgUp and PgDn keys, you can browse through the days of the current month and also through those of other months. If you use the scroll arrows next to the date information, the program will switch to the same day in the following or previous month.

Space has also been allocated in the Month view for setting down notes. Reminders are placed here which apply to a specific day but which are not bound to a fixed time. Of course, you can also enter and alter information here.

8.2 Some remarks concerning calendar planning

Before you begin planning using the Calendar, it is advisable to consider a couple of points.

A great deal of the information in the calendar, such as the number of days in February and the day of the week corresponding to a certain date, can be calculated independently by Windows. However, there are regional and national holidays which a computer does not know automatically, not to mention other personal details like birthdays and summer holidays for instance. You must first register this kind of information.

8.2.1 Schedule

The Calendar provides a timetable which allows you to note down an appointment for any moment of the day. When Calendar has been started up, it is possible to

Some remarks concerning calendar planning 183

register a maximum of 24 appointments, that is, one appointment per whole hour. You can make this standard schedule more precise, but you should consider in advance the schedule which suits your appointments, or the length of time an appointment usually takes. Normally, a division into half-hours is sufficient. Then, it is still possible to make appointments for a quarter of an hour before or after the whole hour. However, the registration of appointments which deviate in this way costs more effort. That is why it is important to choose a schedule in such a way that appointments like this form an exception.

8.2.2 The start of the working day

It is, of course, possible to scrutinize all the hours in the daily list, but you have really no interest in examining the hours between 0.00 and 6.00 when starting the working day. If you go to work at 7 AM, you will wish to see which appointments are scheduled for that time.

Therefore, we shall first adjust a number of settings. Click on *Options* in the menu bar or press Alt-O, and then select *Day Settings*. The following diagram will appear:

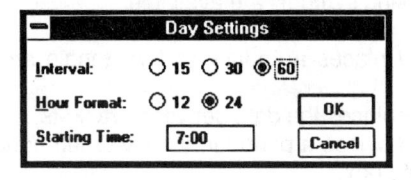

```
┌─────────── Day Settings ───────────┐
│ Interval:      ○ 15  ○ 30  ● 60    │
│ Hour Format:   ○ 12  ● 24    ┌──────┐│
│                              │  OK  ││
│ Starting Time:  │ 7:00 │     └──────┘│
│                              ┌──────┐│
│                              │Cancel││
│                              └──────┘│
└──────────────────────────────────────┘
```

In the *Interval* box, specify 30 by clicking on it or by going there with the cursor keys. Now you are able to make an appointment every half hour. The *Hour Format* can remain unchanged, otherwise 15.00 will be shown as 3.00. The *Starting Time* is important, as we have seen above. Go to this option by pressing Tab twice or click on it using the mouse. The time which you specify here appears as starting time in the Calendar daily timetable. Specify here the time you begin working, or the time you normally deal with the first appointment. Click on *OK* to confirm this or press Enter.

8.3 Defining special days

We shall now register public holidays and personal information, beginning with New Year's Day. Click on the *Show* menu or press Alt-S, and then select *Date*. Specify 1-1-92 as the date. If you make a typing error which invalidates the specified date, Windows will call your attention to this with a message. Acknowledge this message with Enter or *OK* and register the date once more. Calendar will now display a month view of January, the first day being shown inversely. (If you get a day view of January 1st, switch over to the month view using the shortcut key F9.) We shall specify this day as a public holiday by clicking on the *Options* menu from the menu bar (or by pressing Alt-O) and by then selecting *Mark*. A dialogue box will appear with various possibilities for definition.

8.3.1 Marking symbols

Five marking symbols are available.

Symbol 1 places a square or a rectangle around the date.
Symbol 2 places the date between brackets.
Symbol 3 places a period in the lower left-hand corner of the date box.
Symbol 4 places a cross in the upper left-hand corner.
Symbol 5 underlines the date in question. Due to the fact that this underlining coincides with the lower edge of *symbol 1*, these two symbols may not be used together. A combination of symbols of your choice can be assigned to each day.

Defining special days 185

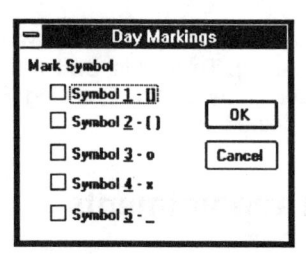

```
┌─────────────────────────────┐
│ ─    Day Markings           │
│ Mark Symbol                 │
│    ☐ Symbol 1 - []          │
│    ☐ Symbol 2 - ( )   ┌──────┐
│                       │  OK  │
│    ☐ Symbol 3 - o     └──────┘
│                       ┌──────┐
│    ☐ Symbol 4 - x     │Cancel│
│                       └──────┘
│    ☐ Symbol 5 - _           │
└─────────────────────────────┘
```

We shall now assign a reference to the various marking symbols. The (impossible) combination of 1 and 5 will receive a meaningless function.

symbol	meaning
1	public holidays
2	regional holidays
3	deadline VAT payment
4	birthdays
5	holidays

According to this table, January 1st should receive *symbol 1*. Click on the corresponding check box or press the Spacebar. The other symbols can be activated using the Tab key. Subsequently, mark your birthday with *symbol 4*. This can be done more quickly using the function keys. First press F4, then specify your birthday, then press F6, click on the *symbol 4* check box, and finally *OK*.

8.3.2 Introducing commentary

In this way, you can mark all public and private holidays and also other important days. Let us examine your birthday once again. You will undoubtedly wish to celebrate it with friends, and you wish to make a note concerning this. Click on the scratch pad in the lower part of the work area, or go there using the Tab key. Then make the desired note. Using the Tab key, you can return to the calendar section.

After all these preparations, you can now seriously begin calendar planning. To do this, switch the Calendar over to the Day view again. Pressing F8 is the quickest means of doing this.

8.4 Registering appointments

As already mentioned, it is possible to note appointments in the standard timetable, but appointments which deviate from this can also be registered.

8.4.1 Appointments conforming to the schedule

Registering appointments which conform to the schedule is very easy. First press F4 to open the Calendar at the desired date. Then go to the desired time using the cursor keys or the mouse, and register the appointment. It is possible to jot down more text than can be shown, with a maximum of eighty characters. If you try to enter more text, you will get the message that the text is truncated or broken off.

8.4.2 Appointments which deviate

Appointments or plans which deviate from the standard schedule are registered in another way. Imagine that you will leave earlier today than you normally do, at 16:40 for instance. Click on *Show* from the menu bar and then select *Today* (Alt-S, T). Now press F7. In the dialogue box which then appears you can specify your departure time as *Special Time*:

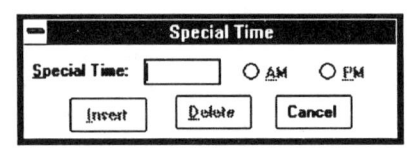

As you will observe, the *AM* and *PM* options are displayed in grey. This means they are not active. These options are only used if you have specified a 12 hour notation in the *Day Settings* option.

Now click on *Insert* or press Enter and you will see in the Day view that the special time has been introduced and that the insertion point is located at that particular time. You can register the appointment immediately.

8.5 Setting an alarm

Of course, you will not wish to have to watch the clock constantly to avoid forgetting your appointments. For this reason, an *Alarm* has been included in the Calendar program. This can remind you of each appointment. The signal is given optically, and may also be given acoustically if required. It is also possible to be reminded of an appointment up to ten minutes beforehand. We shall first regulate these options. Click on *Alarm* (Alt-A) and then on *Controls* (C). Specify here the number of minutes you wish to be warned in advance.

Caution: These settings apply to **all** appointments in your calendar!

If you do not wish to receive an acoustic signal, click on the corresponding check box. The warning will then only be given optically.

Calendar status	warning
active window	dialogue box appears (see diagram next page)
inactive window	title bar flashes
icon	icon flashes

When you have specified the desired settings, click on *OK* or press Enter. You can now determine at which appointments the warning should be given. Place the insertion point at the relevant appointment, click on *Alarm* and then on *Set* or press Alt-A and S. This can be done more quickly by using F5. Press once to activate the warning for the appointment in question. Pressing it again switches it off. This setting can be recognized by the small clock which appears to the left of the appointment if the warning is switched on.

When the system time in your computer indicates that it is time to warn you of the appointment, *Alarm* will warn you using optical signals and with three peeps if required. This flashing continues until you turn it off. As soon as you go to an icon or activate a window, the following dialogue box appears:

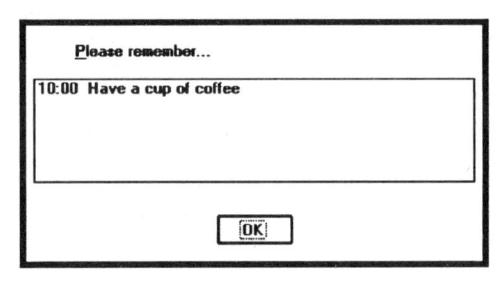

```
Please remember...
10:00 Have a cup of coffee




            [OK]
```

Acknowledge this with *OK* and the warning will be switched off.

8.6 Managing appointments

Sometimes a certain appointment is no longer necessary or is cancelled or postponed. Alterations can easily be made in the Calendar. Editing information which has already been registered is done using the Clipboard with which you are already familiar.

Accordingly, it is possible, for instance, to write notes like 'Pay VAT' or 'Buy present' just once and to then copy them. To do this, mark the written text using the mouse and copy it to the Clipboard using the *Copy* option from the *Edit* menu. Using the *Paste* option from the same menu, you are able to copy the text to all relevant appointments.

If you wish to relocate a certain appointment because this has been postponed, mark the corresponding text using the mouse. Then choose *Edit* and *Cut*. In this way the text is placed in the Clipboard. Using F4 and the cursor keys, select the new time or date. Then use *Edit* and *Paste* to extract the contents of the Clipboard. If an alarm signal has been attached to this appointment, it will not be copied. This must be assigned separately to the new appointment. The old signal should be removed.

Deleting a certain appointment takes place in roughly the same way. Only, in this case, you omit the registration procedure. The *Remove* option from the *Edit* menu is used to delete all appointments on a certain date or on different days. If you select this option, a dialogue box will appear in which you can specify the first and last days of the cancelled appointments.

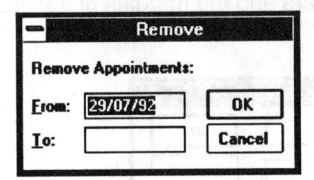

If you only specify a date behind *From*, the appointments on that day alone will be removed.

8.7 Saving the calendar

When the appointments have all been registered, they only need to be saved on disk. Choose the *Save* option from the *File* menu and specify the name, with the path if required, for instance PRIVATE. Then you know that your personal appointments are registered here. The name of the file must conform to the DOS conventions, thus a maximum of eight characters, no spaces etc. If you do not specify an extension, Windows will assign CAL as extension. Calendar then knows that PRIVATE.CAL is a calendar file.

8.8 Printing the calendar

If you wish to take your calendar with you on your travels or to meetings, or if you wish to assign your appointments to your secretary, there is the facility to print your calendar. Only those days with appointments and notes will be printed, so you do not get any empty pages. The appointments with an alarm receive an asterix when printed.

8.8.1 Layout

First determine the layout of your appointment list. Click on *File* and then select *Page Setup* or press Alt-F and T. A dialogue box will appear in which you can specify headers and footers and the margins of the list which is to be printed.

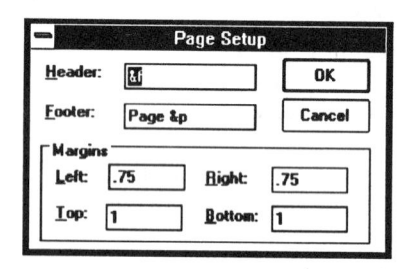

In the headers and footers, certain codes are used for information such as system time and date, page number and the file name of the Calendar. The codes have the following meanings:

Printing the calendar

code	meaning
&l	print the following text left-aligned
&d	current system date
&c	print the following text centered
&f	file name of the current calendar
&r	print the following text right-aligned
&t	current system time
&p	current page number

The header may look like this:

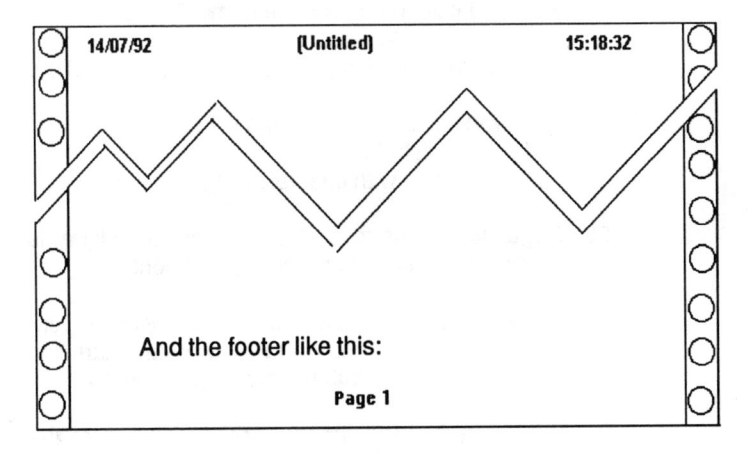

14/07/92   [Untitled]   15:18:32

And the footer like this:

Page 1

The margins are measured in inches. Click on *OK* or press Enter to retain the *Page Setup*.

8.8.2 Printing

Printing can now begin. Go to the *File* menu and select the *Print* option. In the dialogue box which then appears, you must specify the first day in the appointment list which you wish to have printed. The default setting here is the day which is currently displayed in the

Calendar. Only this day will be printed if you do not specify anything behind *To*, just as in the case of deleting appointments. You should specify otherwise the last day of the appointments you wish to have printed.

Note: Check if the printer has been properly installed. You can do this by going to the *Print Setup* option in the *File* menu.

8.9 Exercises 24 to 29

24) Create a new calendar (*File, New*) for this year and mark all public holidays with the marking *Symbol 1*. Save the calendar under the name GENERAL.

25) Specify the following options in the GENERAL calendar:
    - the working day starting time is 8:30
    - 24 hour registration
    - time schedule with intervals of 15 minutes.

26) Regulate the alarm so that an acoustic signal is emitted 5 minutes before an appointment.

27) You are planning to take a short holiday in the period between Christmas and New Year. Mark the days in this period with the marking *Symbol 4*.

28) Return, using the quickest possible method, to the present day and register an appointment ten minutes from the present moment. Register the text: 'Phone Dame Edna'. Activate the alarm for this appointment and reduce the calendar to an icon.

29) When the icon begins blinking, click on it. Then print the current page from your GENERAL calendar. Define the layout in such a way that the header of the printed page receives the calendar name and the footer contains the text: 'Data from:' followed by the time and date of the print. Save this entity.

9 Cardfile

9.1 Application and appearance

The Cardfile accessory functions as a filing cabinet, or to be more precise, various filing cabinets. Just as you would have different filing cabinets for different purposes, you approach Cardfile in exactly the same way.

This program is a small database. Windows assists you in the organization and processing of, and in the search for, information. It cannot, of course, compete with the large professional database systems, but that is not its aim. You will see that Cardfile is perfectly suited to small tasks which come up in daily life. You are not only able to save texts in this small database, but also images. In doing this, Cardfile surpasses many professional database systems.

9.1.1 Icon

The Cardfile application is represented in the Accessories group window by the following icon:

Cardfile

Start up the application in the familiar way by double clicking on the icon. Windows then opens the Cardfile window.

9.1.2 Window

The standard appearance of the Cardfile window is as follows:

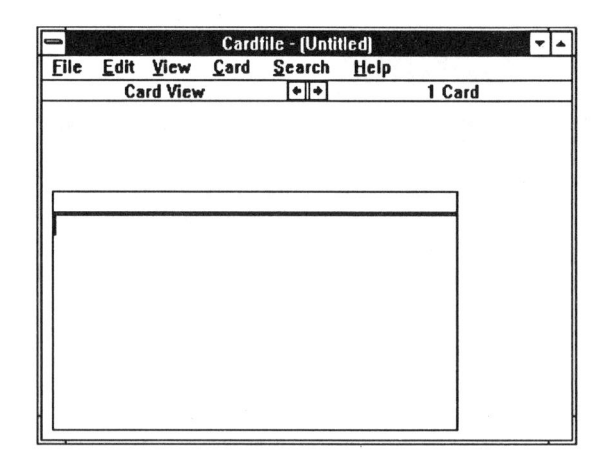

```
┌─────────────────────────────────────┐
│ ═    Cardfile - [Untitled]      ▼ ▲ │
│ File Edit View Card Search Help     │
│    Card View        [◆][◆]   1 Card │
│                                     │
│                                     │
│       ┌───────────────────────┐     │
│       │                       │     │
│       │                       │     │
│       │                       │     │
│       │                       │     │
│       │                       │     │
│       │                       │     │
│       │                       │     │
│       └───────────────────────┘     │
└─────────────────────────────────────┘
```

Under the menu bar, there is another bar in which the status information is displayed. Here, you will see the display mode (*Card View*) and the number of existing cards (*1 Card*). The two scroll arrows enable you, just as in Calendar, to browse through the various cards. This is, of course, only possible when there are several cards.

Under this, there is an index card. This card is subdivided into an index line and an information area. Cardfile always presents an blank card at the start and at the creation of a new cardfile.

9.1.3 Card View

There are two different methods of displaying information in the Cardfile: on Cards or in a List. They differ from each other with respect to the editing possibilities. This option is to be found in the *View* menu. You can recognize the active option by the check mark in front of it. At the moment, this is *Card*.

9.1.4 List View

Now select the List view by clicking on *List*. The window now appears as follows.

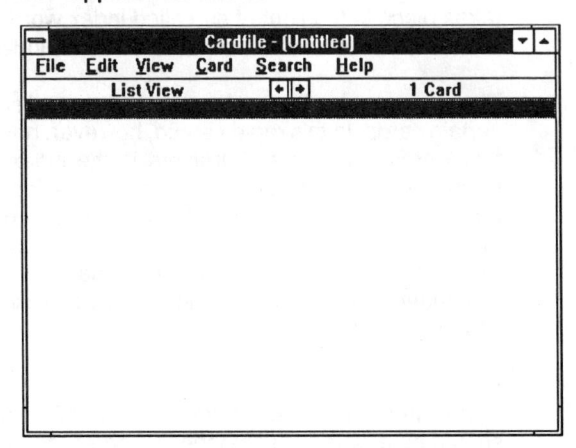

```
┌─────────────────────────────────────────┐
│         Cardfile - (Untitled)       ▼ ▲ │
│ File  Edit  View  Card  Search  Help    │
│         List View      ◄ ►      1 Card  │
│                                         │
│                                         │
│                                         │
│                                         │
│                                         │
│                                         │
│                                         │
└─────────────────────────────────────────┘
```

The information on the status line has changed and the blank card has disappeared. Instead of this blank card, there is now a dark bar. A line is reserved as an index line for every card in the cardfile.

But we shall first get to work with the card. Switch back to *Card* under the *View* menu.

9.2 Organization of the Cardfile

As mentioned, Cardfile can be regarded as a small database. For this reason, we wish to outline a couple of points before we begin on this card indexing system. This is important in order to be able to work optimally with the cardfile later. We shall not begin any theoretical discussion about databases, we shall only deal with a few fundamental aspects of this system.

9.2.1 The index line

If you wish to create a cardfile, the various cards have to be arranged in some kind of order. This classification takes place in the light of so-called index words. These are the first words which are entered in the index line.

These words also have a function in the rapid search for certain cards. In this rapid search, however, not only the first words but all the characters in the index line are utilized. As the name already indicates, the index line is a part of the index for the entire file. This line may contain a maximum of forty characters, including spaces. Thus, in each cardfile, you must consider how the order of sequence of the cards should be determined, and what you will be able to look for.

Example
You wish to create an address file in which the cards should be arranged in alphabetical order regarding surnames. But you also wish to be able to search in terms of postal code and town. The index line should appear as follows:

```
Atkinson JG9 4NY John O'Groats
Cleese LE1 3FT Land's End
```

In another case, you wish to create a file dealing with real estate, classified according to property. A rapid search based on location should also be possible. The index lines should appear as follows:

```
Farmhouse Braintree
Flat Aberdeen
```

The first word or text fragment determines the order of sequence. Numbers are classified according to the first cyphers, not according to their value. If required, they should be registered with pre-zeros.

9.2.2 The information area

The real information which is to be saved is registered in the information area. Each card has room for eleven lines each containing forty text characters. If that is not sufficient, two or more extra cards can be used. The index line must be identical to that in the first card, excepting the extension numbering. Thus:

```
Indexing 01
Indexing 02
Indexing 0n
```

It is possible to record images in the information area (as a supplement to the text if required) as well as text. We shall demonstrate this using the map you made with Paintbrush.

9.2.3 Telephone numbers

For those users who own a Hayes (or compatible) modem, Cardfile offers an interesting extra option. Cardfile is able to automatically dial a telephone number which is registered on one of the cards. We shall return to this presently.

Telephone numbers should, however, be clearly distinguished from other data which include numbers. The software is not able to make this distinction. Cardfile does this as follows: the first series of numbers on a card or index line which contains three or more numbers, possibly with a hyphen, is regarded as being a telephone number and can be used for automatic dialling.

Thus, if you wish to make use of this automatic dialling facility, it is advisable to register the telephone number in the index line to prevent erroneous interpretations within Cardfile.

9.3 Creating a cardfile

We shall begin by creating an address file using the following data:

name	address	telephone
Stan Laurel	123 Eel Avenue BL6 2IP Blackpool	0253-12345
Oliver Hardy	456 Whale Lane MO4 2LY Morecambe	0524-23456
Harold Lloyd	789 Salmon Springs RH3 4PC Rhyl	0745-34567

The above mentioned theory teaches us:

The surnames or company names are chosen as index words. In addition, we have registered the name of the town in the index line to facilitate rapid searching. The telephone numbers are registered at the end of the index line in order to avoid confusion with other numbers.

9.3.1 Processing a blank card

Each time a new cardfile is begun, the blank card has to be filled in. We begin with the first address, because Cardfile does the classification automatically.

We first fill in the index line. To do this, select the *Index* option from the *Edit* menu, or press directly the function key F6. In the dialogue box which then appears, you can specify the name, town and telephone number.

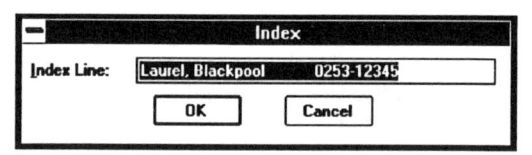

Creating a cardfile

To make it more obvious, we have left a space between the town and the telephone number. If you leave too much space here, there may be too little space for the telephone number. The maximum number of characters for the index line is forty. If there is too little space, remove a couple of characters before filling in the rest.

Now enter the address as shown here:

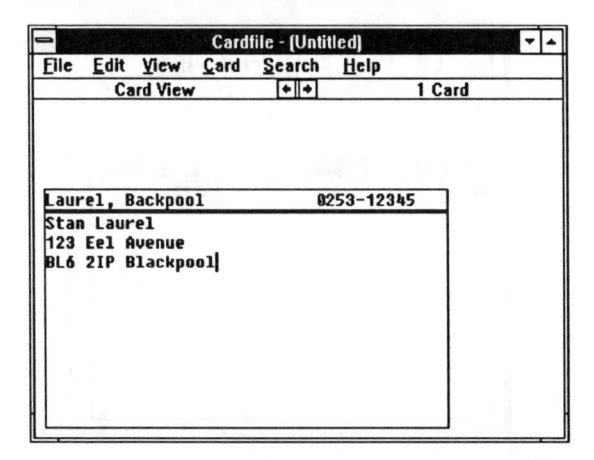

```
┌─────────────────── Cardfile - (Untitled) ──────────▼─▲─┐
│ File  Edit  View  Card  Search  Help                   │
│      Card View          [←][→]           1 Card        │
│                                                        │
│                                                        │
│  Laurel, Backpool            0253-12345                │
│  Stan Laurel                                           │
│  123 Eel Avenue                                        │
│  BL6 2IP Blackpool|                                    │
│                                                        │
│                                                        │
│                                                        │
└────────────────────────────────────────────────────────┘
```

In the Card view, the insertion point is always located in the information area of the card in the foreground. The data can be entered immediately. All additions and corrections take place by setting the insertion point at the desired position and registering the information using the keyboard. Each alteration can be undone by selecting the *Undo* option from the *Edit* menu, as long as the cardfile has not been saved and the card has not yet been classified. It is, thus, still in the foreground.

9.3.2 Adding new cards

For the second and all subsequent addresses, new cards have to be added. To do this, select the *Add* option from the *Card* menu by clicking on it using the mouse. The function key F7 does this quicker. For each new card, a dialogue box first appears to deal with specification of the index line.

```
Hardy, Morecambe 0524-23456
```

If you now press *OK*, a new card which is blank, except for the index line, will appear in the foreground. Introduce the rest of the information.

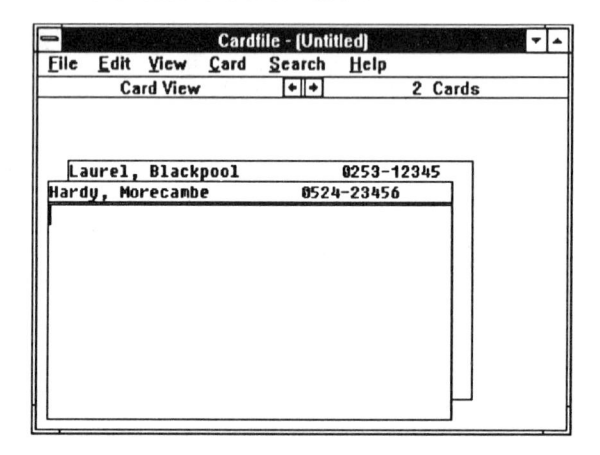

```
┌─────────────────────────────────────────┐
│            Cardfile - (Untitled)      ▼ ▲│
│ File  Edit  View  Card  Search  Help    │
│         Card View      ◄ ►      2 Cards │
│                                         │
│                                         │
│   ┌─────────────────────────────────┐   │
│   │Laurel, Blackpool    0253-12345  │   │
│   │Hardy, Morecambe     0524-23456  │   │
│   │                                 │   │
│   │                                 │   │
│   │                                 │   │
│   │                                 │   │
│   │                                 │   │
│   │                                 │   │
│   │                                 │   │
│   └─────────────────────────────────┘   │
└─────────────────────────────────────────┘
```

Complete the list by registering the information concerning Harold Lloyd from Rhyl. Do this in exactly the same way as described above.

9.3.3 Text cards

The cards which we have filled in up until now contain only text, i.e. the names and addresses of certain persons. Click on the *Edit* option in the menu bar. You will see that in the central part of the menu a check mark is placed next to *Text*.

This means that you can enter text using the keyboard, copy text to the Clipboard and extract it again, and you can delete texts.

However, a card can only contain a limited amount of text: a maximum of eleven lines each containing 40 characters. If you attempt, for instance, to copy a text of more than 440 characters from the Clipboard, this command will not be implemented.

9.3.4 Picture cards

As mentioned, it is also possible to register pictures in the Cardfile. There are many possibilities of combining pictures with the Cardfile. We shall deal with only a few of them here. You are able to copy a picture to a card, you can move it around and you can remove it again.

We shall now create a picture card using the small map which you made previously using Paintbrush. Start up Paintbrush, load the ROADMAP file, mark it using the pick and select the *Copy* option from the *Edit* menu. You may now close Paintbrush again. The map is now in the Clipboard.

Now take Mr. Hardy's card. Press Ctrl-V to copy the contents of the Clipboard to the card.

Note: If the hourglass remains stationary, just move the mouse or press a cursor key.

But you will observe that nothing appears. The reason is obvious: examine the *Edit* menu. A check mark is placed in front of *Text*, therefore Cardfile is not able to record pictures. Using the mouse, click on *Picture* and then on *Paste* in the same menu, or press Ctrl-V again. Now the map will be transferred to the card.

If the map or another picture is too large for the card, that need not be a problem. Even when the cardfile has been saved, you are able to move the picture on the card until the desired fragment becomes visible. Thus, the card resembles a window through which you can see the picture. If necessary, you will have to perform this movement in several steps if the total shift is greater than the dimensions of the card. This also applies in the case of the picture overlapping the text.

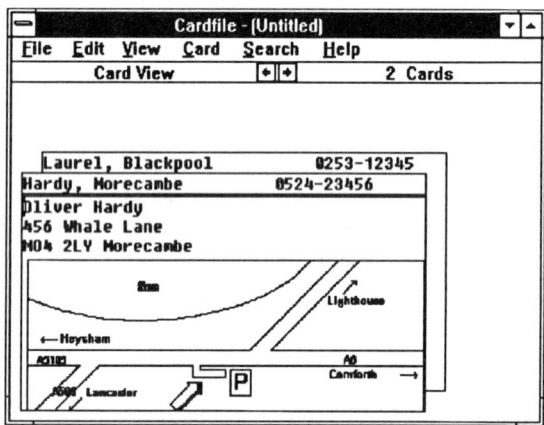

9.3.5 Mixed cards

In Cardfile, you do not have to restrict yourself to exclusively picture or text cards. It is also possible to add text to pictures so that mixed text and picture cards can be created.

To do this, switch over to the *Text* mode once more by clicking on this option in the *Edit* menu. Type the following text:

```
Route to Oliver Hardy
```

The result appears somewhat disorderly, as if you have written upon the plastic which encases the map. In fact, Cardfile works at two levels, one for pictures and one for text. Thus, you must either move the text to another position using spaces or empty lines, or relocate the picture. Do not forget to activate the corresponding mode when you are working with text or picture!

Caution: If you have copied a picture to the 'picture level', it is not possible to copy another picture to the same card. Each new picture replaces the previous one. Size does not play a part in this. If you wish to save more pictures, you must use additional cards. Do not forget to register exactly the same text in the index line, with extension if necessary, so that cards which belong together are placed together in the cardfile.

9.3.6 Working with pictures and objects

It is also possible to make alterations to a picture. To do this, activate the *Object* option in the *Edit* menu. As you will see, this option receives another name when a picture has been placed on the card and the *Picture* option has been activated. This option is now called *Edit Paintbrush Picture Object* and provides the possibility of making alterations in a dynamic way.

Activating this option starts up the program containing the stored picture. The picture can now be edited as a Paintbrush picture. Subsequently, close Paintbrush. Before leaving the program, when asked, you should state that the picture will be altered. You will return automatically to the Cardfile, where you will see that the picture has indeed been altered. If the result is not satisfactory, the *Undo* option in the *Edit* menu enables you to undo the alterations.

Thus, it is not necessary to start up the graphical program separately. Windows does this for you. In addition, the program monitors the alterations made and reminds you if an alteration threatens to be lost.

Extensive information concerning OLE technology and dynamic data exchange can be found in chapter 15 of this book.

9.4 Saving a cardfile

Each small database which you create using Cardfile is saved as a separate file with the extension CRD. Accordingly, it is possible to create cardfiles for various purposes and to save these separately. Do this by selecting the *Save* option from the *File* menu. It is advisable to assign names to the various databases which refer to the contents. The normal DOS rules apply here too: a maximum of eight letters, no spaces etc.

9.5 Printing a cardfile

It is sometimes necessary to have information on paper. In Cardfile, it is possible to either print the card in the foreground, or all the cards consecutively, in the correct order of sequence. When printing, you have to keep in mind the following, in this order:

9.5.1 Check the printer settings

Every time you change the printer settings, such as the print direction, the cartridge font in the case of laser printers, the paper feed etc., these settings remain in force until you switch the printer off and then on again, or until you change the settings manually. Thus, when printing a large number of cards, it is sensible to check the *Print Setup* option in the *File* menu, to see if the current settings are correct.

9.5.2 Adjusting the layout

If you choose the *Page Setup* option from the *File* menu, a dialogue box, with which you are already familiar from Calendar, will appear. In this, you are able to specify the margins in addition to the contents of the headers and footers. Cardfile uses the same codes as Calendar.

9.5.3 Printing

As already mentioned, when printing you have the choice between printing all available cards or only the selected card in the foreground.

If you are planning to print all the cards in a certain database, select the *Print All* option from the *File* menu.

To print one specific card you must bring it into the foreground. In the Card view, this is very simple. Click on the index line in the case of visible cards or use the scroll boxes in the status bar. In this case, you only need to select the *Print* option from the *File* menu.

9.6 Searching in a cardfile

When you are searching through a large cardfile for very specific information, browsing with the help of the scroll boxes is a tedious and time consuming occupation. For this reason, Cardfile possesses two quick and handy search possibilities. Go to the *Search* menu in the title bar. This menu contains the *Go To*, *Find* and *Find Next* options.

9.6.1 Searching through the index

The index is the complete collection of all the index lines in a cardfile. If you select the *List* option from the *View* menu, you will see a fragment of this index.

If you know the index word referring to certain information, you will be able to find the required card quickly, because index words normally occur only once. This also applies to our address file.

To search for a card using a complete or partial index word, we make use of the *Go To* option from the *Search* menu. This option looks through the index. For instance, to look for an address containing an Edinburgh telephone number, register the Edinburgh number 031 in the dialogue box. As soon as a card is found containing the three consecutive numbers 031 in the index line, Cardfile places this card in the foreground.

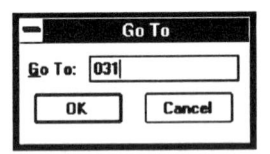

If no card is found containing these numbers, you will receive a message to this effect. The diagram below is the result of a search for the text 'Charlie' which does not appear in an index line.

9.6.2 Searching in the information area

In order to search in the information area, you make use of the *Find* option from the *Search* menu. Specify in the dialogue box what is to be sought. Cardfile will now examine every card to look for the specified text. This may take a little time.

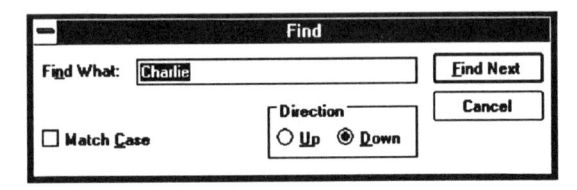

The *Find Next* option is especially handy when Cardfile has found a card but this card is not the one you are looking for. Cardfile then looks for another card in the

Dialling automatically

file containing the same text. Of course, this also happens in the case of searching using the index, if you have specified a part of the index word. If you have specified a complete index word or the beginning of it, for instance, 'Chaplin', this option is superfluous because identical or similar cards are arranged consecutively.

9.7 Dialling automatically

If your computer has a Hayes (or compatible) modem, you no longer have to telephone your acquaintances manually. Cardfile can dial for you automatically.

Imagine you wish to telephone Mr Lloyd in Rhyl. To do this you need to know his number which is to be found on his card. Using F4, activate the dialogue box dealing with index search. Specify the name and town: 'Lloyd Rhyl'. Cardfile supplies the required information.

Then choose the *Card* menu from the menu bar and then the *Autodial* option. The following dialogue box will appear on your screen:

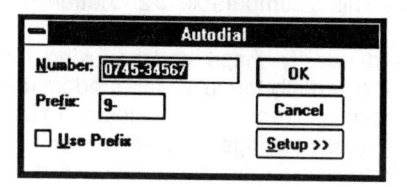

	Autodial	
Number:	0745-34567	OK
Pre**f**ix:	9-	Cancel
☐ **U**se Prefix		**S**etup >>

Lloyd's telephone number is located in the *Number* box. If this is the first occasion that you telephone using the modem and Windows, you must select *Setup*. The dialogue box extends and the following appears:

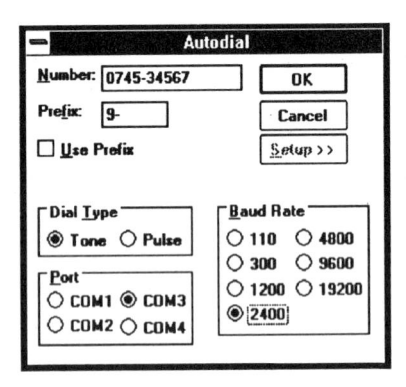

There are three groups of options. In each case, a single option can be activated by clicking on the corresponding check box. In the light of the settings here, Cardfile assumes the following:

- The telephone is connected to a computer operated exchange, a so-called tone exchange.
- The modem is connected to the third serial port of the computer, COM3.
- The data is transported with a speed of 2400 bits per second. This is comparable to 240 letters per second.

You should specify these options using information which can be partially found in your modem manual and which you can also receive on request from British Telecom. When these settings have been specified, click on *OK*. Cardfile will then dial the number. A dialogue box will appear on the screen, asking you to lift the telephone. The person who is being called will not be enchanted by the electronic crackle of the modem in his or her ear. It is self-evident that the modem and the telephone must be connected to the same line.

If everything has gone smoothly, you will have contact within a few seconds.

For additional and more extensive information concerning working with modems and the corresponding set-

Editing a database 209

tings, we refer you to the chapter dealing with Terminal. This communications program makes intensive use of modems and data transport. Most readers will not use the *Autodial* option in Cardfile. For this reason, we shall deal more extensively with all details concerning this in chapter 11.

We have just instructed Cardfile to look for an existing number. This number can also be personally chosen by clicking on it before you select the *Autodial* option from the *Card* menu. A double click using the mouse works quickest.

9.8 Editing a database

In each database, things have to be altered now and again, not only to correct mistakes but also to bring information up to date.

9.8.1 Altering the index line

Occasionally the index line has to be changed, for instance, if someone changes address or receives a new telephone number. In a case like this, click on the *Index* option from the *Edit* menu. The dialogue box which then appears enables you to specify the changes to be made to the card in the foreground.

9.8.2 Altering the information area

In the information area, you are able to carry out all desired changes in the same way as you learned in the Write application. Do not forget to activate the proper mode: *Text* for cards with text and *Picture* for cards with pictures.

9.8.3 Restoring cards

As long as the database has not been saved and the edited card has not been placed in the background, you can restore this card to the state in which it was before the alterations. In this case, select the *Undo* option from the *Edit* menu, or use the shortcut combination Alt-Backspace. The most recent alterations will now be undone. The alterations in the other cards will be retained.

9.8.4 Deleting cards

If you no longer need the information on a card, you can delete this card. Select the *Delete* option from the *Card* menu to delete the card in the foreground. As a safeguard, a dialogue box will appear in which you must confirm that you really do wish to delete the card.

Caution: Cards which have been deleted are **irretrievably** lost!

9.8.5 Duplicating cards

Sometimes different cards contain roughly the same information. This can occur, for instance, if you have separate cards for different contact persons in one firm. Cardfile has a useful facility for cases like this.

Example
We shall add three cards to the present database: Miss Callas, Miss Sutherland and Mrs Pavarotti who all work at Harrods in London.

We shall first add a new card by clicking on the *Add* option in the *Card* option (shortcut F7). Now register the following:

```
Callas London
```

Click on *OK* and enter the name and address of the firm in the information area:

```
Harrods Ltd.
Postbox 1000
LN1 UP2 London
```

Then create cards for the two other contact persons in the firm by duplicating this card. Thus, choose twice in succession the *Duplicate* option from the *Card* menu. Now you only have to alter the index lines of these two cards. You are familiar with this procedure.

9.8.6 Merging cardfiles

It may be necessary for your own clerical management to adopt an existing address file and to make use of it. To prevent having to look for a certain address in two different files, it is advisable to merge these two cardfiles.

When merging two files, you should always first open the file which will later contain the cards. Then choose the *Merge* option from the *File* menu. A dialogue box will appear which you already know from opening a file. Mark the file which is to be merged and click on *OK*. The two files will now be merged in such a way that each card is placed in the proper position. Save the result. You now have one file containing all the addresses.

9.9 Exercises 30 and 31

30) Apply our short theoretical introduction to a file. Specify here the rules concerning the classification and the contents of the index lines.

31) Create a file for books, magazines, videos and CDs.

10 Notepad

10.1 Application and appearance

It occurs regularly that something has to be jotted down quickly: a telephone call, something urgent, a sudden idea etc. Windows provides the Notepad accessory for cases like this.

Notepad is a small text editor which is very suitable in situations when a more powerful word processing program like Word or WordPerfect is not really necessary.

10.1.1 Icon

Notepad is part of the Accessories group. The icon appears as follows:

Notepad

Start up the program with a double click on the icon.

10.1.2 Window

When started up, the standard Notepad window will appear. This consists of a work area, the notepad sheet and the normal window components such as menu bar, scroll bars etc.

You will see by the text in the title bar ('Untitled') that the current sheet is still free and has not yet been saved in a file.

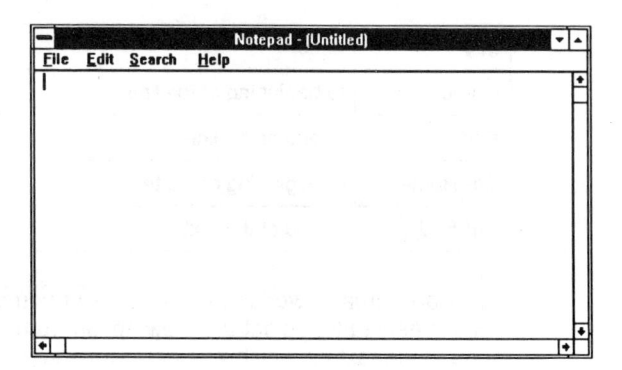

10.1.3 Notepad files

Each window sheet in this application is saved as an individual file which receives the extension TXT unless you specify otherwise.

Notepad is also able to process other files, such as AUTOEXEC.BAT, CONFIG.SYS, WIN.INI, SYSTEM.INI. In this, it is only important that these files are **text files**. These are files which only contain printable ASCII characters and which are frequently concluded by an end-of-file character. In contrast to this, files which also make use of non-printable characters are called **binary files**. For example, all programs are binary files. This kind of file cannot be processed by Notepad.

10.2 Creating a file

When you start up Notepad everything is ready for making a new file. The only thing you have to do is type the desired text in the window. To do this, make use of the keyboard as described previously. Using the scroll bars, you can move the window quickly over the text. In addition to the mouse, the following keys allow you to move the cursor quickly:

key	effect
Home	to beginning of the line
End	to end of the line
Ctrl-Home	to beginning of the text
Ctrl-End	to end of the text

If you are already working on a text and you wish to make a new note, select the *New* option from the *File* menu. If the text on which you were working previously has been altered, a dialogue box will appear which draws your attention to this. Choose *Yes* if you wish to save the changes, *No* if not but nevertheless wish to open a new file, and *Cancel* if you prefer to continue working on the old file.

When entering text, you will observe that the text moves to the left when you reach the right-hand side and continue typing. You begin a new line only when you press the Enter key. This can be prevented by choosing the *Word Wrap* option in the *Edit* menu. Then you begin a new line automatically as soon as the last typed word does not fit into the present line in the window. The lines are automatically adjusted again if you make the Notepad window narrower or broader. The text is always adapted to the current width of the window. When printing, Notepad will keep this in mind. This way of working conforms to the normal break-off procedure in a word processing program.

10.3 Saving files

To save your notes, choose either *Save* or *Save As* from the *File* menu. The latter option will be automatically chosen by the program, even if you choose the *Save* option. Using *Save As* enables you to alter a file and to save the altered version under a different name than the original. The original version remains under its own name.

10.4 Searching in the Notepad

In large texts, a search function can be very useful for finding a certain position in the text. Go to the *Search* menu and select the *Find* option. In the subsequent dialogue box, you can specify the text which should be sought.

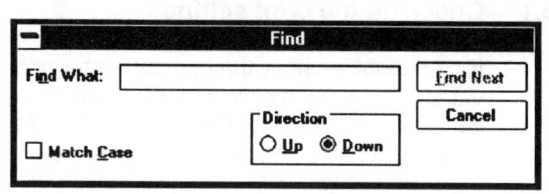

```
┌─────────────────────── Find ───────────────────────┐
│ Find What: [                    ]      [Find Next] │
│                    ┌─Direction─┐       [ Cancel  ] │
│ ☐ Match Case       │ ○ Up ● Down│                  │
│                    └───────────┘                   │
└────────────────────────────────────────────────────┘
```

In the *Match Case* check box, you can specify whether or not the program should pay attention to small and capital letters. If you do not activate this box, Notepad will look for all possible versions.

The *Up* and *Down* options allow you to search either backwards or forwards through the text from the current cursor position. If you wish to search through the whole text, you must first move the cursor to the beginning of the text. Then specify *Down* as search direction. The other way around is also possible, of course, i.e. cursor to the end and then *Up*.

If Notepad has found the text which you were looking for, but it is not the position you required, select from the *Find* menu the *Find Next* option. This can also be done using the shortcut key F3. Notepad then searches in the specified direction for the next occurrence of the text. When there is no (further) occurrence of the text, a message is given to this effect. This is as follows:

```
┌──────── Notepad ────────┐
│  ⓘ   Cannot find "Windows"│
│                         │
│         [OK]            │
└─────────────────────────┘
```

10.5 Printing a file

Printing in Notepad notes takes place in the same way as in other applications from the Accessories group. You are already familiar with this procedure.

10.5.1 Checking the print settings

If you doubt whether the correct printer has been activated in the case of several printers being connected, or if you are not sure that the connected printer has been properly regulated, you should check the printer settings before printing, and alter these if necessary. Choose *Print Setup* from the *File* menu. You can make all the necessary alterations here.

10.5.2 Specifying the page setup

Subsequently, you should determine the layout of the page to be printed. Choose the *Page Setup* option from the *File* menu. The following window will appear on your screen:

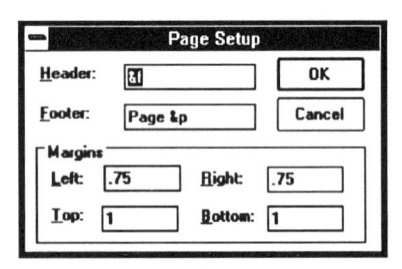

```
┌─────────── Page Setup ───────────┐
│  Header:  [&I]          [  OK  ] │
│  Footer:  [Page &p]     [Cancel] │
│  ┌Margins────────────────────┐   │
│  │ Left: [.75]  Right: [.75] │   │
│  │ Top:  [1]    Bottom: [1]  │   │
│  └───────────────────────────┘   │
└──────────────────────────────────┘
```

You can specify the format of the headers and footers here and the margins of the page to be printed.

This dialogue box is identical in all Accessories applications. Notepad will print the file within the margins specified. If *Word Wrap* has been activated, the text will be printed just as it appears on the screen.

Finally, select the *Print* option from the *File* menu. Notepad will print the file, taking into consideration the settings specified under *Print Setup* and *Page Setup*.

10.6 Altering text

If you wish to make an alteration in a noted text, first open the corresponding file by clicking on the *Open* option from the *File* menu. In the now familiar dialogue box, select a file or fill in the name of a file. The text of the file will appear in the window. Using the keyboard, you can now alter the text by deleting and adding new characters.

Large slices of text should be selected using the mouse. Then, you are able to delete, copy or relocate these fragments using the Clipboard. To relocate a fragment of text, select the *Cut* option from the *Edit* menu. The text will be stored in the Clipboard and can, using the *Paste* option from the same menu, be placed at a new position.

The *Undo* option from the *Edit* menu enables you to undo the most recent alterations. If you click on this having moved a text, this relocation will be undone. If you select this option once more, the text will be inserted again. Thus, this option works as a kind of switch between the present and previous situation.

Finally, if you choose the *Select All* option from the *Edit* menu, you can mark the entire Notepad text in order to execute a certain task. This can also be done using the shortcut keys:

- Ctrl-Home (places cursor at the beginning of the text)
- Shift-Ctrl-End (marks all to the end of text).

When you have marked the whole text in one of these ways, you can then copy it to the Clipboard. If you wish, for instance, to merge two files into one large file, open the second file and, using the *Paste* command from the *Edit* menu, add the contents of the Clipboard to this file.

10.7 Limits to the file size

Using Notepad, you can edit files up to a size of roughly 50,000 characters.

If you try to open a file which is too big for Notepad, you will receive a message to this effect. If you attempt to open the README.WRI text using Notepad, the following window will appear:

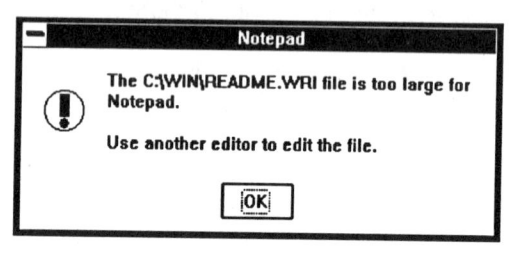

```
┌─────────────────────────────────────────────┐
│                  Notepad                    │
├─────────────────────────────────────────────┤
│     The C:\WIN\README.WRI file is too       │
│  (!) large for Notepad.                     │
│                                             │
│     Use another editor to edit the file.    │
│                                             │
│                   [OK]                      │
└─────────────────────────────────────────────┘
```

10.8 Logbook files

Notepad also provides the possibility of keeping so-called **logbook files**. These are files in which the date and time are registered along with each note.

You can create a logbook by opening a new file and placing the following text at the beginning of the file:

    .LOG

Do not forget the period in front of the letters!

Subsequently, using the *Time/Date* option from the *Edit* menu (or shortcut F5), specify the current date and time on the next line.

Make your note and save it. When you reopen this file, you will observe that the system date and time have been added underneath.

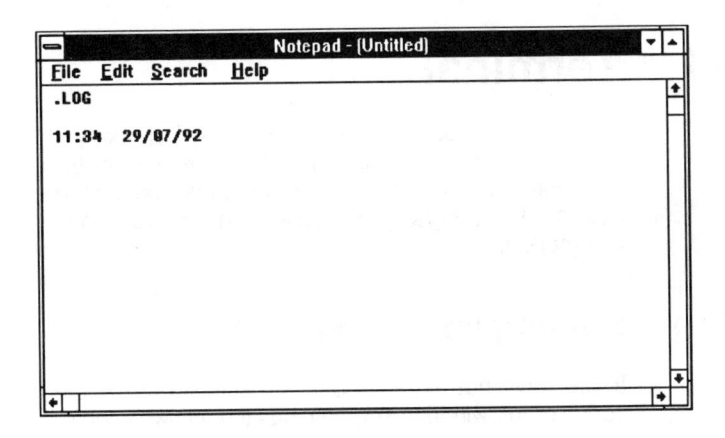

```
┌─────────────────────────────────────────────┐
│ ━             Notepad - (Untitled)     ▼ ▲ │
│ File  Edit  Search  Help                    │
│ .LOG                                        │
│                                             │
│ 11:34  29/07/92                             │
│                                             │
│                                             │
└─────────────────────────────────────────────┘
```

10.9 Exercises 32 and 33

32) Print the Windows file SETUP.TXT. In the layout, specify that the file name should appear as footer and that the page number as header.

33) Create a logbook file under the name TRIPS. This should serve as a register in which only the destination, the number of miles (or kilometres) and the duration of the trip need to be entered after you have opened the file.

11 Terminal

The Terminal application enables you to connect your computer to other computers. This allows you to draw upon information from **online databases** and **bulletin boards**. This program requires extra hardware in terms of a modem.

11.1 Starting up Terminal

If you have not already done so, activate the Accessories group window. Terminal has the following icon:

Terminal

Start up this program by double clicking on the icon. The standard window will be opened. This appears as follows:

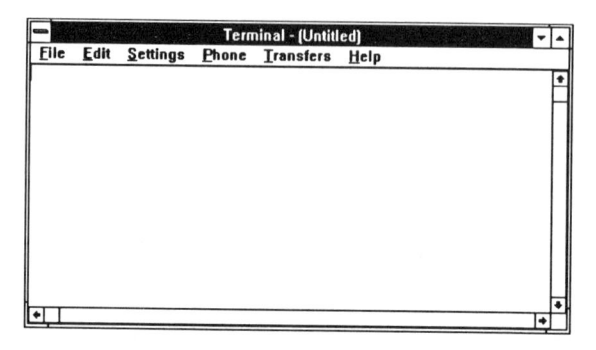

Under the title bar you will see an empty window. In this, the text which is being transported to or from another computer is displayed.

11.2 Hardware requirements

Terminal can only be used when assisted by extra hardware. If connection to other computers is to be made via a telephone line, your computer must be connected to the telephone network.

Modem
Connection to the public telephone network takes place using a special device, called a **modem**. Modem is short for **mo**dulator-**dem**odulator. External modems have three connections: one for the electricity network, another for the telephone network and one for the computer. This last connection is coupled to a free serial interface on your computer. Normally, that is the communications port COM1. There are also internal modems which are placed as a card in the computer.

Null modem cable
If the computer with which you wish to communicate is located in the same room as your computer, you can use a **null modem cable** to link the serial ports of both computers.

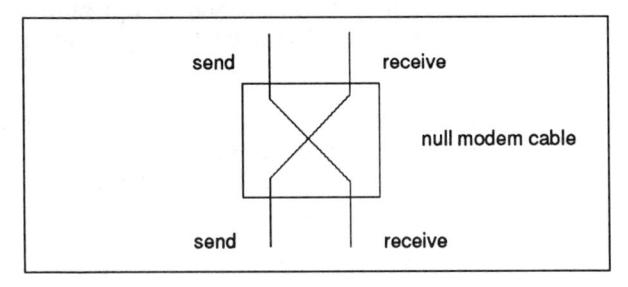

```
       send         receive
            \  /
             \/
             /\
            /  \              null modem cable
       send         receive
```

A null modem cable is necessary, for example, to transport data from a PC to a laptop if this works with different drive formats.

11.3 Other preconditions

In order to be able to communicate with another computer, you must first know how information is transported between computers.

Baud Rate
Data transport takes place via the serial interface. The individual bits of each character are transmitted consecutively via this interface. Your computer has to be adjusted to the speed with which this takes place. This speed is expressed in baud or bits per second and is called **baud rate**.

Start bit, data bits, stop bits
As you know, each character in the computer is made up of a certain number of bits, for instance, seven or eight bits. If you imagine the 0 and 1 bits as an uninterrupted flow through the serial line, which seven or eight bits belong together? The computer is not able to recognize them without some assistance. For this reason, extra information is required to define the beginning and end of each character. The beginning is always marked by a **start bit**. Then comes the fixed number of **data bits**. Finally, there are one or two **stop bits**. Then comes the start bit for the following character etc.

Parity
Occasionally, a computer will interpret line disturbance as being data bits. For this reason, in communication between computers, special methods are used to recognize and to eliminate the effects of these disturbances if possible. One of the most simple methods is to add an extra bit to each character sent, in accordance with a certain convention: the so-called **control** or **parity bit**. Using these bits, the receiver can check the accuracy of the transport according to the same convention.

Data Flow Control
Finally, one has to determine exactly what should happen if the information comes in quicker than the com-

puter can process it. This is often the case if the data is directly printed by the receiver. Therefore, it is necessary to specify just when data should flow from the one computer to the other and when a pause should be inserted. This is called **data flow control**.

Contract, password
How do you receive this information? If you wish to make use of the services of another computer, you must make a contractual agreement. This need not always be expensive - this rather depends upon the services you wish to use. The computer which supplies information is called the **host**. When the contract has been finalized, you are able to receive all the required information from the host. In this, use of a secret code word which you alone know is normal procedure. Otherwise, it is possible for someone else to use the facilities under your name, leaving you with the costs.

11.4 Preparing a session

In Terminal, we call communication with another computer via the modem a **session**. Before telephoning a bulletin board or a public database, you must first know the telephone number, of course. In addition, you must know the amount of data bits, stop bits and the parity with which these computers work. This information must first be registered in the Terminal program.

Open the *Settings* menu and select the *Communications* option. In the subsequent dialogue box, you can specify the desired settings using the corresponding options: *Baud Rate, Data Bits, Stop Bits* and *Parity*.

Caution: When specifying *Baud Rate* you must enter a speed which corresponds to the speed of your modem. Check in the modem handbook which baud rates are supported by your modem.

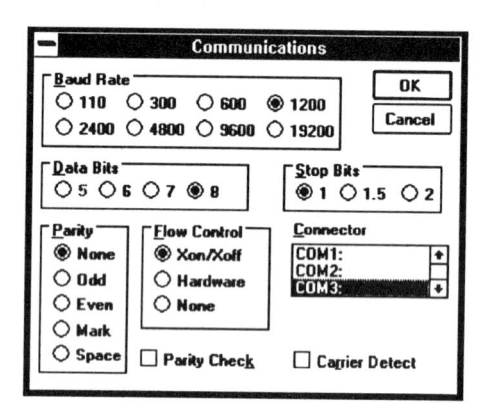

```
┌─────────────────────────────────────────┐
│ ■           Communications              │
├─────────────────────────────────────────┤
│ ┌Baud Rate─────────────────┐  ┌──────┐  │
│ │ ○ 110  ○ 300  ○ 600  ● 1200│ │  OK  │  │
│ │ ○ 2400 ○ 4800 ○ 9600 ○ 19200│ │Cancel│  │
│ └──────────────────────────┘  └──────┘  │
│ ┌Data Bits──────────┐  ┌Stop Bits─────┐ │
│ │ ○ 5 ○ 6 ○ 7 ● 8   │  │ ● 1 ○ 1.5 ○ 2│ │
│ └───────────────────┘  └──────────────┘ │
│ ┌Parity──┐ ┌Flow Control┐ Connector     │
│ │● None  │ │● Xon/Xoff  │ ┌COM1:──────┬┐│
│ │○ Odd   │ │○ Hardware  │ │COM2:      ││
│ │○ Even  │ │○ None      │ │COM3:      ┴││
│ │○ Mark  │ └────────────┘ └───────────┘ │
│ │○ Space │ □ Parity Check  □ Carrier Detect│
│ └────────┘                              │
└─────────────────────────────────────────┘
```

The computer is now adjusted to the settings of the host. If you possess a modem which can automatically dial a telephone number, you must first specify the number to be dialled. This takes place in the *Phone Number* option in the *Settings* menu. When this option has been chosen, the following dialogue box appears. Here, you can enter the required telephone number behind *Dial*.

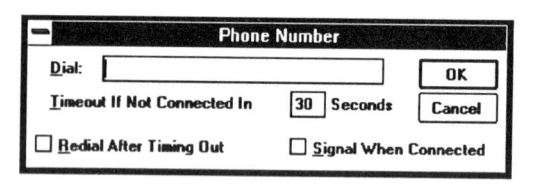

```
┌─────────────────────────────────────────┐
│ ■           Phone Number                │
├─────────────────────────────────────────┤
│ Dial: ┌──────────────────────┐ ┌──────┐ │
│       │                      │ │  OK  │ │
│       └──────────────────────┘ └──────┘ │
│ Timeout If Not Connected In [30] Seconds┌──────┐│
│                                         │Cancel││
│ □ Redial After Timing Out  □ Signal When Connected│
└─────────────────────────────────────────┘
```

One thing must be made clear here: it is not the computer which dials the number, but the modem. The computer, in other words, the Terminal program, only informs the modem of the number. However, Terminal does not only pass on the number, but must also finally set the dialling process in motion. To do this, the special modem command must be known. You can find this command in your modem handbook. Now open the *Settings* menu and then the *Modem Commands* option. The following dialogue box will appear:

Realizing a computer connection 225

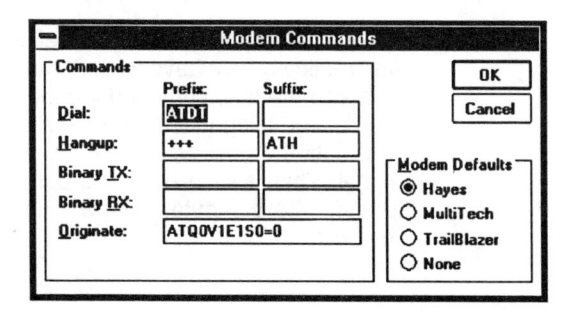

```
┌─ Modem Commands ─────────────────────┐
│ ┌─Commands──────────────────┐  ┌──────┐ │
│ │        Prefix:   Suffix:  │  │  OK  │ │
│ │ Dial:  [ATDT]    [    ]   │  └──────┘ │
│ │ Hangup:[+++ ]    [ATH ]   │  ┌──────┐ │
│ │ Binary TX: [  ]  [    ]   │  │Cancel│ │
│ │ Binary RX: [  ]  [    ]   │  └──────┘ │
│ │ Originate:[ATQ0V1E1S0=0]  │ ┌Modem Defaults─┐│
│ │                           │ │ ◉ Hayes       ││
│ │                           │ │ ○ MultiTech   ││
│ │                           │ │ ○ TrailBlazer ││
│ │                           │ │ ○ None        ││
│ └───────────────────────────┘ └───────────────┘│
└──────────────────────────────────────┘
```

In the *Modem Defaults* options box, choose the modem with which your modem is compatible, or *None*, and fill in the commands for *Dial* and *Hangup*. With *Dial*, specify under *Prefix* the characters which should precede the telephone number, and under *Suffix* the characters which should follow the number.

A number will only be dialled if the modem understands the specified characters.

11.5 Realizing a computer connection

Now that all the necessary settings have been regulated, we can give the command which implements the connection.

Click successively on *Phone* and *Dial*. A dialogue box will show the telephone number to be dialled. In addition, a default setting of 30 seconds is specified, followed by a **time-out**. Normally, a connection should be made within this time. If you have not yet specified a telephone number, a dialogue box will appear automatically. You can specify a number in this box.

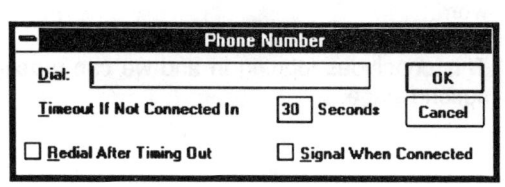

```
┌─ Phone Number ────────────────────────┐
│ Dial: [                    ]   ┌────┐ │
│                                │ OK │ │
│ Timeout If Not Connected In [30] Seconds ┌──────┐│
│                                          │Cancel││
│ □ Redial After Timing Out   □ Signal When Connected│
└───────────────────────────────────────┘
```

Note: If your modem is not able to dial a number automatically, you have to work with a switch between the telephone and the modem. Dial the desired telephone number manually, and wait until the host acknowledges this with a signal. Then switch over and put down the phone. The computer is now connected to the host.

11.6 Session procedure

After this first attempt to work with Terminal, we shall examine a session more closely.

A session like this consists of various stages which are executed one by one in the same order of sequence. Each stage may consist of a large number of separate commands which may occur in different combinations.

11.6.1 Logging in

Each session begins with **logging in**. This entails the following:

- making a connection, using a datanet if required. A separate logging in must take place for this datanet.
- identification to the host, usually a combination of a user name and a password.

In practice, this normally means that the host asks your name. You give your name or another word by which you can be identified. Subsequently, you will be asked to give a password. Often you have to repeat this password.

This concludes logging in and we can proceed to the second stage.

11.6.2 Dialogue

After logging in, it is possible to send commands to the host who will respond to valid commands and will send the results to your computer. Terminal displays these results on your screen. In the case of faulty or invalid commands, a message to this effect will appear on the screen. This message differs according to the host. This message is sent by the host, not by Terminal.

If you wish to give commands to the host, you should wait until the host is ready. The host also waits when you send a command. But how do the sender and receiver know that the other has completed the sending or receiving of the message? Simple: the host sends a prompt, like the one you know from DOS, to conclude the response. You conclude your command by pressing the Enter key.

The stage which we have called **dialogue** here makes up the main phase of a session. The dialogue may also be the preparation of the following stage which, however, may not occur in every session.

11.6.3 Exchanging files

In a dialogue, the information sent and received appears alone on the screen in general. However, it is sometimes necessary to exchange and save entire files. The difference between these two procedures can be compared to the difference between making a telephone call and writing a letter.

If you call up an electronic notice board, a bulletin board, you can ask for a list of files. You can then choose one of these files and have the host send it to you.

Exchanging files always takes place in two stages. Firstly, the host is informed of the file to be sent. This is the dialogue phase in which the host receives the instruction to send or receive something. Subsequently, you must give the Terminal command for sending or receiving the file. Click on the *Transfers* menu. You can choose from the following possibilities:

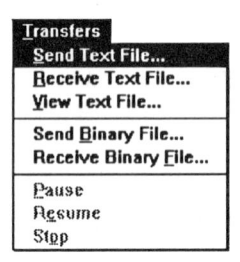

```
Transfers
Send Text File...
Receive Text File...
View Text File...
Send Binary File...
Receive Binary File...
Pause
Resume
Stop
```

The options are self-evident. If you choose one of the first five possibilities, Terminal must know the name of the file which should be displayed, sent or created. When you have chosen one of these options, a list will appear as a window. These windows all resemble one another. However, the largest window will appear if you click on *Receive Text File*. Three check boxes allow you to specify the way in which you wish to save the files. If you select the first check box, the contents of a received file will be added to another file. Click on the second box if the characters to be saved have ASCII codes ranging from 0 to 31. The third box provides the possibility of replacing two or more received consecutive spaces by a tab when saving.

11.6.4 Logging out

The last stage in a session is always **logging out**, in other words, politely taking leave of the host. You cannot just switch the computer off in the middle of a session or break the connection abruptly by hanging up. This may only be done in an emergency.

Just as in the case of logging in, logging out also takes place in two stages:

- taking leave of the host
- breaking the connection; in the case of a datanet session, you must also sign off first.

Signing off differs according to the program. You will mostly find the corresponding option in the menu. When you have made it clear to the other computer that you wish to quit, the other computer will send a message that the connection has been severed. Then you may also break the connection by choosing the *Hangup* option from the *Telephone* menu.

11.7 Printing

Terminal provides two possibilities for printing information during a session. It is possible to print a complete session while it is being carried out. In addition, a part of this information can be printed, namely the information which is shown or has just been shown in the Terminal window.

If you wish to print certain information later, you have to first receive it as a file. Later you can have it printed by Notepad or by another program.

11.7.1 Printing incoming messages immediately

When you have specified which printer should operate in which way, you can connect (or disconnect) the printer to the transmission line by choosing the *Printer Echo* option in the *Settings* menu. Everything which is now received will be simultaneously shown on the screen and printed.

Information which is already visible on the screen when these options are chosen or which appears just at that moment, will not be printed. Accordingly, it is important to give the *Printer Echo* command on time. If you wish to print the whole session simultaneously, you must give the command before beginning the session.

Clicking on *Settings* and *Printer Echo* works as a switch. If printing has been switched on, a check mark is located in front of the *Printer Echo* option. If you click once more on this option, the printer will stop and the check mark will disappear.

11.7.2 Printing text fragments

It is often not really necessary to print the entire session. Mostly you are interested in specific information: a message in the mailbox, or certain information from an online database. Owing to the fact that this type of information is frequently included in other text, you do not know precisely when the required information will be sent. Thus, it can only be printed at the moment that it becomes visible on the screen. In this case, the method of printing described above will not work.

In order to print a text which has already been received, you must select it. Do not worry if the text disappears at the top of the screen. Terminal buffers the text; in other words, the program saves it in its memory. This buffer cannot, however, absorb an unlimited amount of information. For this reason, it is advisable to print the text as quickly as possible when you have observed that this contains the information you require.

Due to the fact that the transmission will mostly continue in a case like this, i.e. the host keeps on sending data, you should first interrupt the session. Click on *Transfers* and *Stop*. During a dialogue, Ctrl-S will also bring this about. This command is transmitted directly to the host.

Then use the scroll bars to mark text or choose the *Select All* option from the *Edit* menu if you wish to print all the data in the buffer. Then you can copy the required information to the Clipboard using the *Copy* option from the *Edit* menu. From here you can save the information and later print it.

You can continue the session by clicking on the *Resume* option in the *Transfers* menu. If you have stopped the session using Ctrl-S, you can resume it using Ctrl-Q.

11.8 Advanced options

Up until now we have exclusively made use of the most important default settings in Terminal. This communications program can, however, perform much more complicated tasks. It is able to execute the first and last stages of a session more or less automatically. In addition, dialogue and data transport can be considerably simplified and expedited. We shall examine the various options and settings more closely below.

11.8.1 Registering telephone numbers

The *Phone Number* option from the *Settings* menu allows you to specify or alter a telephone number. Terminal can pass this number on to the modem.

A telephone number is specified in the text field, along with brackets and hyphens if necessary. Some telephone centrals still work using pauses; these are generated by a comma. Each comma represents two seconds pause. Valid forms of telephone numbers are thus:

```
0219876543
(021)9876543
0219876-543
(021)9876-543
(021),,98,76-,543
```

Connection to the host does not always take place immediately. For this reason, you can give Terminal the command to continue dialling automatically until a connection has been made. First specify in the *Timeout If Not Connected In* box a time between 30 and 39 seconds. If you then activate the *Redial After Timing Out* option, Terminal will make a renewed effort after the specified number of seconds.

In situations like this, you will probably not remain waiting in front of the screen until a connection has been made. Therefore, you should activate the *Signal When Connected* option. The familiar Windows peep will warn you as soon as Terminal has made a connection.

11.8.2 Terminal emulations

Many hosts take for granted certain features of the terminal to and from which they send and receive data. These features deal primarily with the characters which are sent when certain keys are pressed, particularly function keys. Additionally, these features concern the instructions which cause the terminal to react by positioning the cursor correctly, clearing the screen etc.

Terminal can emulate three different types of terminals. Select the *Terminal Emulation* option from the *Settings* menu. In the dialogue box which then appears, one option may be chosen from the three possibilities.

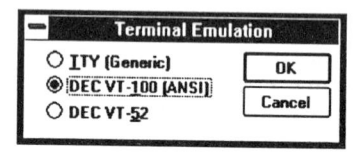

```
┌─────────────────────────────────────┐
│         Terminal Emulation          │
├─────────────────────────────────────┤
│  ○ TTY (Generic)         ┌────────┐ │
│  ● DEC VT-100 (ANSI)     │   OK   │ │
│  ○ DEC VT-52             ├────────┤ │
│                          │ Cancel │ │
│                          └────────┘ │
└─────────────────────────────────────┘
```

Only the host management can tell you which of these options should be chosen. The second option, *DEC VT-100 (ANSI)* is the default option. Most hosts can cooperate with this. If you do not receive information concerning the emulation which should be used, or if you communicate only with mailboxes, select the *TTY (Generic)* option. In this case, no special functions will be supported. Your computer then works as a kind of telex. Only the normal typewriter functions are used. (This is the source of the abbreviation TTY: TeleTYpe.)

11.8.3 Terminal Preferences

To alter the screen display, or to translate the keyboard, choose the *Terminal Preferences* option from the *Settings* menu.

The dialogue box shown below will appear on the screen. The majority of the options can be set to your own preferences.

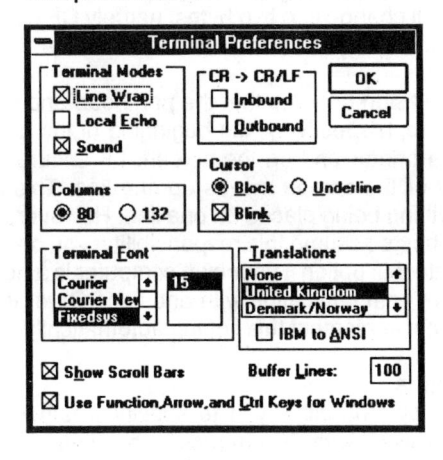

Terminal Modes
The first option in this group *Line Wrap* allows you to determine whether a received line which is longer than the window line should be continued on the next line or not. If this option is not activated, all characters which are situated outside the Terminal window will be lost.

If you activate the *Local Echo* option, the characters which you enter using the keyboard will not only be sent, they will also be displayed on the screen. If the remote computer echoes your keystrokes, leave the local echo off. The Printer Echo can only print the information which appears on the screen. Accordingly, you also decide here whether the information which you have entered should be printed too.

Activate *Sound* if the computer should emit a peep when the host wishes to state a message.

CR->CR/LF
This group contains two operating options. One option allows you to specify how the sign CR (*Carriage Return*, ASCII code 13) should be dealt with in *inbound* messages. The other option deals with *outbound* messages. If the corresponding box has been activated, this one byte will change into two bytes, namely CF (ASCII code 13) followed by LF, (*Line Feed*, ASCII code 10).

The CR sign ensures that the printhead and the cursor return to, respectively, the beginning of the current line on the printer and on the screen. LF ensures that the paper or the screen moves up one line. This prevents everything being placed on one line. However, because most hosts assume this responsibility, you only need to activate this option if your own computer is a host (in the case of communication with another PC), or if the host does not implement this setting automatically.

Columns
These options allow you to specify whether Terminal should work with 80 characters per line or 132. If in doubt, choose 132 to ensure that no information is lost.

Cursor
This group allows you to choose between a normal or blinking block as cursor, or a normal or blinking underlining stripe.

Terminal Font
This list of choices enables you to specify both the font and the size of the letters. Terminal uses these chosen

fonts for the characters displayed on the screen. This setting applies only to the display on the screen, not to the characters which are actually sent.

Translations
This option deals with the special characters used in some countries. Here, you should specify the ISO characterset applicable to the transmitted data.

Show Scroll Bars
This allows you to switch the scroll bars in Terminal on and off. If the scroll bars are switched on, you are able to review and mark certain fragments of text considerably more quickly.

Buffer Lines
Here you can specify the number of lines which Terminal can store temporarily. This may range from 25 (normal screen size) to 400. Thus, it is possible when printing selected text to be able to browse back through 400 lines of text.

11.8.4 Communication parameters

The technical preconditions allowing you to make a connection are specified in the *Communications* option in the *Settings* menu. If erroneous information is registered here, no connection will be possible, or only a rather ramshackle one.

The commands which should be specified here can be found partly in your modem handbook and the remainder can be acquired from the host or from the mailbox.

Caution: Not all conceptual combinations of options are possible. Terminal automatically adopts some options once a certain option has been specified. Therefore, check all groups once again before you confirm the settings using *OK*.

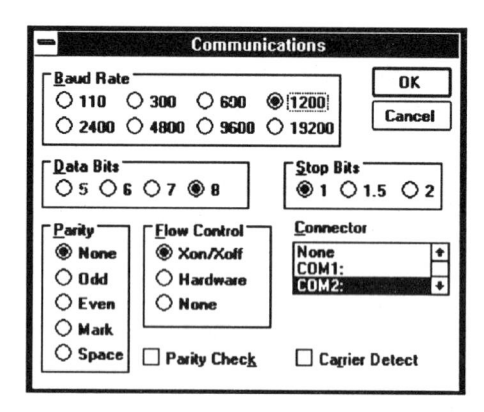

Baud Rate

In the *Baud Rate* option you are able to choose between a number of values which range from 110 to 19,200. The usual speeds for average modems are 300, 1200 and 2400 baud. You should always select the greatest possible speed in the case of a direct computer connection using a null modem cable.

The speed specified here should conform to both that of your own modem and that of the host.

Data Bits

Specify in this group the number of bits which make up each character to be sent. If the information sent contains characters with ASCII values exceeding 127, you are obliged to choose eight data bits, otherwise the characters will arrive in a mutilated condition. In the case of a purely ASCII text, a seven data bits setting is sufficient.

Very occasionally, a transmission of five or six data bits takes place. In communication with a host, the character length will be stated.

Stop Bits

In the *Stop Bits* option group, the length of the end signal for each character is determined (see also section 11.3). The possibilities are 1, 1.5 and 2. Here also, you must comply with the instructions of the host.

Advanced options

Parity
Parity allows you to determine how the control bit should be used. In eight bit applications, choose *None*, then no control bit is added. In the case of *Odd* parity, Terminal will set the control bit in such a way that, including the control bit, an uneven number of bits will always be sent for each character. In the case of *Even* parity, this is always an even amount of bits. With *Mark*, a bit is added which is always set to 7, and with *Space* a bit is added which is always set to 0.

The host also determines the parity.

Flow Control
This refers to the so-called Data Flow Control, in other words, the way in which the transmission is interrupted and continued, for instance, by overloaded receivers. There are three options:

- With *Xon/Xoff*, Terminal uses two special signs, namely the ASCII codes 17 and 19 to interrupt and continue the transmission. This method is also called **software handshake**. Due to the fact that these characters are sent in the same way as the information, they may not occur anywhere else in the information, otherwise this would lead to an unexpected and accidental interruption or continuation of the transmission.
- With *Hardware*, a special serial interface line is used to send the data flow signal. This is also called the **hardware handshake**.
- If you choose *None* there is no control over the data flow. This may, however, lead to loss of data.

Only the option which is also used by the host can be chosen.

Connector
This allows you to select the serial port to which the modem should be connected. If you have two computers which are connected to each other by a null modem cable, select *None* here. Terminal will then automati-

cally check if COM1 is available and will choose COM2 if that is not the case.

Parity Check
If you activate this option, Terminal will judge each character in the light of the parity regulations. If it occurs that the control bit does not comply with the agreed convention, Terminal will display a question mark instead of the character received.

Carrier Detect
This check box enables you to switch on a special hardware operation, comparable to the hardware protocol in *Data Flow Control*. Terminal then checks the modem to see if the computer has been informed, by means of a separate wire in the connection cable, as to whether the connection has been made. This only works, of course, if the modem actually uses this signal. If necessary, consult the modem handbook.

11.8.5 Modem commands

To adapt Terminal to the working methods of your modem, you may have to make certain adjustments using the *Modem Commands* option in the *Settings* menu. This will be no problem if you have one of the following types of modem, which are to be found in the dialogue box:

- Hayes
- MultiTech
- TrailBlazer

Simply click on the required option. If you wish, you may adjust other details before clicking on *OK*.

Caution: A second click on one of the options from the *Modem Defaults* group removes the changes made. The default setting for the selected type is then restored.

Advanced options

For all other modems, click on *None*. The text fields will be cleared and you can fill in the necessary characters for your modem yourself.

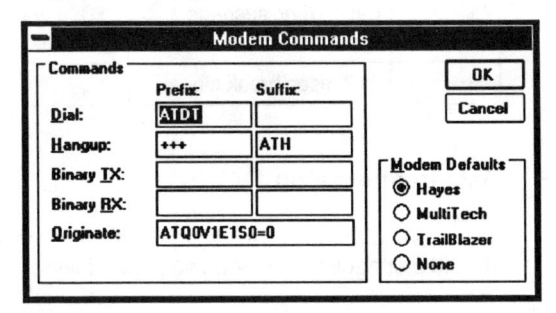

```
┌─                    Modem Commands                    ─┐
│ ┌─Commands─────────────────────┐   ┌──────────┐        │
│ │         Prefix     Suffix    │   │    OK    │        │
│ │ Dial:   │ATDT│    │    │     │   └──────────┘        │
│ │ Hangup: │+++ │    │ATH │     │   ┌──────────┐        │
│ │ Binary TX: │  │   │    │     │   │  Cancel  │        │
│ │ Binary RX: │  │   │    │     │   └──────────┘        │
│ │ Originate: │ATQ0V1E1S0=0│    │   ┌─Modem Defaults─┐  │
│ │                              │   │ ● Hayes         │  │
│ │                              │   │ ○ MultiTech     │  │
│ │                              │   │ ○ TrailBlazer   │  │
│ │                              │   │ ○ None          │  │
│ └──────────────────────────────┘   └─────────────────┘  │
└────────────────────────────────────────────────────────┘
```

Behind *Dial*, specify the command which is required to dial a number. Terminal will later enter the telephone number between the prefix and suffix.

The command which instructs the modem to break the connection should be specified behind *Hangup*. Under *Prefix*, specify the part of the command which gives the modem the cue to switch over to the so-called command mode. This means that the modem interprets all the following signs as being a command and thus will not send them. Under *Suffix*, specify the actual command to hang up.

Binary TX stands for **binary transmission**. Under *Prefix*, specify the command which prepares the transmission of a binary file. Under *Suffix*, the command ending this mode should be registered.

In the same way, at *Binary RX*, the command to receive a binary file and the command to quit this mode should be registered.

The commands dealing with the last option, *Originate*, can be found in the modem handbook. If necessary, comply with Terminal's default setting. You may also use the following codes instead of special operating characters:

code	meaning	example
^A...^Z	Ctrl-A...Ctrl-Z	^M for Enter
^$Dnn	delay of nn seconds	^$D04 wait four seconds
^$B	117 msec break signal	

11.8.6 Data transmission

When sending and receiving files in Terminal, we should distinguish between two sorts of files:

- A **text or ASCII file** contains only characters which occur on a typewriter, thus, letters, numbers, tabs and returns.
- In contrast to this, a **binary file** may contain any character from the code used. With a PC, that is the ASCII code. Binary files can be, for example, program files, files containing graphics or compressed files.

Remember that text files are merely a limited form of binary files. Each file can be sent as a binary file, as long as the host supports the protocols required for this.

Before a transmission can be started, you must specify the particular method which Terminal should use to control the flow of data. This should be done separately for text and binary files. To specify the data flow control for text files, select the *Text Transfers* option from the *Settings* menu. The following window will appear:

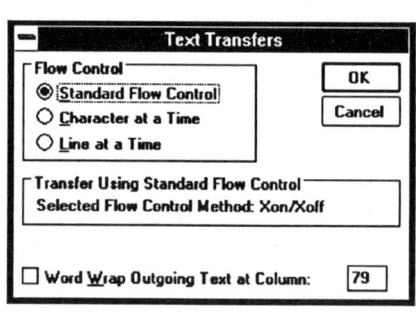

In setting this control, you may choose from three possibilities. *Standard Flow Control* is the first option. This entails that data will be sent as specified in the *Communications* option of the *Settings* menu. This default value is shown in the middle of the dialogue box.

When a text has been created using a word processing program like Write or Notepad, the lines of the text are frequently longer than the screen width of the computer which will receive the text. Because this can lead to problems and even loss of information, you should activate the third option in cases like this. Next to this, you can specify the column where the Word Wrap should take place. Always specify one column less than the amount which is actually available, because Terminal still has to enter the sign for the word wrap (^M).

If you choose the *Character at a Time* option, Terminal will adjust the data in the dialogue box as follows:

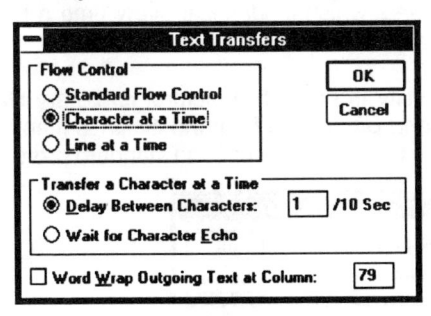

```
┌─────────────── Text Transfers ───────────────┐
│ ┌Flow Control──────────────┐    ┌────────┐   │
│ │ ○ Standard Flow Control  │    │   OK   │   │
│ │ ● Character at a Time    │    ├────────┤   │
│ │ ○ Line at a Time         │    │ Cancel │   │
│ └──────────────────────────┘    └────────┘   │
│                                              │
│ ┌Transfer a Character at a Time──────────┐   │
│ │ ● Delay Between Characters:  [ 1 ] /10 Sec│
│ │ ○ Wait for Character Echo              │   │
│ └────────────────────────────────────────┘   │
│                                              │
│ ☐ Word Wrap Outgoing Text at Column:  [ 79 ] │
└──────────────────────────────────────────────┘
```

In the central part of the window, the choice between two possible types of data transport is provided. The characters will be sent either with a *Delay Between Characters*, shown in tenths of a second, or sending will be delayed until the previous character has been sent back by the host. In this case, choose *Wait for Character Echo*. Using the second method, the character echo is compared to the character sent. Accordingly, an actual control takes place concerning the accuracy of the transmission. This type of control slows down the transmission considerably.

The following diagram shows the dialogue box which appears when you choose the *Line at a Time* option.

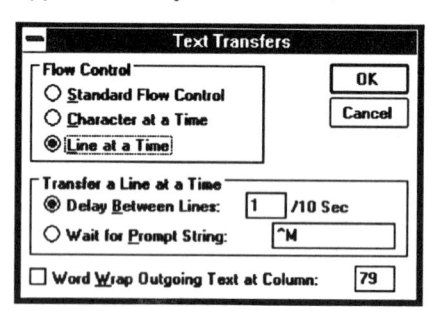

```
┌─────────── Text Transfers ───────────┐
│ ┌─Flow Control─────────────┐  ┌──────┐│
│ │ ○ Standard Flow Control  │  │  OK  ││
│ │ ○ Character at a Time    │  └──────┘│
│ │ ● Line at a Time         │  ┌──────┐│
│ └──────────────────────────┘  │Cancel││
│                               └──────┘│
│ ┌─Transfer a Line at a Time──────────┐│
│ │ ● Delay Between Lines:  [1] /10 Sec││
│ │ ○ Wait for Prompt String:  [^M]    ││
│ └────────────────────────────────────┘│
│ □ Word Wrap Outgoing Text at Column: [79]│
└───────────────────────────────────────┘
```

Here, you may also choose from two options. The first option also works with a delay, but not between individual characters this time. The delay concerns whole lines. The *Wait for Prompt String* option does not wait for an echo, it waits for a precisely defined series of characters which is identical every time a line is sent. Normally ^M is shown for Enter.

To specify the data flow control for binary files, select the *Send Binary File* from the *Settings* menu. You can choose between two common standard protocols.

```
┌──── Binary Transfers ────┐
│ ● XModem/CRC    ┌──────┐ │
│ ○ Kermit        │  OK  │ │
│                 └──────┘ │
│                 ┌──────┐ │
│                 │Cancel│ │
│                 └──────┘ │
└──────────────────────────┘
```

The first protocol, *XModem/CRC*, works with eight data bits, without parity, and the second protocol, *Kermit*, works with either seven or eight bits, thus parity can be specified as even, odd or none. The exact procedures involved in these controls lie outside the scope of this book - the subject matter is too complicated.

A file transmission is started up by choosing one of the active options in the *Transfers* menu. A file window will appear first, allowing you to choose the required file and directory. Information will be displayed in the lower part of the Terminal window. This information includes the file name and the size of the file sent or received. There are also option buttons enabling you to interrupt or stop the transmission.

The following procedure allows you to send parts of a file: click on the *View Text File* option in the *Transfers* menu. As soon as the desired fragment of text is displayed on the screen, click on the *Stop* button. Then mark the desired text and copy this to the *Clipboard* using the *Copy* option from the *Edit* menu. Then, using *Clear Buffer* from the *Edit* menu, you can remove the text from the screen.

If a connection has already been made, the *Paste* option from the *Edit* menu results in the data in the Clipboard being shown on the screen due to local echo. It is then immediately sent to the host. It is also possible to send marked text directly by choosing *Send* from the *Edit* menu after the text has been marked.

11.8.7 Assigning commands to function keys

Terminal has 32 logical function keys available. These have nothing to do with the keyboard function keys. They form four groups of eight switching options to which you can assign functions specified personally.

This assignment is to be found in the *Settings* menu, under the *Function Keys* option. When you click on this, a dialogue box will appear in which you can specify the commands.

The units F1 to F8 do not represent the function keys on the computer. They deal with the eight command options which are displayed in the Terminal window.

![Function Keys dialog box showing F1 through F8 entries with Key Name and Command columns, OK/Cancel buttons, Key Level radio buttons (1-4), and Keys Visible checkbox]

In each of these options, you should specify under *Key Name* the text which should accompany this option. The real instructions should be specified in the *Command* text box. In addition to the codes which you already know from the modem commands, the following codes can also be used:

code	meaning
	dial
	hangup
	switch to options at level 1...4

Thus, you can enter commands which frequently arise during communication with a bulletin board or with another computer. Often the same commands have to be given, particularly at the beginning of a session, but also in the course of it. If you assign this work to these function keys, this saves a great deal of typing and thought. Give logical and meaningful names to these function keys, such as **Login, Name, Password**.

The *Keys Visible* check box at the lower right-hand side of the dialogue box allows you to have the function keys constantly visible at the bottom of the Terminal window. If you do not activate this box, it is still possible to have the function keys appear on the screen when required, by clicking on the *Show Function Keys* option in the *Settings* menu. A second click removes them again from the screen.

A simple click on one of these function keys sends the Terminal command. You operate these function keys using the keyboard and the key combination Ctrl-Alt-F*n*, in which F*n* stands for one of the function keys.

The switch option *Level 1*, in the lower right-hand corner, enables you to switch to the next level. When you click on this, the commands from the next level appear on the screen. When the highest level containing commands has been activated, another click brings the first level round again.

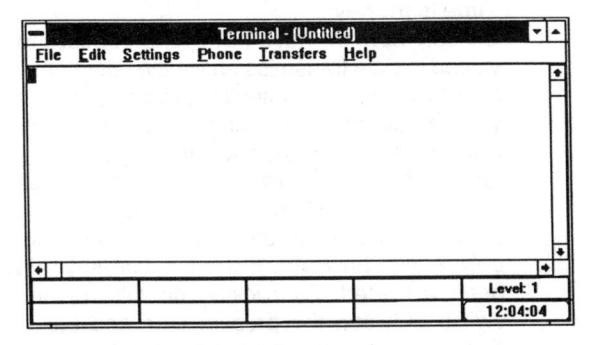

11.9 Saving Terminal files

Settings which have now been made should not have to be worked out again for the following session. That is why we shall now go to the *File* menu and choose the *Save* or *Save As* option. Give a meaningful name to your file. Terminal saves these settings under this name and automatically adds the extension TRM.

11.10 Working with Terminal files

These Terminal files can thus be called up again for a session again later. Each time a file is opened, Terminal reproduces the settings as they were the last time the file was saved.

Opening
A file is opened by selecting the *Open* option from the *File* menu. If you select the *New* option, all the settings in Terminal will be restored to the default values.

Altering
If you wish to make certain changes in an existing file, open the file first. You can then alter the settings by selecting the corresponding options in the *Settings* menu. Do not forget to save the file again afterwards.

Time is money
Up until now we have not spoken about the costs involved in data transmission via the telephone. If you are not dealing with commercially exploited bulletin boards, you do not pay more than the normal telephone rates. But even then, it is advisable to pay attention to the time taken. This is possible using the *Timer Mode* from the *Settings* menu. When this option has been activated, a stopwatch begins in the lower right-hand corner. This only works, however, if the function keys display has been activated. By clicking on this option, you can switch between the present time and the stopwatch. The stopwatch can be set to zero by clicking on the *Timer Mode* option in the *Settings* menu.

11.11 Exercise 34

34) Assign commands which you frequently use to the special function keys.

12 Multimedia

Since the appearance of the 3.1 version, Windows provides the possibility of creating and reproducing sound using the computer. Just as in Terminal, to do this you need to have the necessary hardware available, this time in the form of sound cards.

There are two programs in the Accessories group window which are important in terms of Windows' multimedia function: Sound Recorder and Media Player.

Media Player   Sound Recorder

The one program, Media Player enables you to play music via the computer, and the other, Sound Recorder, provides the possibility of personally recording music or spoken texts. The latter possibility is particularly interesting in combination with OLE technology.

Before these programs can actually be used, two conditions have to be satisfied. Firstly, as mentioned, you need to possess the necessary hardware. In this case, that is a sound card.

Secondly, this card must be made known to Windows by means of a *device driver*, which is an operating program for the card in question. Windows supports most popular cards, such as Ad Lib, the well-known SoundBlaster, the ThunderBoard, the Roland etc. Installation of this program takes place in the Control Panel under the *Drivers* option (see section 5.2.12).

12.1 The Media Player

If you double click on the Media Player icon in the Accessories window, the following window will appear on the screen:

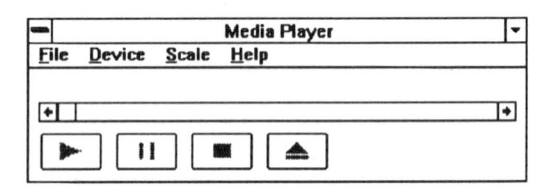

If the proper operating program has not yet been installed, a dialogue box will give a message to this effect and the program will not be started up. You are able to work with the Media Player only when the corresponding operating program has been installed using the Control Panel.

The Media Player is used to reproduce files in which sound has been recorded or in which animation techniques have been applied. In addition, you can run your CD player, for example, using this program.

The contents of the *Device* menu depends on the sort of device you have specified. In this, a distinction is made between a **simple** and a **compound** device.

Simple devices are, for example, CD players. The criterion here is that no special files have to be loaded in order to make the device work. With devices like these, it is also possible to quit the Media Player while the device plays on.

Compound devices have the feature that they 'run' a file. An example of a device like this is a MIDI sequencer, for which you first have to specify a MIDI file. In this case, choose the media device from the *Device* menu. The *Open* dialogue box will appear. Select here the name of the file you wish to play.

If you choose the *Open* option from the *File* menu, you can specify a file to be played using a device. Select the *Exit* option to quit the program. This results in, at the same time, the closing down of animation devices, MIDI sequencers and WAV audio players. A CD player will continue playing, however, even after the program has been ended.

In the *Scale* menu, you are able to switch between *Time* and *Tracks*. Track display can be very useful in the case of a CD player. The scroll box allows you to go to the required track and you can then press Play to have the player begin at the desired position.

You will no doubt recognize, from other sound equipment, the buttons at the lower part of the screen. The left-hand button stands for Play, next to this is the Pause button. The third button in this row is the Stop key and the last, Eject, allows you to eject media objects from a player if applicable.

12.2 The Sound Recorder

When you activate the Sound Recorder program by double clicking on the icon, the following window will appear:

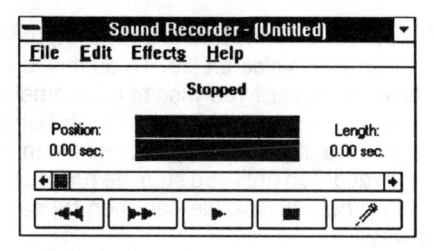

This program enables you to record, play and process sound.

When you have installed the necessary hardware and operating programs, it is very simple to play a sound track. Open the *File* menu and select the *Open* option. In the dialogue box which then appears, you can select a file to be played. By default, the extension WAV is assigned. This is a format for sound files which is supported by Windows.

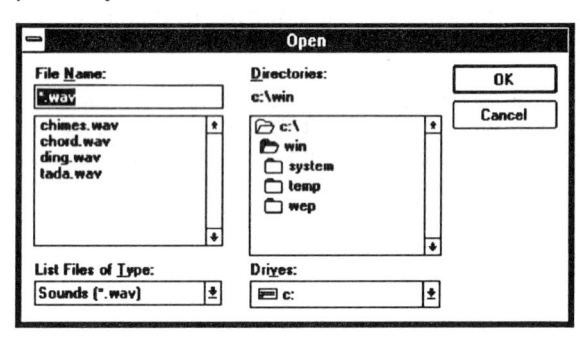

```
┌─────────────────────────────────────────────────┐
│ ─                        Open                   │
├─────────────────────────────────────────────────┤
│ File Name:          Directories:      ┌───────┐ │
│ ┌─────────────┐     c:\win            │  OK   │ │
│ │*.wav        │                       └───────┘ │
│ └─────────────┘     ┌──────────┐      ┌───────┐ │
│ ┌─────────────┐ ↑   │ 🗁 c:\    │ ↑    │Cancel │ │
│ │chimes.wav   │     │ 🗁 win    │      └───────┘ │
│ │chord.wav    │     │ 🗀 system │                │
│ │ding.wav     │     │ 🗀 temp   │                │
│ │tada.wav     │     │ 🗀 wep    │                │
│ │             │ ↓   │          │ ↓              │
│ └─────────────┘     └──────────┘                │
│ List Files of Type: Drives:                     │
│ ┌───────────┬─┐     ┌──────┬─┐                  │
│ │Sounds(*.wav)│±│   │ 🖴 c:  │±│                 │
│ └───────────┴─┘     └──────┴─┘                  │
└─────────────────────────────────────────────────┘
```

When you have made a choice and have loaded a file, click on the Play button (the middle button at the bottom) to start up the file. The word 'Playing' now appears, indicating that the sound track is being played. You can stop the file by pressing the key next to the Play button and this is indicated by 'Stopped' appearing in the window. The other buttons conform to common sound equipment. The left button stands for Rewind and the adjacent button for Forward.

If a microphone is connected to your computer, you are able to place your voice on file. To do this, open a new file (or an existing file if you wish to add something to it). Then press the right-hand button at the bottom of the window, Record. If you then speak into the microphone, this will be recorded until you stop the process by pressing the Stop button. The file can then be saved in the familiar way.

The *Effects* menu enables you to adjust the recorded sound by making it louder or quieter, by speeding it up or slowing it down. Echoes can also be added to recorded sound. Another special effect can be created by playing the recorded sound backwards.

The *Edit* menu also contains possibilities to create special effects. The *Insert File* and *Mix With File* options enable you to merge different files. In the first case, a file is inserted at a position which has been previously determined. In this process, the original recordings remain intact, in other words, the sound tracks are played consecutively. In the second case, one recording is merged with the other and they are played simultaneously. If this has been well thought-out, it can lead to very interesting results.

For many users, the possibility of placing a sound file in a text file using OLE technology will be particularly interesting. Accordingly, a document can acquire a personal tint. The specific possibilities of this new technology are outlined elsewhere in this book. That information should enable you to make personal remarks concerning a text. Someone else, of course, can only make use of this if he or she possesses the proper hardware.

13 Calculator

13.1 Application and appearance

The Calculator enables you to carry out almost all calculations which occur in daily life, from small addition problems to technical calculations and statistical surveys.

13.1.1 Icon

The Calculator is located in the Accessories group. It has the following icon:

Calculator

The Calculator program is started up by double clicking on the icon.

13.1.2 Window

When started up, the Calculator will appear in one of its two forms on the screen, as a standard calculator or as a scientific calculator. The first time Calculator is started up, the standard version appears.

Go to the *View* menu. A check mark is located in front of the *Standard* option, which indicates that the standard version is active. As long as this setting remains unchanged, you will always get this version each time the Calculator is started up.

If you select the *Scientific* option, a more powerful calculator appears.

The standard calculator 253

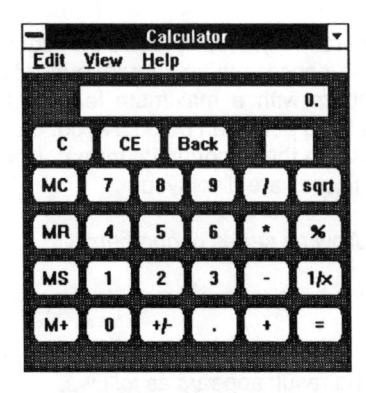

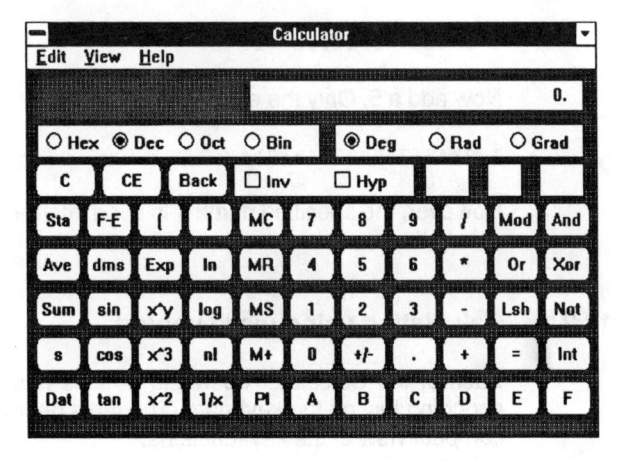

However, switch back to *Standard* for the moment.

13.2 The standard calculator

We shall first examine the standard calculator and its operation more closely. Just as with all other Windows operations, you can operate the Calculator using either the mouse or the keyboard.

The four main calculation methods can be implemented using the standard calculator. In addition, it is possible to calculate percentages, reciprocals and square roots. Calculator also possesses an internal buffer for interim results. Numbers with a maximum length of thirteen figures and a fixed point can be displayed. Larger numbers are shown in the exponential format, in which the first fourteen figures are displayed.

Type in the following series of numbers:

```
1234567890123
```

Now add a 4: Calculator switches over to the exponential display. The result appears as follows:

```
1,2345678901234e+013
```

Now add a 5. Only the exponential is increased:

```
1,2345678901234e+014
```

However, the specified number is used internally for the calculations.

13.2.1 Calculating using the keyboard

Each of the Calculator operating buttons has a corresponding key on the keyboard. The table below gives a compact view of the key functions:

operating button	key(combination)	function
C	Esc	clears display, discontinues current calculation
CE	Delete	clears display alone
Back	Backspace/left arrow	deletes rightmost digit of displayed number
MC	Ctrl-C	memory clear
MR	Ctrl-R	memory recall

MS	Ctrl-M	memory store
M+	Ctrl-P	adds value displayed to any value in the memory
0...9	0...9	numbers
.	. or ,	inserts a decimal point in the displayed number
/	/	divides
*	*	multiplies
+	+	adds
-	-	subtracts
sqrt	@	square root
%	%	calculates percentage
1/x	r	calculates reciprocal
=	= or Enter	shows result of last operation

We shall now perform an exercise using the keyboard. We shall work out the total price of an article, including 17.5% VAT. The article costs £12.95.

Just to be certain, we shall first clear the previous operation (C) and the memory (MC). Then we type in the calculation, setting the VAT in the memory at the same time:

Esc Ctrl-C 12.95 + 17.5% Ctrl-M Enter

Note: Using Ctrl-Insert or Ctrl-C, you can place the result in the Clipboard. Using Shift-Insert or Ctrl-V, you can call it up for use in another application if required.

The result of the above calculation is 15.21625. In the lower right-hand corner, an M has appeared. This means that the memory contains a value. Call up this interim result using Ctrl-R. You will see a VAT value of 2.26625.

13.2.2 Calculations using the mouse

Using the mouse enables you to operate the Calculator in a more intuitive manner. You can 'press' the desired buttons on the Calculator just as you would do with your fingers on a real calculator. Repeat the above calculation, this time using the mouse.

13.3 The scientific calculator

Compared to the standard calculator, the scientific calculator provides considerably more functions, for example, raising to a power, application of trigonometric functions, logarithms, exponential calculations and statistical functions. In addition, the scientific calculator, and this is particularly interesting for computer programmers, is able to work in different number systems and to execute various logical operations.

13.3.1 Simple calculations using the keyboard

The scientific calculator can be operated using the keyboard in the same way as the standard calculator. The table displayed below provides a list of all extra keys and corresponding buttons on the calculator.

Caution: The button used here for calculating reciprocals (1/x) is located differently than on the standard calculator. The buttons for the square root (sqrt) and percentages (%) are omitted from the scientific calculator. These calculations can be executed by a combination of functions:

```
sqrt :   Inv x ^2
%    :   /100 (depending on the operation)
```

The scientific calculator

The keys in question are used by the scientific calculator for other objectives.

button	key	function
Hex	F5	calculates in the hexadecimal number system
Dec	F6	calculates in the decimal system
Oct	F7	calculates in the octal number system
Bin	F8	calculates in the binary number system
Deg	F2	sets trigonometric input for degrees (0...360)
Rad	F3	sets trigonometric input for radians in decimal mode (0...2*PI)
Grad	F4	sets trigonometric input for gradients in decimal mode (0...400)
Dword	F2	shows 32 bits representation of the displayed number
Word	F3	shows the lower 16 bits of displayed number, but does not change the value
Byte	F4	shows the lower 8 bits of the displayed number but does not change the value
Inv	i	sets the inverse functions for sin (arcsin), cos (arccos), tan (arctan), PI (2*PI), x^y (x^(1/y)), x^2 (sqrt), x^3 (x^(1/3)), ln (e^x), log (10^x), Int (fraction), Lsh (Rsh), dms (conversion to degree-minute-second format), Ave, Sum and s
Hyp	h	sets the hyperbolic function for sin (sh), cos (ch), tan (th)
F-E	v	switches over from fixed point display to exponential display
dms	m	converts displayed number to degree-minute-second format
sin	s	calculates the sine
cos	o	calculates the cosine

tan	t	calculates the tangent
(	(	starts one of the 25 levels of parentheses
)	)	closes the current level of parentheses
Exp	x	introduction of exponent to the tenth power in exponential format
ln	n	calculates the natural logarithm
x^y	y	calculates x to the power y
x^3	#	calculates the cube value of x
x^2	@	calculates the square of x
log	l	calculates the common (base 10) logarithm
n!	!	calculates the factorial of the displayed number
PI	p	displays the value of Pi (3,14159265359)
A...F	A...F	hexadecimal numbers A...F (for 10...15)
Mod	%	displays the modulus, or remainder, of division using whole numbers
And	&	calculates bitwise AND
Or	|	calculates bitwise OR
Xor	^	calculates bitwise exclusive OR
Lsh	<	shifts bitwise to the left
Not	~	calculates bitwise inverse
Int	;	displays integer portion of a decimal value

It is better to use the mouse if you have one, since mouse operations are far more simple and straightforward than keyboard operations. However, we do need the corresponding keys from the keyboard to implement automatic calculations. As you will see, the Calculator requires character codes for its operation and these are characters on the keyboard.

13.3.2 Calculations using the mouse

In the course of becoming more familiar with the extensive possibilities of the scientific calculator, we shall only use the mouse in our exercises. Its operation is straightforward and is closest to the natural manner of handling a calculator.

Conversion from one numerical system to another
As you know, characters in the computer are coded for display. For the personal computer, these codes are in the ASCII table (see appendix C). Examine the character A. Here, the ASCII code is 65. We shall now deal with this value in the light of other numerical systems.

Enter this value by pressing the corresponding buttons using the mouse. Now click on the *Hex* switch button. The decimal number 65 is converted to the hexadecimal number 41. Then click on *Bin*. The result is a binary number with the same value: 1000001. This corresponds to the internal coding of the character A in the computer.

As you see, the three switch buttons on the right have changed. Instead of *Deg*, *Rad* and *Grad*, the options *Dword*, *Word* and *Byte* are now shown. These stand for the length of the corresponding binary number: double word, word and byte. If you click on these buttons, the display will be altered but not the value. Enter the number 650,000. Do not forget to click on *Dec* first, otherwise a warning sound will be emitted. This is due to the fact that in the binary system the numbers 5 and 6 are invalid. Then click on *Bin* and consecutively on *Word, Byte* and again on *Dword*. You will observe that only the lower 16 and 8 positions, respectively, are shown. Finally, the display registers the correct value again.

Logical operations
It is also possible to execute logical operations using the scientific calculator. This makes the calculator a useful instrument for computer programmers. We shall deal with this subject matter using three examples.

The button *Lsh* represents **Left Shift**, in other words, this is the button for moving bits to the left. Set the calculator in the decimal system and enter the number 16. Now switch over to the binary system. The binary equivalent will now be displayed. In order to move the individual bits one step to the left, click on *Lsh, 1* and = in succession. As you see, all numbers have moved up one position and a 0 has appeared at the right-hand side.

The benefit of this will be apparent if you switch back to the decimal system. The number 32 is now displayed. Thus, moving one position in the binary system is equivalent to multiplying the number by 2. Try this out. Each time you move the number one position in the binary system, the value is multiplied by 2. Now you can see just how quickly the computer can multiply when the factor is a power of 2, thus 2, 4, 8, 16 etc.

Or represents bitwise OR. In this logical operation, two binary numbers are processed step by step from left to right. In this, the result at a certain position is a 1 if at least one of the numbers at this position contains a 1. If both numbers contain a 0 at a certain position, then the result is also a 0. Enter the ASCII code for the character A, and switch over to the binary system. Write down the binary code quickly on a piece of paper. Now return to the decimal system. Click on *Or* and enter the number 32. Now return to the binary system. Place this binary number under the previous number. Then press =. As you will see, what we described above has indeed taken place:

```
1000001
 100000
-------
1100001
```

If you now switch back to the decimal system, you will see that the result is the number 97. However, you must certainly not conclude that an addition has taken place. The fact that 97 is also the sum of 65 plus 32 is pure coincidence. Repeat this, now using the number 33 instead of 32.

Examine the decimal code 97 in the ASCII table. This represents the character a, thus the corresponding small letter of decimal code 65. This way of working can be used for every letter between 65 and 90. The operation *Or* always produces the corresponding small letter.

Of course, vice versa is also possible: making capitals out of small letters. To do this, use *Xor* with 32. In this, two numbers will be processed bitwise from right to left. The result of the comparison is always a 1 if only one of the numbers has a 1 at a certain position. If they both have a 1 or a 0, the result is 0.

Inverse functions
If you wish to use the inverse function, first click on the *Inv* button. This function remains in force until another button is clicked which has an inverse function. For example, you can calculate the cube root of 27 by entering the number 27, clicking on *Inv* and then on x^3.

13.3.3 Statistical calculations

You are also able to carry out statistical calculations using the scientific calculator. The following calculations are possible with a series of separate values:

- the sum of all values
- the sum of the squares of all values
- the average value
- the average value of all squares
- the standard deviation based on n values
- the standard deviation based on n-1 values

These statistical functions can also be operated using the keyboard:

button	key (combination)	function
Sta	Ctrl-S	activates the statistical program
Ave	Ctrl-A	calculates the average value
Inv Ave	i, Ctrl-A	calculates the average value of the squares
Sum	Ctrl-T	calculates the sum
Inv Sum	i, Ctrl-T	calculates the sum of the squares
s	Ctrl-D	calculates the standard deviation of n-1
Inv s	i, Ctrl-D	calculates standard deviation of n
Dat	Insert	enters displayed number in Statistics box

However, owing to the ease of operation, we shall again make use of the mouse in order to acquaint ourselves with the statistical functions. As an exercise, we shall deal with the fuel consumption of a private car. Based on receipts from petrol stations, the following figures are known:

```
 9.4 l / 100 km
 9.7 l / 100 km
11.2 l / 100 km
 9.1 l / 100 km
 8.9 l / 100 km
```

In order to process these figures, we shall proceed as follows: Firstly, we click on the the *Sta* button (upper left-hand corner) to activate the statistical functions. The following window appears on the screen:

The scientific calculator

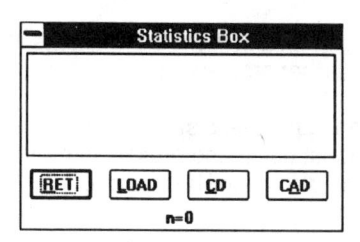

First relocate this *Statistics Box* and the Calculator too, if necessary, so that both windows can be seen simultaneously. Probably the best thing to do is to place them above one another. Switch over to the Calculator by clicking on *Ret* or on the Calculator window. We shall now enter the five different values. Take the first value, enter it and click on *Dat*. The number appears immediately in the Statistics box. Do this with all the consumption figures. The amount of values entered is shown at the bottom of the Statistics box. When you have introduced all the figures, 'n=5' will be shown.

Now you can determine the average value. Click on *Ave*. The average consumption is displayed in the Calculator: 9.66. To calculate the standard deviation, click on *s*: 0.9126883367284.

If we wish to alter basic statistical information, we use the Statistics Box. This is activated by clicking on *Sta* or clicking directly on the window. Due to the fact that the value 11.2 is apparently not representative and only gives a wrong impression of our statistics, we shall remove this piece of information. Mark this number by clicking on it. Then click on *CD*. This value is now removed and 'n=4' is now shown at the botom of the box. There are now only four pieces of information.

If you now calculate the average value again, the result will be 9.275 with a standard deviation of only 0.35.

If you do not wish to completely remove a certain value, but only wish to alter it, delete the former value and enter the new value. The *LOAD* button enables you to transport a marked value from the Statistics Box to the Calculator for further processing.

Before you can apply these statistical functions to your own car, you must delete the present information. Click on *CAD* and the display will be cleared.

13.4 Automatic calculation

We have already mentioned that automatic calculation is possible using the Calculator. To implement this, you have to be familiar with the corresponding key commands. The principle is extremely simple.

Start up Notepad without closing the Calculator, and enter the following problem:

```
12+3=
```

In Notepad, go to the *Edit* menu and activate the *Select All* option. Then select the *Copy* option from the *Edit* menu. Now switch over to the Calculator and select the *Paste* option from the *Edit* menu. The Calculator will work out the result of the problem in no time and show it in the display. Then give the Calculator the command to *Copy* from the *Edit* menu, switch over to Notepad and enter the result using the *Paste* option from the *Edit* menu.

Of course, it is possible to use other applications such as Write and Word for Windows. What really is important is that the selected numbers lead to the correct procedure in the Calculator. We shall demonstrate this using a complicated example. Enter the following line in Notepad or Write, then mark and copy the line:

```
:cq:612:m24:p36:p:rr
```

Switch over to the Calculator and then add the contents of the Clipboard by selecting the *Paste* option from the *Edit* menu. The result is: 0.01388888888889. What has the Calculator done?

In calculations using copying and inserting via the Clipboard, the colon has a special function. Before a letter, the colon means Ctrl and before a number this means function key. Accordingly, ':c' represents Ctrl-C and ':6' represents F6. In the following table, key codes are shown which are only valid if they are taken from the Clipboard:

character	simulated key
q	Esc
\	Insert

Thus, in the series above, the following procedures are implemented:

```
Ctrl-C Esc F6 12 Ctrl-M 24 Ctrl-P 36 Ctrl-P
Ctrl-R R
```

This is equivalent to (see table):

```
MC C Dec 12 MS 24 M+ 36 M+ MR 1/x
```

Thus, firstly the memory and the display are cleared. Then the decimal system is chosen, 12 is placed in the memory using MS, then 24 and 36 are added to the memory and the result is called up using MR. Finally, the reciprocal result is calculated.

13.5 Exercises 35 to 38

35) Add up the following hexadecimal numbers: 3F56AD, FF65 and 451A.

36) What is the result of the logical operation 10010010 And 10110000?

37) Calculate the statistical data of the following series of values: 11.3 17.33 9.7 14.23.

38) Enter the characters in Notepad which automatically calculate the previous exercise.

14 Recorder

14.1 Application and appearance

The Recorder in the Accessories group enables you to automize routine procedures very simply. The Recorder, as the name suggests, records operations using the mouse and the keyboard. These operations are stored in memory so that they can be repeated in exactly the same order of sequence at any chosen moment. We call this type of registration a **macro**.

The Recorder icon has the following appearance:

Recorder

Start up the Recorder program by double clicking on the icon.

The standard window will appear. The available macros will be displayed in the window under the menu bar.

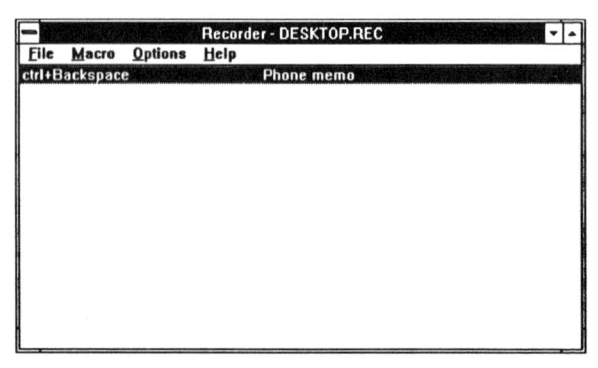

Recorder - DESKTOP.REC
File Macro Options Help
ctrl+Backspace   Phone memo

Next to each macro, the name and key combination needed to call up the macro are registered.

As mentioned, macros are recorded key strokes, mouse movements and clicks on the mouse buttons. Macros like these can be quite large, up to a maximum of 64 Kb. In addition, it is possible to *nest* macros. This occurs if, while recording a macro, you use a key combination which includes another macro. In this case, only the key combination, which is in fact the playback command, is recorded and not the keystrokes and mouse operations which the evoked macro simulates. Accordingly, it is also possible that this macro evokes another macro. These evocations can be nested up to a maximum of four levels. Thus, in total, five macro levels are possible.

Recorded macros are stored by the Recorder in files with the extension REC, unless you personally assign a different extension. The Recorder can only load one file at a time. Therefore, all the macros which should be available at the same time must be saved in the same file. This applies of course especially to nested macros.

Although it is possible to start up other Windows applications such as Calculator and Notepad several times, only **one version** of Recorder can be run at one time.

14.2 Macro planning

Before we create the first macro, we wish to examine several aspects of macros more closely. Just like film directors, we have to imagine the final presentation and the influence a macro will have on the surroundings, in this case, on Windows and the various group and application windows.

Mouse operations
The Recorder is indeed able to record operations from both mouse and keyboard, but, in certain situations, mouse operations may lead to problems. If, for example, you click on the title bar of a window to activate it while recording a macro, it is not clear where the window will be placed when the macro is later played

back. Perhaps the window will be moved or reduced to an icon. Or maybe a macro made using a VGA card will be used later on a computer with a Hercules card. Due to the varying resolutions, all windows have different sizes. Thus, it is very important to consider which operations should be recorded, particularly in the case of the mouse. For this reason, the Recorder has three recording options:

- Clicks and Drags, meaning mouse operations
- Everything, meaning clicks and drags plus keyboard
- Ignore mouse, meaning only keyboard.

Due to the fact that all operations in Windows applications can be carried out using the keyboard, there is no real reason to include the mouse in the macro, except if you wish to record a demo (more about this later).

Application macros
A mouse operation can be recorded in relation to the **window** or in relation to the **screen**. In the first case, the co-ordinates will move along with the relocation of the window. Accordingly, a macro which includes mouse operations will also function with relocated windows. In this case however, only operations of this one window may be recorded.

General macros
This restriction does not apply to general macros. These are recorded in relation to the whole screen, so that various applications can be started up, edited and closed again.

14.3 Recording macros

It would be rather handy, in between times, to be able to jot down a telephone memo while working with Windows. Normally, you would have to switch over to the Notepad, open a new notation file and enter the date and time. We shall now automize these operations with a key combination.

Recording macros

Due to the fact that this macro should be able to run in all applications, it should be recorded relative to the entire screen. In order to avoid any problems which could arise, we shall only record commands from the keyboard and not from the mouse.

1) Start up Notepad, if is not already running.
2) Switch over to the Recorder.
3) Select the *Record* option from the *Macro* menu.

The following window will appear on the screen. Introduce the information shown here:

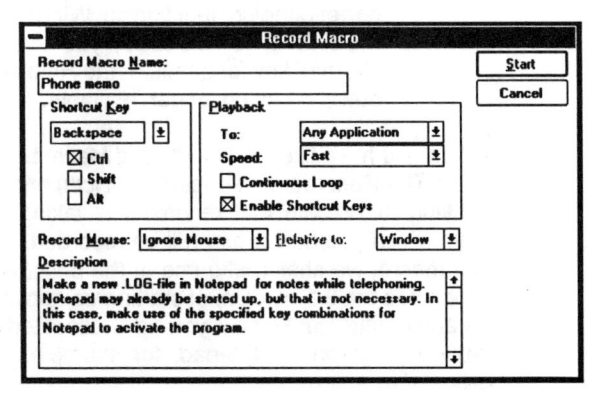

```
┌─────────────────────── Record Macro ───────────────────────┐
│ Record Macro Name:                              ┌────────┐ │
│ [Phone memo                        ]            │ Start  │ │
│ ┌─Shortcut Key──┐ ┌─Playback──────────────────┐ ├────────┤ │
│ │ [Backspace ±] │ │ To:    [Any Application ±]│ │ Cancel │ │
│ │  ☒ Ctrl       │ │ Speed: [Fast            ±]│ └────────┘ │
│ │  ☐ Shift      │ │  ☐ Continuous Loop        │            │
│ │  ☐ Alt        │ │  ☒ Enable Shortcut Keys   │            │
│ └───────────────┘ └───────────────────────────┘            │
│ Record Mouse: [Ignore Mouse ±] Relative to: [Window ±]     │
│ Description                                                │
│ ┌────────────────────────────────────────────────────────┐ │
│ │ Make a new .LOG-file in Notepad for notes while tele-  │ │
│ │ phoning. Notepad may already be started up, but that is│ │
│ │ not necessary. In this case, make use of the specified │ │
│ │ key combinations for Notepad to activate the program.  │ │
│ └────────────────────────────────────────────────────────┘ │
└────────────────────────────────────────────────────────────┘
```

Either the *Record Macro Name* or the *Shortcut Key* text box must be filled in, otherwise the Recorder cannot perform the recording. Some possible shortcut keys are:

- Esc
- F1-F6
- CapsLock
- NumLock
- ScrollLock
- Insert
- Home
- End
- PgDn
- PgUp
- cursor up, down, right, left

- Tab
- Backspace
- Enter
- Spacebar

All these keys can be used as shortcut keys, either singly or in combination with Shift, Ctrl or Alt. Thus, there are 136 possibilities, which should be sufficient.

Note: Remember that Windows and Windows applications already use a number of these keys as shortcut keys. If this is the case, the corresponding function in Windows is neutralized. If, for instance, you use F1 as a shortcut key for a macro, the Help key in Windows, F1, is no longer available.

When you have filled in the *Record Macro* box, click on *Start*. The Recorder is reduced to an icon and keeps on blinking to indicate that recording is taking place. All keys which you now press will be recorded. In filling in this macro, we shall make use of the possibility, available since the 3.1 version, of starting up applications by means of shortcut keys. If you have allocated a unique key combination to Notepad, for example, Ctrl-Alt-N, proceed as follows:

- Press Ctrl-Alt-N to start up the Notepad program.
- Fill in '.LOG' in Notepad and press Enter and F5.
- The macro is now completed and you can close the recording. You can do this by clicking on the blinking icon, but it is better to do so by pressing Ctrl-Break. This latter method is preferable owing to the reasons mentioned previously. Besides, we have specified that mouse operations should be ignored.
- A dialogue box will now appear containing three option buttons. You may choose to cancel the recording, to resume recording or to save the macro. Choose *Save Macro*, then *Save* from the *File* menu. You may assign the name DESKTOP, for example, in order to indicate that this deals with macros which automize clerical tasks.

14.4 Playing back macros

A macro can be played back in two ways:

- If the macro has not yet been loaded, click on *Open* in the *File* menu to load the file containing the desired macro. Mark the macro by clicking on it using the mouse and select the *Run* option from the *Macro* menu. A double click on the macro name is also sufficient.
- If you have assigned a shortcut key to the desired macro, you only have to press this shortcut key.

The execution will be influenced by the settings which you have specified in the *Playback* box in the *Record Macro* window. This is where you specify when and how the macro should be played back. If you select *Same Application*, Windows will automatically switch to that application and will implement the macro there.

The macro can be played back at two speeds, either as rapidly as possible or at the speed at which it was recorded.

Activation of the *Continuous Loop* option results in the playback being automatically repeated when the macro ends. In this case, you have to interrupt the macro using Ctrl-Break otherwise it will continue indefinitely.

The *Enable Shortcut Keys* option button allows you to specify that the macros should be played back using the shortcut keys. This concerns nested macros.

14.5 Changing macros

The contents of macros, thus the specified keystrokes and mouse operations, cannot be altered. If an alteration should be necessary, the entire macro must be recorded once again. It is possible to change the **properties** of the macros. Select the macro whose properties have to be adjusted. Then click on the *Properties* option from the *Macro* menu.

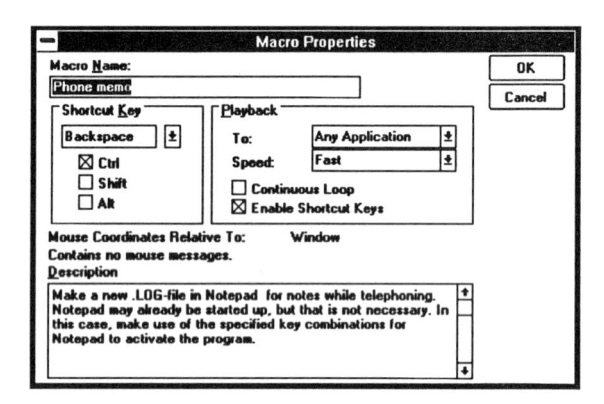

```
┌─────────────────────────────────────────────────┐
│ ─                    Macro Properties            │
│ Macro Name:                              ┌──────┐│
│ ┌──────────────┐                         │  OK  ││
│ │Phone memo    │                         └──────┘│
│ ┌─Shortcut Key──┐ ┌─Playback──────────┐  ┌──────┐│
│ │ ┌──────────┐ │ │     ┌────────────┐│  │Cancel││
│ │ │Backspace │±│ │ To: │Any Appl...│±│  └──────┘│
│ │ └──────────┘ │ │     └────────────┘│          │
│ │  ☒ Ctrl      │ │Speed:┌──────┐ ±   │          │
│ │  ☐ Shift     │ │      │Fast  │     │          │
│ │  ☐ Alt       │ │      └──────┘     │          │
│ │              │ │ ☐ Continuous Loop │          │
│ │              │ │ ☒ Enable Shortcut Keys       │
│ └──────────────┘ └───────────────────┘          │
│ Mouse Coordinates Relative To:  Window           │
│ Contains no mouse messages.                      │
│ Description                                      │
│ ┌──────────────────────────────────────────────┐│
│ │Make a new .LOG-file in Notepad for notes ... ││
│ │Notepad may already be started up, but ...    ││
│ │this case, make use of the specified key ...  ││
│ │Notepad to activate the program.              ││
│ └──────────────────────────────────────────────┘│
└─────────────────────────────────────────────────┘
```

Apart from the settings dealing with what should be recorded and the manner of recording, everything can be changed retrospectively. This applies to the name of the macro, to the shortcut key and to the playback options.

14.5.1 Changing options

There are also default settings in the Recorder which can be changed. To do this, select the *Options* menu. The following options will appear:

```
Options
 √ Control+Break Checking
 √ Shortcut Keys
 √ Minimize On Use
   Preferences...
```

The first three options have a check mark. This means that they are active. You can remove these check marks by clicking on them once more. Another click restores the check mark.

If you make the *Control + Break Checking* option inactive, it is no longer possible to break off a recording operation in Recorder or to interrupt a playback operation.

Making the *Shortcut Keys* option inactive may be useful if you are working with an application which uses exactly those keys for special functions which are also in use for calling up macros. Then the macros can only be evoked using the corresponding option in the *Macro* menu.

As long as the *Minimize on Use* option is active, the Recorder will be reduced to an icon when a macro has been played back. If you make this function inactive, the Recorder window remains active.

Now select the *Preferences* option. In the dialogue box which subsequently appears, you are able to adjust the default settings concerning the recording of a macro. The settings which you now specify will remain in force until you alter them again.

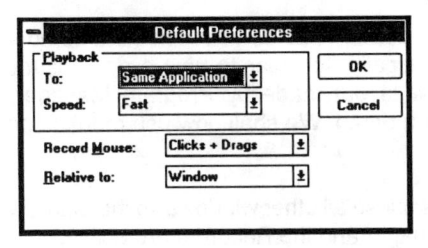

14.5.2 Deleting macros

If you wish to make room in a Recorder file for new macros or if you wish to employ a shortcut key which is already in use, you can delete superfluous macros. This is very simple. Select the macro which is to be deleted. Use the scroll bars if necessary. Then click on *Macro* and *Delete*. Confirm this using *OK*.

14.5.3 Merging macros

If you wish to have certain macros available simultaneously, these macros have to be stored in the same file. If that is not the case, click on the *Merge* option in the *File* menu. The familiar dialogue box dealing with the opening and saving of files will appear. You can now select a file to add it to the current file.

In each Recorder file, a particular shortcut key can only be assigned to one macro. For this reason, the functions of shortcut keys in an appended file are automatically removed. Thus, these have to be specified again. The shortcut keys of macros which are already employed remain in force. A box will inform you of this. That is also the case if two macros have the same name. Then one of the names has to be changed or a shortcut key has to be assigned.

14.6 Creating macros to use as demos

The Recorder enables you to make a demo which runs automatically. In order to give a demonstration of the window layout made by Program Manager, we shall create a demo. We shall now use mouse operations to do this.

- First close all other windows so that only the Program Manager and the Recorder are active.
- Select *Macro* and *Record*.
- Fill in the dialogue box. Specify 'demo1' as the macro name and Ctrl-cursor down as the shortcut key. The playback options remain the same. In the *Record Mouse* box, choose *Everything* and in the *Relative To* box, choose *Window*.
- Begin recording. The Recorder icon blinks, indicating that from now onwards everything is being recorded. Be careful when using the mouse.
- Move the mouse slowly to the title bar and place the mouse on *Window*.
- Click on *Cascade*. Wait for roughly ten seconds in order to give the next user a little time.
- Then drag the mouse slowly to *Window* once more, click on *Window* after a moment, wait and then drag the mouse from *Cascade* to *Tile*.

- After a moment's pause, press Ctrl-Break and save the macro.

Now start up the macro by pressing the shortcut key Ctrl-cursor down.

Probably, you will not really be satisfied with the result, since the macro runs only once and is too quick, despite the pauses which we have inserted. We shall alter this. Select the *Properties* option from the *Macro* menu. Change the *Playback* options. Activate the *Continuous Loop* option button by clicking on it and choose *Recorded Speed* as playback speed. Start the macro again. The playback display is probably a great deal better now.

14.7 Exercise 39

39) Create a macro which performs a calculation assisted by the Calculator. This result should be transferred to another application, just as we have seen with the Calculator in combination with the Notepad.

15 Integrating Windows applications: working with OLE technology

Since the 3.1 version of Windows, the so-called OLE technology is supplied as a standard part of the program. OLE is short for *Object Linking and Embedding*. Working with OLE objects can take place directly using the *Edit* menu from applications which provide this possibility, or by using the *Object Packager* program from the Accessories group.

15.1 Linked and embedded objects

Just as in the case of DDE, Dynamic Data Exchange, the OLE technology also deals with the linkage of data from different programs and files. This does not merely refer to an association, it also means that information from one application can be quickly altered in a different application. Information (a document or a picture or a section of these) which has been recorded as an entity at a certain position is called an **object**.

In this a distinction is made between **linked** and **embedded** objects.

An embedded object
An embedded object is a document or picture (or a section of these) which has been created in another document in another application. When you embed, a copy of the information from the source document is made and transferred to the destination document. You no longer have any connection to the document from which you transferred the information. When you edit an embedded object, the source document is not affected.

A linked object
In the case of a linked object, the document in question

(or picture or section of this) is not brought into the other application, but is represented by an icon at a certain position. The object remains in the application in which it was created. When you edit a linked object, you are actually editing the information in the source document.

15.2 The Object Packager

We shall first deal with the *Object Packager* program. Subsequently, in the light of practical examples, we shall review the linkage of data from different programs.

The *Object Packager* icon has the following appearance:

Object Packager

A double click on the icon starts up the program. The following window appears:

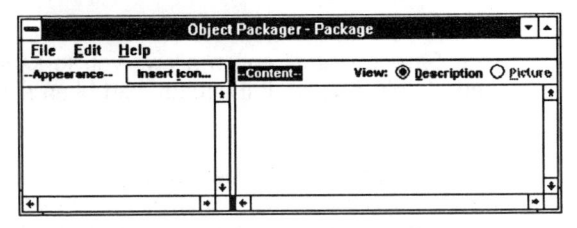

The Object Packager, as you will observe, consists of two adjacent windows. In the left-hand window (the icon window), the icon belonging to the program which contains the linked or embedded object is shown. In the right-hand window (the contents window), the name of the document containing the object is displayed. A picture of the object can also be displayed here.

The File menu

Using the *Import* option from the *File* menu, you can open a chosen file in the Object Packager. This may also be a file from an application which does not support the linking or embedding of OLE objects. In the icon window, the icon of the program in which the object was created is shown. In the contents window the name of the file is shown.

The *New* option clears the information in both windows. If changes have been made, you will get the chance to save these first.

If you open the Object Packager from an application, the *Update* option enables you to adjust an OLE object in the document in which it was opened. If we open the Object Packager directly, this option is no longer available.

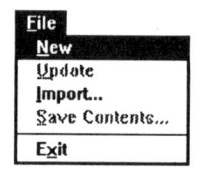

```
File
  New
  Update
  Import...
  Save Contents...
  Exit
```

The *Save Contents* option allows you to save an imported object again, if it already had been saved as a file.

The *Exit* option closes the Object Packager. You can also double click on the system menu. Alterations which have not yet been saved may still be retained.

The Edit menu

The options in the *Edit* menu implement the transport functions in the Object Packager. The interaction with the Clipboard takes place here and, thus, also the interaction with the applications which supply or receive the OLE objects.

When you have loaded a file using the *Import* option from the *File* menu as described above, you can transfer the file using the *Copy Package* option from the *Edit* menu to the Clipboard. It can then be extracted from the Clipboard by another application.

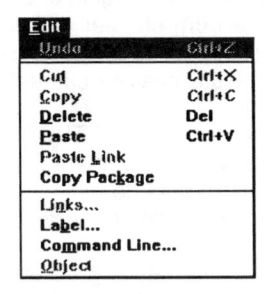

```
Edit
Undo            Ctrl+Z
Cut             Ctrl+X
Copy            Ctrl+C
Delete          Del
Paste           Ctrl+V
Paste Link
Copy Package
Links...
Label...
Command Line...
Object
```

If you wish to make an OLE object from a part of a document, use the original application (the *source application*) to copy the information required to the Clipboard. In the Object Packager, select the *Content* window. Then choose the *Paste* option from the *Edit* menu. This allows you to adopt the contents of the Clipboard. In this case, the object will be embedded. If you wish to link the object, choose the *Paste Link* option.

Choose *Copy Package* to transfer the object to the destination application.

We shall now, using examples from chapters 3 and 4, illustrate the procedures used in linking information. In this case, it is merely a simple example, but it should be sufficient to show the full range of linkage possibilities.

15.3 A familiar example: the letterheading from Paintbrush and Write

If we now again implement the merging of the Write file and the Paintbrush file from chapter 4, but this time using the OLE technique, we are able to see that a number of interesting results can be obtained.

Start up Paintbrush and open the LETTHEAD.BMP file. Select the frame containing the letterheading and copy it to the Clipboard. Then open Write with a *New* file, and choose the *Paste Link* option from the *Edit* menu.

Just as in chapter 4, the letterheading will appear in the upper part of the window. Until now, it does not seem as if there is any difference.

Now we shall return to Paintbrush (Alt-Tab). The information in the letterheading is rather meagre. It seems as if the letterheading originated in the pre-telephone era. Due to the fact that the firm Lindberg and Partners now possesses a modern well-equipped office, with telephone and fax, we shall extend the letterheading to include the following information:

```
Telephone    01-1234567
Telefax      01-2345678
```

To do this, select the text tool (abc) in the toolbox at the left-hand side of the window. Select a suitable font for the letterheading by using the *Fonts* option from the *Text* menu.

Type the above text in the free space in the window. Using the pick (upper right-hand corner of the toolbox), define the text and place it in the lower right-hand corner of the letterheading.

Now switch over to Write using Alt-Tab and observe the result: the firm possesses a telephone and telefax here also.

A familiar example: ...

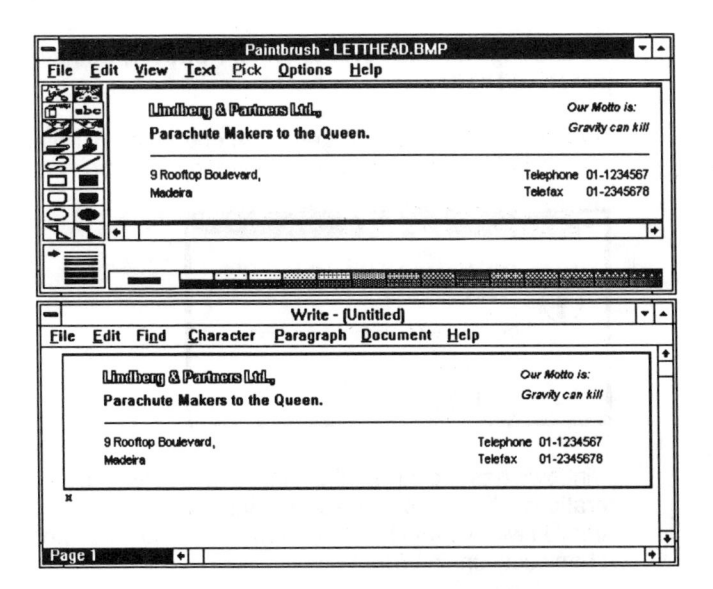

Subsequently, save the file in Write under a recognizable name, for instance, 15-1.WRI (chapter 15, first text file). Exit Write by choosing the *Exit* option from the *File* menu or by double clicking on the Control Menu button.

Switch over to Paintbrush again using Alt-Tab (or via the Task List).

Now that we examine the letterheading more critically, we notice that it has become a bit more impressive as a letterheading, but nevertheless something is still missing. The recipient only knows that he/she has to pay within 30 days. There is no mention of the bank to which the invoice sum should be payed.

In the same way as outlined above, we shall register a banking company in the letterheading:

Bank account: Misland Bank 123456789

In order to check whether Write has also assumed this alteration, just as in the case of the telephone numbers, we shall again switch over to Write. However, we have just closed Write....

No panic, start up the program and open the 15-1 file. The following dialogue box will appear on the screen:

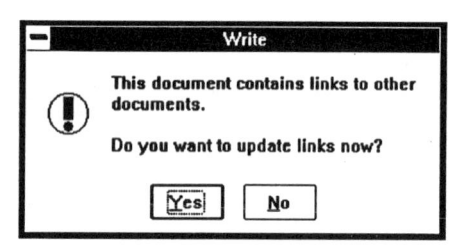

> **Write**
>
> (!) This document contains links to other documents.
>
> Do you want to update links now?
>
> [Yes]   [No]

Windows has registered the linkage and asks if the alterations should be processed. Answer this with Yes and you will observe that the letterheading now also has a bank account in Write.

You can use this technology personally in (more useful) file combinations, for instance, in linkages between spreadsheets and text files. Information in an Excel table probably changes as regularly as clockwork. The table in a filed report will alter automatically.

Appendix A
Installation

The Setup installation program is so well-constructed that it is unnecessary to deal with it extensively. Keeping the following supplementary remarks in mind, installation should be no problem.

- Installation can only take place on a computer with a harddisk. There must be a minimum of 6 Mb available on harddisk but 8 Mb is recommended. For the enhanced mode, 10Mb is best.
- If you have a mouse, it is advisable to connect it before installation, owing to the fact that Windows is already being started up during the installation.
- Place disk nr. 1 in the chosen drive, switch to this drive by typing A: or B: and give the SETUP command.
- Subsequently, you will be given the choice between *Express Setup* and *Custom Setup*. It is advisable to choose the first option. Choose *Custom Setup* only when you are reasonably familiar with basic principles of Windows. In the first case, almost everything will take place automatically, in the second case, you must specify certain points. No accidents will occur, in the case of *Custom Setup*, if you follow the instructions which appear on the screen.
- SETUP will check the hardware present during the installation (the graphic card, network etc.). When using *Custom Setup*, check if this information is correct.
- Read the instructions given by SETUP carefully and follow them precisely.

If, in retrospect, it is obvious that you have missed something, you can use *Windows Setup* from Main to make additions or alterations without having to install Windows all over again.

This may apply, for example, to the keyboard layout which Setup may install to a setting other than the one you wish. This layout, by the way, can be altered in the Control Panel, using the *International* option (Keyboard Layout).

Note: Do not attempt to copy the files directly from the disks to the harddisk. They are compressed and, therefore, have to be expanded before they are available as working programs. If, nevertheless, it is necessary to work without using Setup, proceed as follows:

■ Copy EXPAND.EXE from disk nr. 3 to the harddisk. This program converts compressed files into working programs.
■ Place the source disk in one of the drives.
■ Give the following command, followed by Enter:

```
EXPAND A:file name C:file name
```

In this case, A: is the source drive (may also be B:) and C: is the harddisk to which the files are being copied. The files are copied to the harddisk and expanded.

Appendix B
Practical tips

In this appendix, you will encounter remarks and tips geared to solving problems.

Screendumps
It is impossible to transport a copy of the screen directly to the printer. To do this, some intermediate steps are necessary:

a) Press the PrintScreen key for a copy of the entire screen
b) Press Alt-PrintScreen for a copy of the active window.

In both cases, the information is copied to the Clipboard, and from there it can be transferred to other programs, for instance, to Write or Paintbrush. It is possible to print information from these programs.

Keep in mind that Paintbrush is not able to admit the entire contents of the screen. It can only deal with that part which fits into the drawing area. Accordingly, it is advisable to remove the toolbox and the palette if you wish to admit new information. If the area is still not large enough, the following trick may help:

- Select the *Zoom Out* option from the *View* menu (Ctrl-O).
- Select the *Paste* option from the *Edit* menu twice. Do not pay any attention to the checked pattern which appears on the screen.
- Select the *Zoom In* option from the *View* menu.

The entire contents of the screen have now been transferred and may be edited.

Placing a new graphic card
If a new graphic card has been placed, Windows may

not start up owing to the fact that the program attempts to use a wrong display mode. In that case, start up the Setup program from the DOS command line using the SETUP command. Then specify the graphic card the computer is now using. In most cases, you need to have the installation disk containing the screen drivers available, since Setup will be needing these. If you have a SuperVGA card, you should use the Windows screen driver. This is generally superior to the card supplied by the manufacturer.

Note: Other changes in the hardware should also be registered with Windows via the Setup program.

VGA with monochrome monitor

If you have a normal VGA card and a monochrome monitor, you do not actually have to choose the *VGA with Monochrome display* option. If this option is selected, only black and white are used. This means, for instance, that the three-dimensional effect of the option buttons is not visible. You can quite simply select the normal *VGA* option. In this case, the colours will be displayed in different tints of grey and the windows layout is more pleasant.

Speeding up Windows

You can speed up Windows using the following measures:

- Compress the harddisk regularly. To do this, you need a program which can undo the fragmentation of the files on the harddisk.
- Test which Windows mode runs quickest on your computer. This can be the standard mode in some cases.
- The general rule of thumb is: the more memory, the quicker the programs run.
- A fast processor in the computer alone is not enough. A fast graphic card and a fast harddisk are equally important. In general, the various system components should be geared to one another.

- Use a permanent exchange file in the 386 enhanced mode.
- If available, activate the 32 bit Disk Access option in the 386 enhanced mode by selecting this box in the *Virtual Memory* window.

Creating an exchange file

If you run Windows in the 386 enhanced mode, the hard-disk can be used to save parts of programs if there is a shortage of available memory capacity. Normally, this saving is done in a file which Windows creates each time the program is started up. Addressing this file is, however, rather slow. Assisted by the Control Panel, it is possible to create a permanent exchange file which can be addressed extremely quickly. The disadvantage is that a file like this permanently occupies several Megabytes. Creating a file like this takes place as follows:

- Activate the Control Panel in the Main group of the Program Manager.
- Go to the *386 Enhanced* option and press Enter or click using the mouse.
- Click on the *Virtual Memory* button and then on *Change*. The following window will appear on the screen (the numbers will probably be different on your screen):

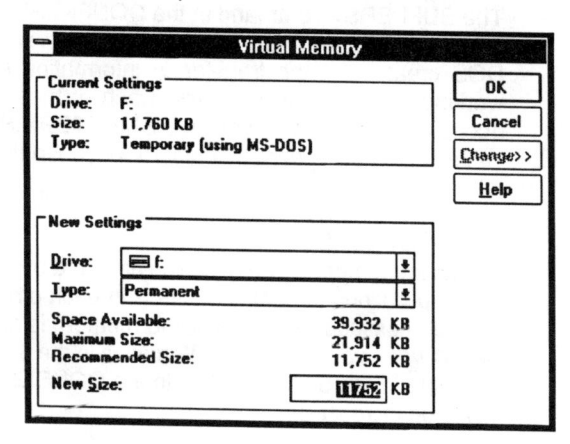

```
┌─ Virtual Memory ─────────────────────────┐
│ ┌─ Current Settings ───────┐   ┌──────┐  │
│ │ Drive:  F:               │   │  OK  │  │
│ │ Size:   11,760 KB        │   ├──────┤  │
│ │ Type:   Temporary        │   │Cancel│  │
│ │         (using MS-DOS)   │   ├──────┤  │
│ └──────────────────────────┘   │Change>>│ │
│                                ├──────┤  │
│                                │ Help │  │
│                                └──────┘  │
│ ┌─ New Settings ─────────────────────┐   │
│ │ Drive:  [■ f:            ▼]        │   │
│ │ Type:   [Permanent       ▼]        │   │
│ │                                    │   │
│ │ Space Available:      39,932 KB    │   │
│ │ Maximum Size:         21,914 KB    │   │
│ │ Recommended Size:     11,752 KB    │   │
│ │                                    │   │
│ │ New Size:             [11752] KB   │   │
│ └────────────────────────────────────┘   │
└──────────────────────────────────────────┘
```

- Select the drive and choose the *Permanent* option in the *Type* drop-down list. Specify the size of the exchange file. Windows is very helpful here and advises about the possible and desired size of the exchange file.

A file which has been created in this way can also be altered and deleted using the same procedures.

Making the mouse driver inactive

If you only use the mouse in Windows, you may delete the corresponding commands from the CONFIG.SYS and AUTOEXEC.BAT files. By doing this, you can gain extra memory since Windows uses its own mouse drivers.

Speed of the various modes

The two different modes in which Windows runs (standard and 386 enhanced), differ not only in the amount of available memory, they also differ in running speed. If you have a 386 computer with more than 2 Mb memory and you work almost exclusively with Windows programs, it can be useful to work in the standard mode because this is quicker than the 386 mode in some respects. To compare these modes, you could examine the speeds of loading and saving in the different modes.

Setting BUFFERS

The BUFFERS= command in the CONFIG.SYS file enables you to specify the number of buffers which MS-DOS creates for the transfer of information between working memory and harddisk. Each of these buffers occupies 528 bytes. If you use SMARTDRV.SYS this value need not be greater than 10, because this driver takes the onus of the buffering.

Setting STACKS

Stacks are temporary areas which are used by MS-DOS and applications to communicate with each other. If the internal message that the stacked memory is full is displayed when you are running Windows in the 386 mode, the value in the STACKS= line in the CONFIG.SYS file has to be increased.

Specifying the TEMP Environment Variable

Many programs, when running, create temporary files which are deleted when the program is closed. The TEMP Environment Variable determines the directory in which these files are stored. The DOS command SET enables you to specify this directory. Normally, this command is located in the AUTOEXEC.BAT file, so that the execution of this process takes place each time the program is started up.

An alteration in the standard setting can be useful if the computer has two harddisks with different speeds or if a RAM disk has been added. In cases like these, the TEMP environment variable should be placed on the faster harddisk or on the RAM disk. The command in the AUTOEXEC.BAT appears as follows:

```
SET TEMP=D:\TEMP
```

Choosing the background

Using Paintbrush, you can design the screen background to your own requirements. Mark the screen area using the pick or scissors and save it using the *Copy To* option from the *Edit* menu. In this, use one of the bitmap options (1 colour, 16 colours etc.). To establish the new drawing as the background, choose the *Desktop* option from the Control Panel in order to register the new drawing as the *Wallpaper*. If you select the *Center* option, the wallpaper will appear only once in the middle of the screen. If you choose the *Tile* option, the pattern will be constantly repeated until it fills the entire screen.

Although this can lead to admirable results, you have to keep in mind that this process will cost you roughly 200 Kb. If there are problems with memory capacity, it is advisable to first remove the wallpaper or the pattern of the Desktop in the Control Panel.

Window operation using the mouse

The quickest way to close windows is to double click on the Control menu button in the upper left-hand corner. A double click on the title bar enlarges windows to their maximum size and also restores them to the original size.

Starting up programs

Programs in Windows can be started up in various ways. A summary is given below. Program Manager and File Manager provide identical possibilities, apart from the fact that the Program Manager uses icons and the File Manager uses file names.

- double click on the icon or name
- using a specified shortcut key combination of Ctrl-key, Alt-key together with a key personally chosen
- select the icon or program name and press Enter
- select the icon or program name and choose the *Open* option from the *File* menu
- select the *Run* option from the *File* menu. Then specify in the text box the name of the program to be started up (for example, NOTEPAD). Parameters can also be specified here if required. You can search for programs using *Browse*.

Specifying another shell

When you start up Windows, the Program Manager is loaded as the 'distribution' centre. All other programs are started up from here and Windows is also closed here. But it is also possible to use any program of your choice instead of the Program Manager to do this. However, it is only meaningful to use the File Manager instead of the Program Manager. To make this alteration, open the SYSTEM.INI file using Sysedit or the Notepad, and go to the following line:

```
SHELL=PROGMAN.EXE
```

Change this to:

```
SHELL=WINFILE.EXE
```

The next time Windows is started up, the File Manager will be loaded instead of the Program Manager.

Doubly addressing a file

Due to the fact that it is possible to keep several programs active simultaneously in Windows, it can easily occur that, for example, you may be working on the same text in two Write windows. In addition, it sometimes occurs that the alterations made in the text are occasionally saved on top of each other. You can prevent this by introducing the SHARE command to the AUTOEXEC.BAT file. If you then attempt to address a text more often, a message will appear stating that the file is being edited under another program.

Specifying colours

The colours of most Windows components can be determined using the Control Panel. However, in the case of a couple of these components, it is only possible to change them by making alterations in the WIN.INI file. Use the Notepad or Sysedit to do this. In the file, look for the line with the following heading:

```
[COLORS]
```

The colours of the Windows screen components are stated here. The names of the elements which can be changed using the Control Panel are given. For instance, using Active Title= enables you to specify the colour which the active title bar will receive.

```
component=red_value green_value blue_value
```

The colour values are integers which specify the relative intensities of red, green and blue. The settings range from 0 (low intensity) to 255 (maximum intensity).

You can make specifications in the file concerning the following components if desired:

ButtonFace, ButtonShadow, ButtonText, GrayText, Hilight, and HilightText.

Example:

```
GrayText=255 0 0
```

Accordingly, options which cannot be activated are displayed not in grey, but in red. Keep in mind that the components must be written as one word.

File Manager layout

In contrast to the Program Mananger, the File Manager does not record the previous layout and proportions of the windows. Each time the program is started up, they have to be specified again. Therefore, it is interesting to create a macro for this task. In addition, if you automatically load the Recorder each time Windows is started up, the macro will be constantly available.

Example of a Desktop

The most ideal layout of the Desktop is, of course, a matter of personal taste. We only wish to give an example of the possibilities here.

The Program Manager does not occupy the entire screen, but leaves enough space at the bottom to display the other program icons. In additon, a double click on this area will activate the Task List.

The Clock and Write programs are automatically loaded when Windows is started up. The Recorder will also be started up automatically so that macros are immediately available.

Using the Control Panel we have placed the icons at a distance of 70 from one another in order to display as many icons as possible in a window at one time.

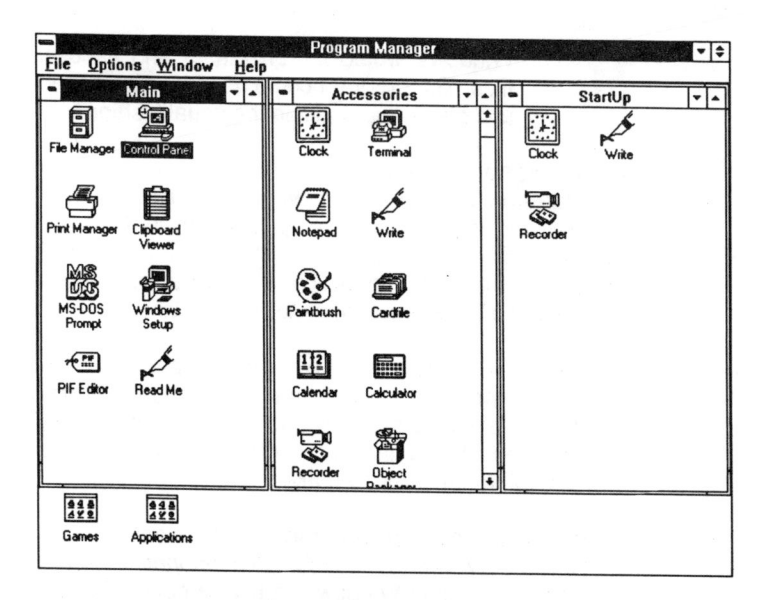

Editing system files

The configuration of MS-DOS and Windows takes place with the help of the CONFIG.SYS, AUTOEXEC.BAT, WIN.INI and SYSTEM.INI files.

These files can be easily opened using the Sysedit program which is to be found in the SYSTEM subdirectory of Windows. This program loads the above mentioned files automatically. If you need to make alterations to these files frequently, it is advisable to include Sysedit in one of the group windows, for instance, in Main.

Renaming directories

The File Manager enables you to rename directories and files by using the *Rename* option from the *File* menu. Click on the directory or file, choose the *Rename* option and register the new name. Caution: only a name for a directory may be registered, not for a complete path.

Note: Do not give the directory in which Windows is located another name. If you should do so,

Windows would be unable to find its own files. The program could no longer be closed and started up again in the usual fashion.

Installing applications
Programs for Windows can be very simply installed with the help of the Windows Setup program in the Main group. In this, the entire harddisk is examined if required. All programs with which Windows is familiar are included in a list. Pay attention to the following:

Windows does not check whether a program is already installed or not. Windows does not recognize the programs with absolute certainty due to the fact that it only reviews the DOS file names. That is why Windows asks you to confirm the guess it makes.

Adding and removing Windows components
Using the *Add/Remove Windows Components* option, fixed components of Windows can be removed from or added to the disk in a simple manner. For instance, if you have absolutely no interest in the Accessories group you can remove them from the menus.

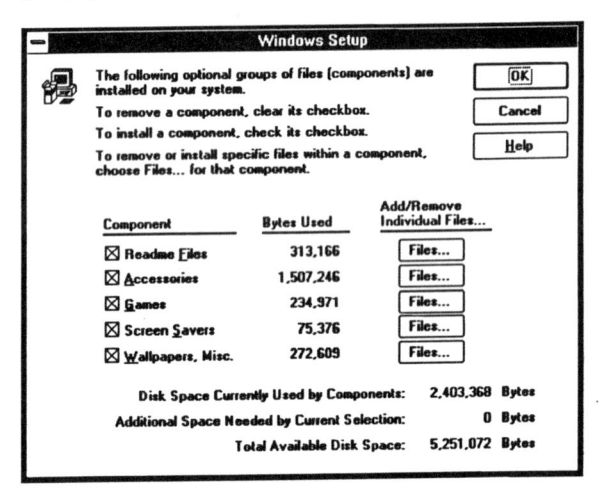

```
┌─────────────────────────────────────────────────────────────┐
│                       Windows Setup                         │
├─────────────────────────────────────────────────────────────┤
│  The following optional groups of files (components) are    │
│  installed on your system.                    [   OK   ]    │
│  To remove a component, clear its checkbox.                 │
│                                               [ Cancel ]    │
│  To install a component, check its checkbox.                │
│  To remove or install specific files within a  [  Help  ]   │
│  component, choose Files... for that component.             │
│                                                             │
│                                   Add/Remove                │
│   Component         Bytes Used    Individual Files...       │
│                                                             │
│   ☒ Readme Files      313,166     [ Files... ]              │
│   ☒ Accessories     1,507,246     [ Files... ]              │
│   ☒ Games             234,971     [ Files... ]              │
│   ☒ Screen Savers      75,376     [ Files... ]              │
│   ☒ Wallpapers, Misc. 272,609     [ Files... ]              │
│                                                             │
│      Disk Space Currently Used by Components: 2,403,368 Bytes│
│      Additional Space Needed by Current Selection:    0 Bytes│
│                  Total Available Disk Space:  5,251,072 Bytes│
└─────────────────────────────────────────────────────────────┘
```

WINHELP

Each time you select the *Help* menu the WINHELP.EXE program is started up containing the corresponding necessary help file. You can switch over from here to other help files by using the *Open* option from the *File* menu.

Appendix C
ASCII character set

Caution: Windows does not use the ASCII character set. It uses the ANSI character set (see appendix D). For this reason, it is occasionally necessary to convert texts if they are adopted by Windows programs from DOS programs, and vice versa. The conversion function is usually supplied by the Windows program.

Dec	Hex	Chr	Dec	Hex	Chr	Dec	Hex	Chr	Dec	Hex	Chr
0	0		32	20		64	40	@	96	60	`
1	1	☺	33	21	!	65	41	A	97	61	a
2	2	☻	34	22	"	66	42	B	98	62	b
3	3	♥	35	23	#	67	43	C	99	63	c
4	4	♦	36	24	$	68	44	D	100	64	d
5	5	♣	37	25	%	69	45	E	101	65	e
6	6	♠	38	26	&	70	46	F	102	66	f
7	7	•	39	27	'	71	47	G	103	67	g
8	8	◘	40	28	(	72	48	H	104	68	h
9	9	○	41	29	)	73	49	I	105	69	i
10	A	◙	42	2A	*	74	4A	J	106	6A	j
11	B	♂	43	2B	+	75	4B	K	107	6B	k
12	C	♀	44	2C	,	76	4C	L	108	6C	l
13	D	♪	45	2D	-	77	4D	M	109	6D	m
14	E	♫	46	2E	.	78	4E	N	110	6E	n
15	F	☼	47	2F	/	79	4F	O	111	6F	o
16	10	►	48	30	0	80	50	P	112	70	p
17	11	◄	49	31	1	81	51	Q	113	71	q
18	12	↕	50	32	2	82	52	R	114	72	r
19	13	‼	51	33	3	83	53	S	115	73	s
20	14	¶	52	34	4	84	54	T	116	74	t
21	15	§	53	35	5	85	55	U	117	75	u
22	16	▬	54	36	6	86	56	V	118	76	v
23	17	↨	55	37	7	87	57	W	119	77	w
24	18	↑	56	38	8	88	58	X	120	78	x
25	19	↓	57	39	9	89	59	Y	121	79	y
26	1A	→	58	3A	:	90	5A	Z	122	7A	z
27	1B	←	59	3B	;	91	5B	[	123	7B	{
28	1C	∟	60	3C	<	92	5C	\	124	7C	|
29	1D	↔	61	3D	=	93	5D	]	125	7D	}
30	1E	▲	62	3E	>	94	5E	^	126	7E	~
31	1F	▼	63	3F	?	95	5F	_	127	7F	⌂

ASCII character set

Dec	Hex	Chr	Dec	Hex	Chr	Dec	Hex	Chr	Dec	Hex	Chr
128	80	Ç	160	A0	á	192	C0	└	224	E0	α
129	81	ü	161	A1	í	193	C1	┴	225	E1	β
130	82	é	162	A2	ó	194	C2	┬	226	E2	Γ
131	83	â	163	A3	ú	195	C3	├	227	E3	π
132	84	ä	164	A4	ñ	196	C4	─	228	E4	Σ
133	85	à	165	A5	Ñ	197	C5	┼	229	E5	σ
134	86	å	166	A6	ª	198	C6	╞	230	E6	µ
135	87	ç	167	A7	º	199	C7	╟	231	E7	τ
136	88	ê	168	A8	¿	200	C8	╚	232	E8	Φ
137	89	ë	169	A9	⌐	201	C9	╔	233	E9	Θ
138	8A	è	170	AA	¬	202	CA	╩	234	EA	Ω
139	8B	ï	171	AB	½	203	CB	╦	235	EB	δ
140	8C	î	172	AC	¼	204	CC	╠	236	EC	∞
141	8D	ì	173	AD	¡	205	CD	═	237	ED	ø
142	8E	Ä	174	AF	«	206	CE	╬	238	EE	∈
143	8F	Å	175	B0	»	207	CF	╧	239	EF	∩
144	90	É	176	B1	░	208	D0	╨	240	F0	≡
145	91	æ	177	B2	▒	209	D1	╤	241	F1	±
146	92	Æ	178	B3	│	210	D2	╥	242	F2	≥
147	93	ô	179	B4	┤	211	D3	╙	243	F3	≤
148	94	ö	180	B5	╡	212	D4	╘	244	F4	⌠
149	95	ò	181	B6	╢	213	D5	╒	245	F5	⌡
150	96	û	182	B7	╖	214	D6	╓	246	F6	÷
151	97	ù	183	B8	╕	215	D7	╫	247	F7	≈
152	98	ÿ	184	B9	╣	216	D8	╪	248	F8	°
153	99	Ö	185	BA	║	217	D9	┘	249	F9	·
154	9A	Ü	186	BB	╗	218	DA	┌	250	FA	·
155	9B	¢	187	BC	╝	219	DB	█	251	FB	√
156	9C	£	188	BD	╜	220	DC	▄	252	FC	ⁿ
157	9D	¥	189	BE	╛	221	DD	▌	253	FD	²
158	9E	₧	190	BF	┐	222	DE	▐	254	FE	■
159	9F	ƒ	191	C0	┐	223	DF	▀	255	FF	

Appendix D
ANSI character set

Dec	Hex	Char	Dec	Hex	Char	Dec	Hex	Char	Dec	Hex	Char
0	0	·	32	20		64	40	@	96	60	`
1	1	·	33	21	!	65	41	A	97	61	a
2	2	·	34	22	"	66	42	B	98	62	b
3	3	·	35	23	#	67	43	C	99	63	c
4	4	·	36	24	$	68	44	D	100	64	d
5	5	·	37	25	%	69	45	E	101	65	e
6	6	·	38	26	&	70	46	F	102	66	f
7	7	·	39	27	'	71	47	G	103	67	g
8	8	·	40	28	(	72	48	H	104	68	h
9	9	·	41	29	)	73	49	I	105	69	i
10	A	·	42	2A	*	74	4A	J	106	6A	j
11	B	·	43	2B	+	75	4B	K	107	6B	k
12	C	·	44	2C	,	76	4C	L	108	6C	l
13	D	·	45	2D	-	77	4D	M	109	6D	m
14	E	·	46	2E	.	78	4E	N	110	6E	n
15	F	·	47	2F	/	79	4F	O	111	6F	o
16	10	·	48	30	0	80	50	P	112	70	p
17	11	·	49	31	1	81	51	Q	113	71	q
18	12	·	50	32	2	82	52	R	114	72	r
19	13	·	51	33	3	83	53	S	115	73	s
20	14	·	52	34	4	84	54	T	116	74	t
21	15	·	53	35	5	85	55	U	117	75	u
22	16	·	54	36	6	86	56	V	118	76	v
23	17	·	55	37	7	87	57	W	119	77	w
24	18	·	56	38	8	88	58	X	120	78	x
25	19	·	57	39	9	89	59	Y	121	79	y
26	1A	·	58	3A	:	90	5A	Z	122	7A	z
27	1B	·	59	3B	;	91	5B	[	123	7B	{
28	1C	·	60	3C	<	92	5C	\	124	7C	|
29	1D	·	61	3D	=	93	5D	]	125	7D	}
30	1E	·	62	3E	>	94	5E	^	126	7E	~
31	1F	·	63	3F	?	95	5F	_	127	7F	·

Dec	Hex	Char	Dec	Hex	Char	Dec	Hex	Char	Dec	Hex	Char
128	80	·	160	A0		192	C0	À	224	E0	à
129	81	·	161	A1	¡	193	C1	Á	225	E1	á
130	82	·	162	A2	¢	194	C2	Â	226	E2	â
131	83	·	163	A3	£	195	C3	Ã	227	E3	ã
132	84	·	164	A4	¤	196	C4	Ä	228	E4	ä
133	85	·	165	A5	¥	197	C5	Å	229	E5	å
134	86	·	166	A6	¦	198	C6	Æ	230	E6	æ
135	87	·	167	A7	§	199	C7	Ç	231	E7	ç
136	88	·	168	A8	¨	200	C8	È	232	E8	è
137	89	·	169	A9	©	201	C9	É	233	E9	é
138	8A	·	170	AA	ª	202	CA	Ê	234	EA	ê
139	8B	·	171	AB	«	203	CB	Ë	235	EB	ë
140	8C	·	172	AC	¬	204	CC	Ì	236	EC	ì
141	8D	·	173	AD	-	205	CD	Í	237	ED	í
142	8E	·	174	AE	®	206	CE	Î	238	EE	î
143	8F	·	175	AF	¯	207	CF	Ï	239	EF	ï
144	90	·	176	B0	°	208	D0	Ð	240	F0	ð
145	91	·	177	B1	±	209	D1	Ñ	241	F1	ñ
146	92	·	178	B2	²	210	D2	Ò	242	F2	ò
147	93	·	179	B3	³	211	D3	Ó	243	F3	ó
148	94	·	180	B4	´	212	D4	Ô	244	F4	ô
149	95	·	181	B5	µ	213	D5	Õ	245	F5	õ
150	96	·	182	B6	¶	214	D6	Ö	246	F6	ö
151	97	·	183	B7	·	215	D7	×	247	F7	÷
152	98	·	184	B8	¸	216	D8	Ø	248	F8	ø
153	99	·	185	B9	¹	217	D9	Ù	249	F9	ù
154	9A	·	186	BA	º	218	DA	Ú	250	FA	ú
155	9B	·	187	BB	»	219	DB	Û	251	FB	û
156	9C	·	188	BC	¼	220	DC	Ü	252	FC	ü
157	9D	·	189	BD	½	221	DD	Ý	253	FD	ý
158	9E	·	190	BE	¾	222	DE	Þ	254	FE	þ
159	9F	·	191	BF	¿	223	DF	ß	255	FF	ÿ

Index

386 enhanced (Control Panel) . . 139
386 enhanced mode . . 99, 139, 150

adding cards (Cardfile) 199
airbrush (Paintbrush) 61
alarm (Calendar) 187
aligning text (Write) 107
altering text (Notepad) 217
application window 20
appointments (Calendar) . . 186, 188
arranging windows 38
arrow keys 19, 33
ASCII file, see text file
associating documents with
 programs 48
associating documents with
 programs (File Manager) . . . 172
Auto arrange 40
automatic calculation (Calculator) . 264
automatic dialling (Cardfile) 197, 207

baud rate (Terminal) 222, 236
binary files 213
binary files (Terminal) 240
BMP 62
box (Paintbrush) 71
browse 44
brush (Paintbrush) 71
~ shapes (Paintbrush) 87
BUFFERS 288

Calculator 252
 automatic calculation 264
 functions 257
 logical operators 259
 numerical systems 259
 scientific 256
 standard 253
 statistical calculations 261
Calendar 178
 alarm 187
 appointments 186, 188
 commentary 185
 headers and footers 190
 hour format 183
 month view 181
 printing 190
 saving 189
 special days 184
 starting time 180
Cardfile 193
 adding cards 199
 automatic dialling 197, 207
 deleting cards 210
 duplicating cards 210
 editing data 209
 entering data 198
 index line 196
 information area 197
 layout 204
 List menu 195
 merging files 211
 mixed cards 202
 objects 203
 picture cards 201
 printing 204
 restoring cards 210
 saving 204
 searching 205
 telephone numbers 197
 text cards 200
 View menu 194
Cascade 38
centering text (Write) 107
changing macros (Recorder) . . 271
character styles (Write) 105
circles (Paintbrush) 79
clipboard 98
Clock 175
 analogue 176
 digital 177
 fonts 176
 setting 177
colour 291
colour (Control Panel) 122
colour (Paintbrush) . . 55, 58, 60, 87
combining text and pictures
 (Write) 117

command button 31
commentary (Calendar) 185
communication parameters
  (Terminal) 235
COMx 127
connection (Terminal) 225
Control menu 29
Control menu box 22
Control menu button 28
Control Panel 121
  386 enhanced 139
  colour 122
  desktop setup 128
  drivers 142
  fonts 126
  international 137
  keyboard speed 132
  mouse 128
  network 139
  ports 127
  printers 132
  sound 143
  wallpaper 131
copying files (File Manager) . . .166
correcting text (Write) 95
currency format 138
cursor 15, 17
cursor (Paintbrush) 57
cursor (Write) 94
cursor keys 19
cursor movements (Write) 95
curves (Paintbrush) 79
cut, copy and paste (Write) . . .100

Data Flow Control
  (Terminal) 222, 237
data transmission (Terminal) . . .240
date format 138
DDE 13, 276
deleting cards (Cardfile) 210
deleting files (File Manager) . . .168
demos (Recorder) 274
desktop 15, 20
desktop setup (Control Panel) . .128
device driver (Multimedia) 247
dialogue (Terminal) 227
directories (File Manager) 169
directory structure (File Manager) 160

directory windows (File Manager) 158
disk commands (File Manager) . 169
disk operations (File Manager) . 171
dots (in menus) 32
drivers (Control Panel) 142
drop-down list 124
duplicating cards (Cardfile) . . . 210
Dynamic Data Exchange,
  see DDE

Edit menu (Write) 99
editing data (Cardfile) 209
ellipsis 32
embedded object
EMS 155
enlarging windows 23
entering data (Cardfile) 198
erasing (Paintbrush) 60, 66
exchange file 287
exchanging files (Terminal) . . . 227
EXPAND.EXE 284

file attributes (File Manager) . . 165
File Manager 158
  associating documents and
    programs 172
  copying files 166
  deleting files 168
  directories 169
  directory structure 160
  directory windows 158
  disk commands 169
  disk operations 171
  file attributes 165
  moving files 167
  root directory 160
  settings 173
file size limits (Notepad) 218
filled box (Paintbrush) 86
find (and replace) (Write) 101
flip horizontal/vertical (Paintbrush) 80
fonts (Clock) 176
fonts (Control Panel) 126
fonts (Paintbrush) 76
formatting text (Write) 107
function keys (Terminal) 243

graphic cards 285

Index

group 35
~ windows 37
creating ~s 43
deleting ~s 43
description 42
properties 42

headers and footers (Calendar) . 190
headers and footers (Notepad) . 216
headers and footers (Paintbrush) 84
headers and footers (Write) . . . 113
Help 51
hidden files 165
high memory 155
hour format (Calendar) 183
hyphenation (Write) 111

icons 15
arranging 40
changing 46
moving 37
image attributes (Paintbrush) . . 86
indenting (Write) 107
index line (Cardfile) 196
information area (Cardfile) 197
insertion point 17
installation 283
installing applications 294
international (Control Panel) . . . 137
italics (Write) 105

justifying text (Write) 107

keyboard 17, 31
keyboard layout 137
keyboard speed (Control Panel) . 132

layout (Cardfile) 204
layout (Write) 105
line (Paintbrush) 71
lines (Paintbrush) 59
linesize box (Paintbrush) 56
linked object
List menu (Cardfile) 195
logbook files (Notepad) 218
logging in (Terminal) 226, 228
logical operators (Calculator) . . 259

macro planning (Recorder) . . . 267
Main 35
maximize button 22, 25
media player (Multimedia) 248
menu bar 22
merging files (Cardfile) 211
minimize button 22, 24, 37
mixed cards (Cardfile) 202
modem (Terminal) 221
modem commands
(Terminal) 225, 238
monochrome monitor 286
month view (Calendar) 181
mouse 15
click 17
click speed 128
cursor 17
drag 17, 22
swap buttons 128
~ pointer 16
moving files (File Manager) . . . 167
MSP 64
Multimedia 247
device driver 247
media player 248
sound card 247
sound recorder 249
multitasking 139, 154

network (Control Panel) 139
Notepad 212
altering text 217
file size limits 218
headers and footers 216
logbook files 218
page setup 216
printing 216
saving files 214
searching 215
null modem cable (Terminal) . . 221
number format 138
numerical systems (Calculator) . 259
object 276
Object Linking and Embedding,
see OLE
Object Packager 277
objects (Cardfile) 203
OLE 276

Index

opaque relocation (Paintbrush) . 74
opening files (Paintbrush) 63
opening files, dialogue boxes . . 65
operating modes 149
option buttons 82

page endings (Write) 114
page layout (Write) 113
page setup (Notepad) 216
page setup (Paintbrush) 84
Paintbrush 55
   airbrush 61
   box 71
   brush 71
   brush shapes 87
   circles 79
   colour 55, 58, 60, 87
   cursor 57
   curves 79
   erasing 60, 66
   filled box 86
   flip horizontal/vertical 80
   fonts 76
   headers and footers 84
   image attributes 86
   line 71
   lines 59
   linesize box 56
   opaque relocation 74
   opening files 63
   page setup 84
   palette 56
   pick 71, 80
   polygon 85
   printing 82
   printing quality 83
   rectangles 59
   saving files 62
   saving/loading part of image . . 89
   scissors 71
   showing cursor position . . . 75
   size of image 86
   summary of tools 90
   text 76
   toolbox 56
   transparent relocation 74
   Undo option 67
   zoom in 69

zoom out 69
palette (Paintbrush) 56
parity (Terminal) 222, 237
PCX 63
phone number (Terminal) . 224, 231
pick (Paintbrush) 71, 80
picture cards (Cardfile) 201
PIF Editor 147
pixel oriented image 67
playing back macros (Recorder) 271
polygon (Paintbrush) 85
port (Terminal) 237
ports (Control Panel) 127
preparing a session (Terminal) . 223
Print Manager 136, 143
print queue 144
printer, installing 133
   port 134
   settings 135
printers 132
printers (Control Panel) 132
printing (Calendar) 190
printing (Cardfile) 204
printing (Notepad) 216
printing (Paintbrush) 82
printing (Terminal) 229
printing (Write) 95, 116
printing quality (Paintbrush) 83
Program Manager 19, 35
programs
   copying ~ to another group . . .45
   deleting ~ from a group 50
   description 42
   moving to another group 43
   properties 42
   starting 51
   starting automatically 52
   starting ~ as an icon 50
protocols (Terminal) 242

quitting Windows 20, 53

Recorder, ... 266
   changing macros 271
   demos 274
   macro planning 267
   playing back macros 271
   recording macros 268

Index

shortcut keys 269
recording macros (Recorder) . .268
rectangles (Paintbrush) 59
reducing windows 23
restoring cards (Cardfile) 210
restoring windows 24
root directory (File Manager) . . .160
ruler (Write) 105

saving (Calendar) 189
saving (Cardfile) 204
saving (Write) 115
saving documents (Write) 95
saving files 62
saving files (Notepad) 214
saving files (Terminal) 245
saving files, dialogue boxes . . . 64
saving/loading part of image
 (Paintbrush) 89
scissors (Paintbrush) 71
screen saver 130
screendumps 285
scroll bar 22, 25
scroll box 22, 25
scroll pointer 22, 25
searching (Cardfile) 205
searching (Notepad) 215
selecting text (Write) 97
settings (File Manager) 173
settings, save 51
shortcut keys 31, 52, 156
shortcut keys (Recorder) 269
showing cursor position
 (Paintbrush) 75
size of image (Paintbrush) 86
sound (Control Panel) 143
sound card (Multimedia) 247
sound recorder (Multimedia) . . .249
spacing (Write) 107
special days (Calendar) 184
speeding up Windows 286
STACKS 288
standard mode 149
start/data/stopbits (Terminal) . .222
start/stopbits (Terminal) 236
starting (Terminal) 220
starting (Write) 93
starting time (Calendar) 180

starting Windows 19
Startup group 52
statistical calculations
 (Calculator) 261
sub- and superscript (Write) . . . 106
summary of tools (Paintbrush) . .90
switching to another program 32, 119
system files 165
SYSTEM.INI 121

tabs (Write) 109
Task List 119
telephone numbers (Cardfile) . . 197
Terminal 220
 baud rate 222, 236
 binary file 240
 communication parameters . . 235
 connection 225
 Data Flow Control 222, 237
 data transmission 240
 dialogue 227
 exchanging files 227
 function keys 243
 logging in 226, 228
 modem 221
 modem commands . . . 225, 238
 null modem cable 221
 parity 222, 237
 phone number 224, 231
 port 237
 preparing a session 223
 printing 229
 protocols 242
 saving files 245
 start/data/stopbits 222
 start/stopbits 236
 starting 220
 terminal emulation 232
 terminal modes 233
 text file 240
 time-out 225
text (Paintbrush) 76
text blocks (Write) 98
text cards (Cardfile) 200
text file (Terminal) 240
text files 213
Tile 39
time format 138

time-out (Terminal) 225
title bar 22
toolbox (Paintbrush) 56
transparent relocation
(Paintbrush) 74
True Type fonts 76, 126

underline (Write) 105
Undo option (Paintbrush) 67

vector oriented image 67
VGA card 286
View menu (Cardfile) 194
virtual memory 139, 141

wallpaper (Control Panel) 131
WIN.INI 121
window 15
word wrapping 93
Write 93
  aligning text 107
  bold 105
  centering text 107
  character styles 105
  combining text and pictures . .117
  correcting text 95
  cursor 94
  cursor movements 95
  cut, copy and paste 100
  Edit menu 99
  find (and replace) 101
  formatting text 107
  headers and footers 113
  hyphenation 111
  indenting 107
  italics 105
  justifying text 107
  layout 105
  page endings 114
  page layout 113
  printing 95, 116
  ruler 105
  saving 115
  saving documents 95
  selecting text 97
  spacing 107
  starting 93
  sub- and superscript 106
  tabs 109
  text blocks 98
  underline 105
WYSIWYG 93

XMS 155

zoom in (Paintbrush) 69
zoom out (Paintbrush) 69